Everything You Ever Wanted to Know about Heaven . . .
But Never Dreamed of Asking

PETER KREEFT

Everything You Ever Wanted to Know about Heaven . . .

But Never Dreamed of Asking

First Complete Edition

IGNATIUS PRESS   SAN FRANCISCO

Portions previously published by
Harper & Row Publishers
San Francisco
and Fitzhenry & Whiteside, Ltd.
Toronto

Quotations from the Bible, unless otherwise indicated in the notes,
are from the Revised Standard Version of the Bible,
copyrighted 1946, 1952, 1971, and 1973.

Cover by Riz Boncan Marsella

ISBN 978-0-89870-297-2
Library of Congress catalogue number 89-82372
Printed in the United States of America

for John
God's first gift, good and true
a strong and soaring eagle,
an ocean silent and deep

for Jenny
white wave,
lovely lioness,
leaping, conquering all obstacles

for Katherine
the quiet beauty of a great flowering tree,
an infinitely precious diamond
reflecting light on all things with her love

for Elizabeth
a queen, a rose, a treasure saved and cherished,
a swift river watering the world's dryness with her life

Of these four masterpieces
written by God with human hands
I am unutterably proud.

NOTE

Throughout this book I have insisted on capitalizing Heaven, Hell, and Purgatory, as well as pronouns referring to the deity, contrary to current convention. My justification for the first is that these places are quite as real and substantial as Kokomo or Timbuktu; and the second is justified practically, for clarity's sake, as well as theologically, out of respect and adoration (which are also contrary to current convention!).

CONTENTS

Introduction

"Will my dead cat be alive in Heaven?"

"Can I get to Heaven without being religious?"

"Why won't Heaven get boring?"

"What kind of body will I have in Heaven?"

"Is there sex in Heaven?"

"Why can't you get there in a rocket ship?"

"Can you time travel in Heaven?"

"Is Heaven here on earth?"

Can anyone answer such questions? Is this book possible?

Everyone asks such questions, consciously or unconsciously. For next to the idea of God, the idea of Heaven is the greatest idea that has ever entered into the heart of man, woman, or child.

But wait. Right here at the beginning we run into a problem. My uncle put it this way:

"I hear you're writing a book. What's it about?"

"Heaven."

"Heaven, eh? Do you have some thoughts about it?"

"Of course I have some thoughts about it. How could I write a book about it if I didn't? Isn't that a silly question?"

"No, I don't think so. Follow my thought for a minute—these thoughts of yours: they've entered into your mind and heart, right?"

"Of course. What are you driving at?"

"Just this: according to the Bible, your book must be wrong."

"What? How can you say that? You haven't even read it yet. In fact, I haven't even written it yet!"

"Well, the Bible describes Heaven this way: 'Eye hath not seen, nor ear heard, neither have entered into the heart of man, the things which God hath prepared for them that love him.'[1] And your thoughts *have* entered into the heart of man. Therefore your thoughts can't be the truth about Heaven."

He had me there. I almost threw the manuscript away.

But then I thought of the answer, weeks later. I thought of the other great idea, the idea of God. It too is the idea of something (or rather Someone) that "eye hath not seen, nor ear heard, neither have entered into the heart of man." "For my thoughts are not your thoughts, neither are your ways my ways, saith the Lord. For as the heavens are higher than the earth, so are my ways higher than your ways, and my thoughts than your thoughts."[2] Yet that fact has not stopped us from writing millions of books and billions of words about God.

Many of those words are silly or stupid.

Most of them are secondhand platitudes.

But some are helpful and enlightening.

And a few are even awesomely wise and wonderful.

Perhaps the same is true of our words about Heaven. And perhaps all four kinds of words are found in this book.

What's Different about This Book

"Of making many books there is no end; and much study is a weariness of the flesh."[3] Why is this one necessary?

Because there are only three kinds of books about Heaven, and this one is of a fourth kind.

[1] 1 Corinthians 2:9 (KJV).
[2] Isaiah 55:8–9 (KJV).
[3] Ecclesiastes 12:12 (KJV).

First and best, there are the classics, the great old books written by the saints and sages. Unfortunately, these are rarely read today, and many are out of print. Also, they require the understanding of some premodern philosophical and theological language and techniques of reading that many modern readers have lost (unless they have had teachers like Mortimer Adler or read books like *How to Read a Book*).[4] By all means put this book down and read instead Saint Thomas Aquinas' treatise on the resurrection in the *Summa Theologiae*—if you can find it and if you can understand it.[5]

The other two kinds of books available are current books, which are pretty sharply divided into the popular versus the scholarly, the inspirational versus the professional. This division can be unhealthy for both kinds, for it tends to reduce inspirational books to sentiment and cliché with little intellectual bite, and scholarly books to detached dullness and technicality with little existential bite. The first do not speak to our minds and the second do not speak to our hearts or our lives: a case of heat without light or light without heat. That is why I constantly turn back to the blazing sunlight of a Saint Augustine or a Saint Bernard of Clairvaux.[6]

Very few orthodox Christians in this century have combined (1) the inspirational and the scholarly, (2) ancient wisdom and modern language, and (3) imagination and Christian orthodoxy. Among these few, C. S. Lewis stands out as unmistakably the prime example.[7] He has probably influenced

---

[4] New York: Simon & Schuster, 1972.

[5] *Summa Theologiae*, III (Supplement), 69–99.

[6] St. Augustine, *Retractions*, chap. 16; *One Book on Faith and the Creed* (*De fide et symbolo liber unus*). St. Bernard of Clairvaux, *Sermon* XXXI, 1 (on the Beatific Vision); XXXIII, 4 (on the blessed dead); XI, 4 (on the state of blessedness).

[7] See Joe R. Christopher and Joan K. Ostling, *C. S. Lewis: An Annotated Checklist of Writings about Him and His Works* (Kent, Ohio: Kent State University Press, 1974); Peter Kreeft, *C. S. Lewis: A Critical Essay* (Front Royal, Virginia: Christendom College Press, 1988).

more unbelievers to believe and deepened and toughened the faith and understanding of more believers than any other writer of the twentieth century.

But Lewis never wrote a theological study of Heaven, although he did write (1) a great little poetic fantasy about it, *The Great Divorce*, a kind of twentieth-century miniature of *The Divine Comedy*; (2) an unutterably moving and unforgettable sermon about it, "The Weight of Glory"; and (3) two highly imaginative and intelligent chapters on it in his two most ambitious theological books, *The Problem of Pain* and *Miracles*.[8] In the spirit of those writings, this book is an attempt to write the sort of book Lewis might have written about Heaven. (If you hear a softly satirical chuckle from far, far away yet very close, that is Lewis listening to such presumption: "He that sitteth in the heavens shall laugh."[9]) But this is not a book about Lewis, a summary of his thoughts; it is about Heaven. It looks along Lewis, not at him (to use one of his own very useful distinctions).[10] It uses his eyes and mine in binocular vision.

Rather, the vision is multi-ocular. Many other and greater explorers have discovered this "undiscovered country"[11] in the past. But their travelers' tales are not well known today. The old maps are not read. If some of my discoveries, like Lewis', are rediscoveries of Augustine's explorations, or Aquinas', well and good; I have traveled in the company of giants. Like the medievals, we should remember that we are "dwarfs standing on the shoulders of giants. If we see farther than the ancients, it is only because we have their shoulders to stand on."[12] It is better to be right than to be original, and

[8] C. S. Lewis, *The Problem of Pain* (New York: Macmillan, 1962); C. S. Lewis, *Miracles* (New York: Macmillan, 1955).

[9] Psalm 2:4 (KJV).

[10] C. S. Lewis, "Meditation in a Toolshed" in *God in the Dock* (Grand Rapids, Mich.: Eerdmans, 1970), pp. 212–15.

[11] Shakespeare, *Hamlet*, act III, scene 1.

[12] Bernard of Chartres as reported by John of Salisbury, *Metalogicon*, III, 4.

the surest way to be unoriginal is to care nothing about being right and to care only about being original, while "if you simply try to tell the truth (without caring twopence how often it has been told before) you will, nine times out of ten, become original without ever having noticed it."[13] Good philosophy is piggyback thinking: you stand on my shoulders, I stand on Lewis', Lewis stands on MacDonald's,[14] Mac-Donald stands on Augustine's, Augustine stands on Saint Paul's, Saint Paul stands on Christ's. That far up, you see far. We need a Great Chain of Thinking to see the Great Chain of Being. Here is one small link.

[13] C. S. Lewis, *Mere Christianity* (New York: Macmillan, 1960), p. 190.

[14] C. S. Lewis, ed., *George MacDonald: An Anthology* (New York: Macmillan, 1978), especially p. xxxii: "I have never concealed the fact that I regard him as my master."

Part I

Heaven and Us

Chapter One

What Difference Does Heaven Make?

If a thing makes no difference, it is a waste of time to think about it. We should begin, then, with the question, What difference does Heaven make to earth, to now, to our lives?

Only the difference between hope and despair in the end, between two totally different visions of life; between "chance or the dance".[1] At death we find out which vision is true: does it all go down the drain in the end, or are all the loose threads finally tied together into a gloriously perfect tapestry? Do the tangled paths through the forest of life lead to the golden castle or over the cliff and into the abyss? Is death a door or a hole?

To medieval Christendom, it was the world beyond the world that made all the difference in the world to this world. The Heaven beyond the sun made the earth "under the sun" something more than "vanity of vanities".[2] Earth was Heaven's womb, Heaven's nursery, Heaven's dress rehearsal. Heaven was the meaning of the earth. Nietzsche had not yet popularized the serpent's tempting alternative: "*You* are the

---

[1] Thomas Howard, *Chance or the Dance?* (San Francisco: Ignatius Press, 1989).
[2] Ecclesiastes 1:3, 2.

meaning of the earth."[3] Kant had not yet disseminated "the poison of subjectivism"[4] by his "Copernican revolution in philosophy",[5] in which the human mind does not discover truth but makes it, like the divine mind. Descartes had not yet replaced the divine I AM with the human "I think, therefore I am" as the "Archimedean point", had not yet replaced theocentrism with anthropocentrism.[6] Medieval man was still his Father's child, however prodigal, and his world was meaningful because it was "my Father's world" and he believed his Father's promise to take him home after death.

This confidence towards death gave him a confidence towards life, for life's road led somewhere. The Heavenly mansion at the end of the earthly pilgrimage made a tremendous difference to the road itself. Signs and images of Heavenly glory were strewn all over his earthly path. The "signs" were (1) nature and (2) Scripture, God's two books, (3) general providence, and (4) special miracles. (The word translated "miracle" in the New Testament [sēmeion] literally means "sign".)[7] The images surrounded him like the hills surrounding the Holy City.[8] They, too, pointed to Heaven. For instance, the images of saints in medieval statuary were seen not merely as material images of the human but as human images of the divine, windows onto God. They were not merely stone shaped into men and women but men and

---

[3] Nietzsche, *Thus Spake Zarathustra*, trans. R. J. Hollingsdale (Baltimore, Md.; Penguin, 1961), p. 42.

[4] C. S. Lewis, "The Poison of Subjectivism", *Christian Reflections* (Grand Rapids, Mich.: Eerdmans, 1967), pp. 72–81.

[5] Kant, *Critique of Pure Reason*, preface to the second edition. Cf. Francis H. Parker, *The Story of Philosophy* (Bloomington, Ind.: Indiana University Press, 1972), pp. 270 ff.

[6] Descartes, *Discourse on Method*, part 4; *Meditations* 1.

[7] William F. Arndt and F. Wilbur Gingrich, *A Greek-English Lexicon of the New Testament and Other Early Christian Literature* (Chicago: University of Chicago Press, 1957), pp. 755–56.

[8] Psalm 125:2.

women shaped into gods and goddesses. Lesser images too were designed to reflect Heavenly glory: kings and queens, heraldry and courtesy and ceremony, authority and obedience—these were not just practical socio-economic inventions but steps in the Cosmic Dance, links in the Great Chain of Being, rungs on Jacob's ladder, earthly reflections of Heaven. Distinctively premodern words like *glory, majesty, splendor, triumph, awe, honor*—these were more than words; they were lived experiences. More, they were experienced realities.

The glory has departed. We moderns have lost much of medieval Christendom's *faith* in Heaven because we have lost its *hope* of Heaven, and we have lost its hope of Heaven because we have lost its *love* of Heaven. And we have lost its love of Heaven because we have lost its sense of Heavenly glory.

Medieval imagery (which is almost totally biblical imagery) of light, jewels, stars, candles, trumpets, and angels no longer fits our ranch-style, supermarket world. Pathetic modern substitutes of fluffy clouds, sexless cherubs, harps and metal halos (not halos of *light*) presided over by a stuffy divine Chairman of the Bored are a joke, not a glory. Even more modern, more up-to-date substitutes—Heaven as a comfortable feeling of peace and kindness, sweetness and light, and God as a vague grandfatherly benevolence, a senile philanthropist—are even more insipid.

Our pictures of Heaven simply do not move us; they are not moving pictures. It is this aesthetic failure rather than intellectual or moral failures in our pictures of Heaven and of God that threatens faith most potently today.[9] Our pictures of Heaven are dull, platitudinous and syrupy; therefore, so is our faith, our hope, and our love of Heaven.

It is surely a Satanic triumph of the first order to have taken the fascination out of a doctrine that must be either a fascinating lie or a fascinating fact. Even if people think of Heaven

---

[9] Alan Watts, *Behold the Spirit* (New York: Vintage, 1971), p. 154.

as a fascinating lie, they are at least fascinated with it, and that can spur further thinking, which can lead to belief. But if it's dull, it doesn't matter whether it's a dull lie or a dull truth. Dullness, not doubt, is the strongest enemy of faith, just as indifference, not hate, is the strongest enemy of love.[10]

It is Heaven and Hell that put bite into the Christian vision of life on earth, just as playing for high stakes puts bite into a game or a war or a courtship. Hell is part of the vision too: the height of the mountain is appreciated from the depth of the valley, and for winning to be high drama, losing must be possible. For salvation to be "good news", there must be "bad news" to be saved from. If all of life's roads lead to the same place, it makes no ultimate difference which road we choose. But if they lead to opposite places, to infinite bliss or infinite misery, unimaginable glory or unimaginable tragedy, if the spirit has roads as really and objectively different as the body's roads and the mind's roads, and if these roads lead to destinations as really and objectively different as two different cities or two different mathematical conclusions—why, then life is a life-or-death affair, a razor's edge, and our choice of roads is infinitely important.

We no longer live habitually in this medieval mental landscape. If we are typically modern, we live in ennui; we are bored, jaded, cynical, flat, and burnt out. When the skies roll back like a scroll and the angelic trump sounds, many will simply yawn and say, "Pretty good special effects, but the plot's too traditional." If we were not so bored and empty, we would not have to stimulate ourselves with increasing dosages of sex and violence—or just constant busyness.[11] Here we are in the most fantastic fun and games factory ever invented—modern technological society—and we are bored, like a spoiled rich kid in a mansion surrounded by a thousand

[10] Rollo May, *Love and Will* (New York: Norton, 1969).
[11] Pascal, *Pensées*, trans. Krailsheimer (New York: Penguin Books, 1985), pp. 132–39.

expensive toys. Medieval people by comparison were like peasants in toyless hovels—and they were fascinated. Occasions for awe and wonder seemed to abound: birth and death and love and light and darkness and wind and sea and fire and sunrise and star and tree and bird and human mind—and God and Heaven. But all these things have not changed, we have. The universe has not become empty and we, full; it has remained full and we have become empty, insensitive to its fullness, cold hearted.[12]

Yet even in this cold heart a strange fire kindles at times—something from another dimension, another *kind* of excitement—when we dare to open the issue of Heaven, the issue of meeting God, with the mind and heart together. Like Ezekiel in the valley of dry bones,[13] we experience the shock of the dead coming to life.

> You have had a shock like that before, in connection with smaller matters—when the line pulls at your hand, when something breathes beside you in the darkness. So here; the shock comes at the precise moment when the thrill of *life* is communicated to us along the clue we have been following. It is always shocking to meet life where we thought we were alone. "Look out!" we cry, "It's *alive!*" And therefore this is the very point at which so many draw back—I would have done so myself if I could—and proceed no further with Christianity. An "impersonal God"—well and good. A subjective God of beauty, truth and goodness inside our own heads—better still. A formless life-force surging through us, a vast power that we can tap—best of all. But God Himself, alive, pulling at the other end of the cord, perhaps approaching at an infinite speed, the hunter, king, husband—that is quite another matter. There comes a moment when the children who have been playing at burglars hush suddenly: was that a *real* footstep in the hall? There comes a moment when people who have been dabbling

---

[12] C. S. Evans, *Despair* (Downers Grove, Ill.: InterVarsity Press, 1971), p. 12.

[13] Ezekiel 37.

in religion ("Man's search for God"!) suddenly draw back.
Supposing we really found Him? We never meant it to come
to *that*![14]

When it does come to that, we feel a strange burning in the
heart, like the disciples on the road to Emmaeus.[15] Ancient,
sleeping hopes and fears rise like giants from their graves.
The horizons of our comfortable little four-dimensional universe crack, and over them arises an enormous bliss and its
equally enormous absence. Heaven and Hell—suppose, just
suppose it were really, really true! What difference would that
make?

I think we know.

Heaven: Realism or Escapism?

But the question of Heaven is more than this. It is not just a
question about the difference it makes to *us*, a question about
our desire, *our* hopes, *our* future. It is a realistic question, a
question above objective reality. It is the question: How big
is reality?

That is the primary question. *My* greatness depends on
reality's greatness. If reality does not extend to Heaven, I cannot either. Even if I am a small fish, I am greater if I am a
small fish in a big reality-pond than if I am a big fish in a
small reality-pond. That is why C. S. Lewis makes the surprising judgment that "it is more important that heaven should
exist than that any of us should reach it".[16]

To see what difference Heaven makes in this "realistic"
way, to see what Heaven means to reality, take the sum total
of all past and present human experience, the entire universe,
all of space and time and history and matter and mind—every-

---

[14] C. S. Lewis, *Miracles* (New York: Macmillan, 1955), pp. 113–14.
[15] Luke 24:32.
[16] C. S. Lewis, *Surprised by Joy* (New York: Harcourt, Brace & World,
1955), p. 211.

thing anyone has ever experienced. Add to it all future possibilities that we or any other creatures can or may experience on earth or in space or on other planets for billions of years to come until all the stars grow cold. Add an infinite number of evolutionary cycles, big bangs, and new universes if you like. Let us call this quantity of reality X. It is a partially unknown quantity but also partially known. Now let us ask of X: *Is that all there is?* Heaven is the negative answer to that question. There is more.

Our spontaneous reaction to this prophetic announcement should be an ecstatic "Bravo!" Our deepest need is for reality, for more and ever more reality. The ontological thirst, the thirst for being, is our deepest thirst.[17] In every desire, even for truth and goodness and beauty, we desire being; we desire that the object be real. Self-generated fantasies satisfy only imaginary needs.[18] Our spirit, unlike God, is not independent and self-contained; it cannot feed upon itself or fecundate itself or actualize itself. We need reality as our spirit-food. We eat reality. Knowing is a kind of eating: a spiritual assimilation.[19]

Eventually, if only at death, we must meet reality face to face. So we had better begin rehearsing now. If Heaven is not real, every honest person will disbelieve in it simply for that reason, however desirable it is, and if it *is* real, every honest man, woman, child, scientist, theologian, saint, and sinner will want to believe in it simply because it is real, not just because it is desirable.[20] Our deepest desire is not for the desirable but for the real—if we are honest.

---

[17] Mircea Eliade, *The Sacred and the Profane*, trans. Willard Trask (New York: Harcourt, Brace, 1959), introduction. Cf. also *Myth and Reality*, trans. Willard Trask (New York: Harper & Row, 1963).

[18] Cf. Frank J. Sheed, foreword to *The Confessions of St. Augustine* (Kansas City, Mo.: Sheed, Andrews & McMeel, 1970), p. vii.

[19] Nicolas of Cusa, *De Docta Ignorantia*, III, ix.

[20] C. S. Lewis, "Man or Rabbit?" in *God in the Dock* (Grand Rapids, Mich.: Eerdmans, 1970), pp. 108–13; *The Great Divorce* (New York: Macmillan, 1975), chap. 5; *The Screwtape Letters* (New York: Macmillan, 1957), pp. 11–12, 50–52, 120.

The question of Heaven, then, is a realistic question, not an escapist question. Anyone can misuse the idea of Heaven as an escape from the reality of earth. But that is a misuse, not a proper use, and misuse presupposes use, as counterfeit money presupposes real money. In another book (*Heaven: The Heart's Deepest Longing*, especially chapter 5, "What Difference Does Heaven Make to Monday Morning?") I tried at some length to prove the point that Heaven is not escapist; let us consider here only the apotheosis of the attitude of escapism: suicide. If Heaven exists and is so great, why not escape earth right away and get there as quickly as possible?

Escapism and Suicide

First of all because you don't get there that way. The God who revealed Heaven also forbade suicide, and *all* the medically dead and resuscitated patients who had committed suicide and had seen something of the next life reported hellish rather than Heavenly experiences.[21] They saw that suicide was a disastrous mistake, that all the problems they had tried to escape followed them, but after death they could no longer do anything to change them.

This does not mean that we may not hope for the salvation of a suicide. In *Descent into Hell* Williams showed how a suicide may eventually attain salvation.[22] But it means that his or her salvation is always despite, never because of, the suicide. Suicide is not the road to Heaven.

God forbade suicide for a good reason: it would be like deserting our post, as Socrates put it.[23] Or, to vary the

[21] Raymond Moody, *Reflections on Life after Death* (New York: Bantam, 1977), pp. 18–22; Maurice Rawlings, M.D., *Beyond Death's Door* (New York: Bantam, 1979), pp. 85–104.

[22] Charles Williams, *Descent into Hell* (Grand Rapids, Mich.: Eerdmans, 1949).

[23] Plato, *Phaedo*, 61c–62d.

metaphor, it would be like trying to get into college from elementary school by burning down the high school. The reason against suicide is the same as the reason against skipping grades in school. It is not an external, arbitrary command from God but an internal, necessary law of our nature. That is why God gave us the powerful "first instinct of nature", self-preservation: to keep us in school, to keep us from being dropouts. What can be learned here, must be learned here.

What we learn here, what we do here, is freely to create in time the baseline of our eternal identities. We shape our souls here, and the dimension of eternity is added to that shape in Heaven. It is as if earthly squares become heavenly cubes; earthly triangles, heavenly pyramids; earthly circles, heavenly spheres. The shape into which we shape ourselves now is the shape of our eternal selves; only the size (that is, the dimension) is changed.

That is why Heaven is not a distraction from earth and why the point of this book about Heaven is not escape from living here and now but is precisely *how* to live here and now. For these two dimensions of our identity, time and eternity, earth and Heaven, are not an either-or but a both-and, like the two natures of Christ.

The natural tendency of uncorrected thinking is to separate: divine *or* human, heavenly *or* earthly, eternal *or* temporal. Thus originated the twin ancient heresies of Docetism and Arianism (still very much alive under many different names), which first separated the two natures of Christ, then affirmed one at the expense of the other. For Docetism, Christ was rather like Clark Kent: a Superman only disguised as a man, human only in appearance (*doceo*).[24] For Arianism, Christ was like Buddha, merely a perfect man with godlike thoughts.[25]

[24] Robert Farrar Capon, *Hunting the Divine Fox* (New York: Seabury, 1975), pp. 90–91.

[25] For a Socratic dialogue attempting to refute this very old and very current heresy, cf. Peter Kreeft, *Between Heaven and Hell* (Downers Grove, Ill.: InterVarsity Press, 1982).

The same two heresies pull apart the Bible, which, like Christ, is "the Word of God in the words of men".[26] Fundamentalism is like Docetism: it tends to overlook the human and to see the Bible as miraculously dictated by God word for word. Modernism is like Arianism: it overlooks the divine and reduces God's word about us to our words about God. The origin of both is the same: separating the divine and the human, Heaven and earth, forgetting that in the Bible, as in Christ, the human becomes divinized by the divine becoming humanized. In Christ, Heaven is not escapism and earth is not worldliness. For Christ brings the Kingdom of Heaven to earth. More, He *is* the Kingdom of Heaven.

[26] Ralph Martin, *Reading Scripture as the Word of God* (Ann Arbor, Mich.: Servant Publications, 1969).

Chapter Two

Fourteen Questions about Heaven

1. *Will We Know Everything in Heaven?*

Of course not. Why would someone think that? There are two reasons, and the first one is simply a confusion between Heaven and divinity. We will remain human in Heaven, therefore finite, therefore our knowledge will remain finite. True, we will share in divine life, but this is just a *share*. In fact, we share in divine life now, if we are reborn in Christ; our souls nurture a fetal Christ. But I have not observed that fact generating omniscience in myself or any other.

When you come to think of it, knowing everything would be more like Hell than Heaven for us. For one thing, we need progress and hope: we need to look forward to knowing something new tomorrow. Mystery is our mind's food. If we truly said, "I have seen everything",[1] we would conclude, as did the author of Ecclesiastes, "all is vanity".[2] For another thing, the more knowledge, the more responsibility.[3] Only omnipotence can bear the burden of omniscience; only God's shoulders are strong enough to carry the burden of infinite knowledge without losing the joy.

[1] Ecclesiastes 1:14.
[2] Ecclesiastes 12:8.
[3] James 3:1; Luke 12:48.

The second reason we may think our heavenly knowledge is infinite is the theory that on earth we have already an access, a potency, for all knowledge; that the brain is a "reducing valve", not a generator.[4] Perhaps the Fall lowered the curtain between us and all truth, which we now see "through a glass, darkly";[5] and in Heaven the curtain will rise again. Thus, the knowledge we now have is both a memory[6] and a prophecy of Paradise.

But even if this theory is true it does not entail our omniscience. Even if there is no curtain in Heaven, even if our consciousness there dashes against no wall or limit, still we remain like the tiny figures in a Chinese landscape: small subjects in an enormously larger objective world. Even if we then escape from the tiny hut in which we are now imprisoned and through whose smudged windows or chinks in whose walls we now must look—even if we wander freely in the country of light—we are in the light, not the light in us. Our first and last wisdom in Heaven is Socratic, just as it is on earth: to know how little we know. If there is no end of the need for humility in the moral order (the saint is the one humble enough not to think he is a saint), the same is true of the intellectual order (the wise man is the one humble enough to know he has no wisdom). It all depends on the standard of judgment: by earthly standards most of us are moderately saintly and moderately wise; by Heavenly standards all of us, even in Heaven, are children. And by the standard of the *infinite*, inexhaustible perfection of God, we remain children forever. Happy children, fulfilled children, but children.

[4] William James, *The Varieties of Religious Experience* (New York: New American Library, 1959), p. 324; Aldous Huxley, *The Doors of Perception* (New York: Harper & Row, 1963), pp. 22–24.

[5] 1 Corinthians 13:12 (KJV).

[6] Pascal, *Pensées*, trans. Krailsheimer (New York: Penguin Books, 1985), 117, 131.

Perhaps this will be one of the supreme tests: would we choose the childlikeness of Heaven or the promise of "maturity", of "humanity come of age" in Hell? Will we suffer gladly the blow and shock to our pride that is Heaven's gift of eternal childhood (thus eternal hope and progress) or will we insist on the "successes" of "self-actualization" that Heaven denies us and Hell offers us? If the latter, we will find despair instead of hope, ennui instead of creative work, and the emptying out of all our joy. Jesus' teaching, "Unless you turn and become like children, you will never enter the kingdom of heaven",[7] is not something to be outgrown. Saint Bernard of Clairvaux, when asked which are the four most important virtues, replied, "Humility, humility, humility, and humility."[8] It is only the foolish egotist who thinks that our smallness relative to the infinite riches of objective reality is a problem to be overcome.

2. Will We All Be Equal in Heaven?

By God's grace, no! How awful *that* would be—almost as awful as knowing everything. Having no heroes,[9] being unable to look up to anyone, would be Hell, not Heaven.

We modern egalitarians are tempted to the primal sin of pride in the opposite way from the ancients. The old, aristocratic form of pride was the desire to be better than others. The new, democratic form is the desire not to have anyone better than yourself.[10] It is just as spiritually deadly and does not even carry with it the false pleasure of gloating superiority. Flat, boring, repetitive sameness is simply not the structure

---

[7] Matthew 18:3.

[8] *De gradibus humilitatis*, I, 1.

[9] Ernest Becker, *The Denial of Death* (New York: Macmillan, Free Press, 1973).

[10] C. S. Lewis, "Screwtape Proposes a Toast" in *The Screwtape Letters and Screwtape Proposes a Toast* (New York: Macmillan, 1961).

of reality in a theistic universe,[11] either on earth or in Heaven.

However, in Heaven, as on earth, *each* of us will be or do something no one else will be or do as well. No one will be superfluous.

> If He had no use for all these differences, I do not see why He should have created more souls than one. . . . Your soul has a curious shape because it is a hollow made to fit a particular swelling in the infinite contours of the divine substance, or a key to unlock one of the doors in the house with many mansions . . . each of the redeemed shall forever know and praise some one aspect of the divine beauty better than any other creature can.[12]

God's justice is not ours. It surprises ours in a double way. On the one hand, the one-hour workers receive the same pay as the all-day workers, in Christ's parable.[13] "He has put down the mighty from their thrones, and exalted those of low degree; he has filled the hungry with good things and the rich he has sent empty away."[14] "Every valley shall be exalted, and every mountain and hill shall be made low."[15] But on the other hand, to him who already has, more will be given, and "from him who has not, even what he has will be taken away".[16] Human justice is outraged by both halves of Christ's paradoxical justice.

Justice does not mean equality. In a poem, in the universe, in mathematics, in architecture—everywhere there is natural justice, justice means inequality, yin and yang, male and female, higher and lower, East and West, light and darkness, land and water. No flat, dull repetition but uniqueness. In human relationships too, justice does not mean equality, but

---

[11] C. S. Lewis, *Miracles* (New York: Macmillan, 1955), pp. 18, 140–42.
[12] C. S. Lewis, *The Problem of Pain* (New York: Macmillan, 1962), p. 147.
[13] Matthew 20:1–16.
[14] Luke 1:52–53.
[15] Isaiah 40:4 (KJV).
[16] Matthew 13:12.

treating equals equally *and unequals unequally*.[17] Is it just to treat a pig like a man? If so, it is also just to treat a man like a pig. One of the astonishing blind spots of modernity is its unquestioning fixation on equality.

Of course there are degrees of perfection in Heaven; it is quite the divine style. There are degrees of perfection in everything God created (though not in everything we create). Equality is a man-made legal fiction designed as a wall of defense against tyranny, a medicine against a disease.

> "We must all be guarded by equal rights from one another's greed, because we are fallen. Just as we must all wear clothes for the same reason. But the naked body should be there underneath the clothes, ripening for the day when we shall need them no longer. Equality is not the deepest thing, you know."
>
> "I always thought that was just what it was. I thought it was in their souls that people were equal."
>
> "You were mistaken. . . . That is the last place where they are equal. Equality before the law, equality of incomes—that is all very well. Equality guards life; it doesn't make it. It is medicine, not food . . ."
>
> "But surely in marriage . . . ?"
>
> "Worse and worse. . . . Courtship knows nothing of it; nor does fruition. . . . It is not your fault. They never warned you. No one has ever told you that obedience—humility—is an erotic necessity."[18]

Why is there no jealousy in this hierarchical, aristocratic, nonegalitarian Heaven of authority and obedience? Because all are cells in the same body. The kidney does not rebel because it is not the eye.[19] Jealousy is the principle of Hell. There is no Hell in Heaven.

[17] St. Thomas Aquinas, *Summa contra Gentiles*, III, 142, 2.
[18] C. S. Lewis, *That Hideous Strength* (New York: Macmillan, 1965), p. 148.
[19] I Corinthians 12:14–26.

3. Do the Blessed in Heaven See Us Now?

The living often say they feel the dead present and watching them. Is this illusion or fact?

It is fact. The Bible says we are surrounded by "a great cloud of witnesses".[20] The context is speaking of the dead. They are alive. For God is "not God of the dead, but of the living; for all live to him".[21]

Reason confirms revelation here. Does their love for us cease? Does it not rather increase in purity and power? And do not their vision and understanding also increase?

"The Communion of Saints" means not only (1) love and understanding among the blessed in Heaven and (2) love and understanding among the redeemed on earth but also (3) love and understanding between those two groups, the Church Militant and the Church Triumphant, temporarily separated by death.[22]

What difference does this make? Well, what difference does it make to you if you believe you are being watched by a thousand living human eyes? Multiply this consequence by millions and by the increase in love and understanding in Heaven. Throw in literally innumerable angels,[23] all of them sharing mightily in God's love and knowledge. Then you have the difference it makes: the exponent of infinity.

The link connecting the Church Militant with the Church Triumphant, the link connecting Heaven and earth, is the incarnate Christ. We participate in what Christ does, and Christ links Heaven and earth. He is still on earth as well as in Heaven (1) by His Spirit and (2) in His Mystical Body, the Church, His people. Christianity does not worship an absent Christ. And just as He can be on earth even when He has

---

[20] Hebrews 12:1.

[21] Luke 20:38.

[22] The Catholic Encyclopedia, vol. IV, p. 171.

[23] Hebrews 12:22; St. Thomas Aquinas, Summa Theologiae, I, 50, 3.

gone to Heaven, so can we—in Him. The cells in the one Body are all living cells, but only a very few of them are living on earth.

4. Do Ghosts Come from Heaven?

First of all, Scripture strictly forbids us to call them up[24] as Saul called up the ghost of the prophet Samuel by means of the Witch of Endor's necromancy. Because of this deed, he lost his kingdom and perhaps his soul.[25]

The reason for the stricture is probably protection against the danger of deception by evil spirits. We are out of our depth, our knowledge, and our control once we open the doors to the supernatural. The only openings that are safe for us are the ones God has approved: revelation, prayer, His own miracles, sacraments, and primarily Christ Himself. He has made a straight and safe road for us from earth to Heaven, through the dark woods of the innumerable, unknowable, and unpredictable spiritual forces that are to us as fire to an infant or a juggernaut to an ant. The danger is not physical but spiritual, and spiritual danger always centers on deception. The Devil is "a liar and the father of lies".[26] He disguises himself "as an angel of light".[27]

Nevertheless, without our action or invitation, the dead often *do* appear to the living. There is enormous evidence of "ghosts" in all cultures. What are we to make of them? Surely we should not classify the appearances of the wives of C. S. Lewis and Sheldon Vanauken, just to take two Christian examples, as demonic?

We can distinguish three kinds of ghosts, I believe. First, the most familiar kind: the sad ones, the wispy ones. They

---

[24] Deuteronomy 18:10–11; Isaiah 8:19.
[25] 1 Samuel 28.
[26] John 8:44.
[27] 2 Corinthians 11:14.

seem to be working out some unfinished earthly business, or suffering some purgatorial purification until released from their earthly business.[28] These ghosts would seem to be the ones who just barely made it to Purgatory, who feel little or no joy yet and who need to learn many painful lessons about their past lives on earth.

Second, there are malicious and deceptive spirits—and since they *are* deceptive, they hardly ever *appear* malicious. These are probably the ones who respond to conjurings at seances. They probably come from Hell. Even the *chance* of that happening should be sufficient to terrify away all temptation to necromancy.

Third, there are the bright, happy spirits of dead friends and family, especially spouses, who appear unbidden, at God's will, not ours, with messages of hope and love. They seem to come from Heaven. Unlike the purgatorial ghosts who come back primarily for their own sakes, these bright spirits come back for the sake of us the living, to tell us all is well. They are aped by evil spirits who say the same, who speak "peace, peace, when there is no peace".[29] But deception works only one way: the fake can deceive by appearing genuine, but the genuine never deceives by appearing fake. Heavenly spirits always convince us that they are genuinely good. Even the bright spirits appear ghostlike to us because a ghost of any type is one whose substance does not belong in or come from this world. In Heaven these spirits are not ghosts but real, solid, and substantial because they are at home there. "One can't be a ghost in one's own country."[30]

That there are all three kinds of ghosts is enormously likely. Even taking into account our penchant to deceive and to be deceived, our credulity and our fakery, there remain so many trustworthy accounts of all three types of ghosts—trustworthy

[28] Shakespeare, *Hamlet*, act I, scene 5, lines 9–22.

[29] Jeremiah 6:14; 8:11.

[30] C. S. Lewis, *The Silver Chair* (New York: Macmillan, 1953), p. 205.

by every ordinary empirical and psychological standard—that only a dogmatic a priori prejudice against them could prevent us from believing they exist.[31] As Chesterton says, "We believe an old apple-woman when she says she ate an apple; but when she says she saw a ghost we say, 'But she's only an old apple-woman.'"[32] A most undemocratic and unscientific prejudice.

5. Will We Have Emotions in Heaven?

Emotions move us; we do not move them. They are a form of passivity. We will be far more active in Heaven than we ever were before, since our spirits (which are activity) will rule rather than being ruled by our bodies (which are passivity). Nevertheless, we will *have* bodies, therefore passivity, therefore emotions, though they will not be at the unfree whim of heredity, environment, animal instinct, propaganda, others' demands, and the many other forces that presently condition us.

Even when our spirits are perfectly free, they can feel. Even now, it is the spirit that feels, not just the body. It is a prejudice imported from Greek philosophy, not a notion found in Scripture, that feelings should be dominated by rational thought. The center of the self, which the Greeks located in reason,[33] Scripture locates in the "heart", that which loves. This center is no more a *feeling* than it is *thinking*; it is the prefunctional root of both,[34] or it is a deeper feeling and a deeper thinking: "the heart has its reasons which the reason does not know".[35]

But since our thinking and our feeling are equal functions

---

[31] C. S. Lewis, *Miracles*, chap. 1.

[32] G. K. Chesterton, *Orthodoxy* (New York: Dodd, Mead, 1946), p. 279.

[33] Aristotle, *Nicomachean Ethics*, X, 7.

[34] Hermann Dooyeweerd, *A New Critique of Theoretical Thought*, trans. David Freeman (Phillipsburg, N.J.: Presbyterian & Reformed Publishing Co., 1953). Cf. Proverbs 23:7; 4:23.

[35] Pascal, *Pensées* (trans. Krailsheimer), 423.

of the heart, we will retain our feeling in Heaven just as we will retain our thinking. All our humanity is perfected, not diminished, in Heaven.

6. Will We Feel Sorrow in Heaven for Those in Hell?

We seem to face a dilemma here. On the one hand, Scripture assures us that "God shall wipe away all tears from their eyes; and there shall be no more death, neither sorrow, nor crying, neither shall there be any more pain: for the former things are passed away".[36]

On the other hand, the blessed dead seem sometimes to manifest sorrow, like Mary at LaSallette, weeping for the sins of the world.[37] And C. S. Lewis says, "as there may be pleasures in Hell (God shield us from them), there may be something not all unlike pains in Heaven (God grant us soon to taste them)."[38] What could this mean?

Might it be that the sorrow appears only during our first, purgatorial stage? At this point the pains of separation may affect not only the earthly bereaved lover but also the heavenly beloved. As Lewis says, "I can't help suspecting the dead also feel the pains of separation (and this may be one of their purgatorial sufferings)."[39] But this would not explain the tears of Mary, who is certainly beyond Purgatory.

Might it be that the sorrow is only an appearance, like angels' bodies, put on for our sake? But the purpose of appearance should be to teach, not to deceive, if the appearance comes from Heaven.

To solve this problem let us look at the greatest suffering, that which is made possible by love. The more you love, the

[36] Revelation 21:4 (KJV).

[37] A Woman Clothed with the Sun, ed. John J. Delaney (Garden City, N.Y.: Doubleday, 1961).

[38] C. S. Lewis, The Problem of Pain, p. 152.

[39] C. S. Lewis, A Grief Observed (New York: Bantam, 1976), p. 64.

more you can suffer. That fact creates the following problem: Does God the Father suffer? The affirmative answer to that question has been declared a heresy (Patripassianism);[40] yet how can God love us, and remain aloof and invulnerable? As Kierkegaard says, the unhappiness that comes from the inability of lovers to understand each other is

> infinitely more profound than that [unhappiness] of which men commonly speak, since it strikes at the very heart of love. . . . This infinitely deeper grief is essentially the prerogative of the superior . . . in reality, it belongs to God alone. . . . Men sometimes think that this might be a matter of indifference to God, since he does not stand in need of the learner [us]. But in this we forget—or rather, alas! we prove how far we are from understanding him; we forget that God loves the learner.[41]

The dilemma, then, is this: If God cannot suffer, how can He really love us? But if He can suffer, how is He God? To answer this question would also be to answer the question of whether and how we can suffer in Heaven, for Heavenly children resemble their Heavenly Father.

The answer requires us to distinguish between two ingredients of earthly love and caring, an active and a passive ingredient, that are together in fact but distinguishable in thought. Say a parent loves a child who has done something harmful to himself. The parent's love speaks two words to the child. The first word, the word of active caring for the other, says, "How could you do this to yourself?" The second word, the word of passivity and vulnerability, says, "How could you do this to me?" God loves us with the first love only, and the blessed in Heaven will love as God loves. We

[40] *The Catholic Encyclopedia* (1921), vol. X, p. 449. Cf. Helen Waddell, *Peter Abelard* (New York: Viking, 1959), p. 265.

[41] Søren Kierkegaard, *Philosophical Fragments*, chap. 2 in *A Kierkegaard Anthology*, ed. Robert Bretall (New York: Modern Library, 1946), pp. 164, 166.

cannot blackmail God. We cannot make Him wring His hands by holding our breath until we turn blue in the face.[42] He truly loves and cares, yet He is invulnerable—not by being aloof but by being supremely active, not passive.[43]

If our spirits are similar enough to God, we too can love without sorrow or vulnerability because we love only with the active feeling of caring, not the passive feeling of being hurt. For our spirits then are not controlled by our bodies, by heredity and environment. C. S. Lewis' experience of his dead wife's presence and love was like that:

> It was quite incredibly unemotional. . . . Yet there was an extreme and cheerful intimacy. An intimacy that had not passed through the senses or the emotions at all. . . . Can that intimacy be love itself—always in this life attended with emotion, not because it is itself an emotion, or needs an attendant emotion, but because our animal souls, our nervous systems, our imaginations, have to respond to it in that way? If so, how many preconceptions I must scrap! A society, a communion, of pure intelligences would not be cold, drab and comfortless. . . . It would, if I have had a glimpse, be—well, I'm almost scared at the adjectives I'd have to use. Brisk? cheerful? keen? alert? intense? wide-awake? Above all, solid. Utterly reliable. Firm. There is no nonsense about the dead.
>
> When I say "intellect" I include will. Attention is an act of will. Intelligence in action is will *par excellence*. What met me was full of resolution.[44]

Yet on the other side of the dilemma, will Heaven lack the greatest of all beauties of earthly art, the beauty of sorrow, of great tragedy? Nothing of value is simply lost in Heaven; all is preserved and transformed. Earthly indicators are to be read (though with caution) as pointers to Heavenly realities.

---

[42] C. S. Lewis, *The Great Divorce* (New York: Macmillan, 1975), p. 120.

[43] Ibid., p. 121: "The action of Pity will live forever; but the passion of Pity will not." See St. Thomas Aquinas, *Summa Theologiae*, I, 3, 1; *Summa contra Gentiles*, I, 16, 5, on God as purely active.

[44] C. S. Lewis, *A Grief Observed*, pp. 85–88.

And on earth, pain and pleasure are strangely akin at their peak, like death and life. When a thing is enormously beautiful, it hurts. What Heavenly fact is imaged in this earthly mystery?

Perhaps the ultimate fact of all, the nature of God, the inner life of the Trinity as a system of self-dying, self-giving.[45] Perhaps this is the deepest reason of all for pain on earth, and the solution to the "problem of evil": Why does a good and loving God allow so much earthly suffering? To train us for Heaven's joyful suffering and to enact, to incarnate, to manifest the ultimate law of reality on our human level: the law of death and life, blessed self-death (no longer blessed for fallen creatures) leading to eternal life. "All pains and pleasures we have known on earth are early initiations in the movements of that dance."[46] This is the supreme joy in all existence, the joy of God's inner life of self-giving, the secret forever incomprehensible to the rebel, angelic or human, who says "Better to reign in Hell than serve in Heaven".[47]

7. Will We Be Free to Sin in Heaven?

Here is another dilemma. If we answer no, we seem to lack something: free will. If we answer yes, we lack something else: moral perfection. The Heavenly question thus lands us squarely into an earthly and present issue concerning the nature of freedom and of morality and may help us to puncture one of modernity's most pervasive and destructive illusions: the association of freedom with rebellion and of obedience with unfreedom.

Suppose we change the question so as to avoid the ambiguity of the word *freedom*. Are we able to sin in Heaven? If not, it seems we are programmed and determined rather than free. If so, if temptation is possible in Heaven, Heavenly security

[45] C. S. Lewis, *The Problem of Pain*, p. 152.
[46] Ibid., p. 153.
[47] Milton, *Paradise Lost*, book I, line 262.

against sin is gone. One of the best things to look forward to at death, say the saints,[48] is that "he who has died is freed from sin".[49] If there is even a possibility of sin in Heaven, that possibility may be actualized, for if the actualization of a possibility is impossible, then it is not a possibility but an impossibility.

How can we preserve both free will and sinlessness in Heaven? Once again, God is our model and solution: we solve this pseudoproblem in the same way God does. He is both free and sinless. How? Let us judge our freedom by His, rather than vice versa.

What do we mean by "freedom"? Sometimes (1) *political* freedom, freedom from tyranny, oppression, or the denial of our rights; sometimes (2) *physical* power, ability to act, freedom from hindrance; and sometimes (3) *spiritual* power to choose ("free will"). Of course we will have all three in Heaven, but why won't we be able to sin, since we will have free will?

Because we will also have a fourth freedom, the most important one of all: freedom from sin, from what makes us not ourselves. We will be free to be the true selves God designed us to be, free to be determined by God. This determination does not remove our freedom but *is* our freedom, for even now freedom is not simply indetermination; it is freedom to be determined by final causes (purposes) rather than efficient causes (things and events that already exist and act upon us). Our free will means that our present is determined by our future rather than by our past. Final causes are at present only mental pictures and desires. To say we are determined by final causes means that we, like God, create by knowing; that as creative artists our knowledge antecedes and determines the truth of its object, the work of art, rather than conforming to

---

[48] St. Alfonso Liguori, *Preparations for Death*, ed. Rev. Eugene Grimm (Baltimore, Md.: John Murphy & Co., 1926).

[49] Romans 6:7.

its object, as scientific and empirical knowledge does. But we are objects to God (though subjects to the world); we too, therefore, are true only when we conform to God's knowledge of us, God's artistic plan for our identity. Since our highest freedom means freedom to be ourselves, we are most free when we are most obedient to God's will, which expresses His idea of us. Thus freedom and obedience coincide. To obey God is to be free in the most radical sense: free to be me, free from inauthenticity, free from false *being*, free from the alien within, not just free from the alien without, the oppressor.

This explains a paradox frequently met in earthly experience: that at the moment of freest choice it feels most like destiny, and at the moment of most destined choice it feels freest. Caesar's crossing the Rubicon, choosing someone to marry, a conversion decision—these all feel *both* more free *and* more destined than ordinary choices. C. S. Lewis' explanation of this principle is that it is all of us that chooses; nothing is left over.[50] Therefore there is nothing in us that opposes the choice; it is certain; it is wholly determined. But it is also wholly free because it is wholly *self*-determined. The whole self chooses, the divided will[51] is healed.

The answer to our question, then, is that "freedom to sin" is a self-contradictory concept. Sin is inauthenticity and freedom is authenticity; sin is our false self and freedom is our true self. Sin is part of Hell and freedom is part of Heaven. The question cannot be resolved, only *dis*solved, because it confuses Hell with Heaven.

8. *What Will We Possess in Heaven?*

Nothing and everything. Saint Francis of Assisi and others devoted to poverty understand this paradox. Saint Paul speaks

---

[50] C. S. Lewis, *Surprised by Joy* (New York: Harcourt, Brace & World, 1955), pp. 229, 237.
[51] St. Augustine, *Confessions*, VIII, 8–9.

of "having nothing, and yet possessing all things"[52] because possessed by God: "all [things] are yours; and you are Christ's; and Christ is God's."[53]

Heaven is pure communism. There is no private property in Heaven. (Earthly communism, even when not atheistic, is another "too-soon" mistake of Utopianism.) "In Heaven there is no ownership. If any there took upon him to call anything his own, he would straightway be thrust out into hell and become an evil spirit."[54] For the ultimate possession is the self, and if even that is given away, nothing else can be held (because there is no *holder*); and that *is* given away:

> The golden apple of selfhood, thrown among the false gods, became an apple of discord because they scrambled for it. They did not know the first rule of the holy game, which is that every player must by all means touch the ball and then immediately pass it on. To be found with it in your hands is a fault; to cling to it, death. But when it flies to and fro among the players too swift for eye to follow, and the great master Himself leads the revelry, giving Himself eternally to His creatures in the generation, and back to Himself in the sacrifice, of the Word, then indeed the eternal dance "makes heaven drowsy with the harmony."[55]

As MacDonald says, "the heart cannot hoard",[56] only the hand. As Marcel says, the true self cannot possess or have anything because I do not *have* my own body as my body *has* things: I *am* my body.[57]

[52] 2 Corinthians 6:10 (KJV).

[53] 1 Corinthians 3:21, 23.

[54] *Theologia Germanica*, LI.

[55] C. S. Lewis, *The Problem of Pain*, p. 153.

[56] George MacDonald in C. S. Lewis, ed., *George MacDonald: An Anthology* (New York: Macmillan, 1978), p. 119 (no. 287).

[57] Gabriel Marcel, *Being and Having*, trans. Katherine Farrer (Boston: Beacon Press, 1951), pp. 137, 237.

No one can possess goodness, truth, beauty, love, life, light, God. But Heaven *is* these things. Therefore no one can possess Heaven. Whenever, even now, we think of truth or goodness as something we *have* we become self-righteous, narrow, and defensive. To *have* truth is to be dogmatic; to *have* goodness is to be proud; to *have* beauty is to be vain; to *have* joy is to be miserable with fear of losing it. God, I AM, pure subject, is the only Haver. He cannot be had, nor can His attributes or His Kingdom of Heaven.

Thus, we must learn detachment to enter Heaven. Willy-nilly, death detaches us from everything, even ourselves. We must learn to "die before you die. There is no chance after." [58] Learning detachment from the world, which *can* be possessed, is our training for learning detachment from the desire to possess Heaven, which cannot be possessed. Asked whether he thought he would possess any of his beloved library books in Heaven, C. S. Lewis replied, "Only those I gave away on earth." [59]

9. *Will We Wear Clothes in Heaven?*

Those who claim to have caught glimpses of Heaven report a strange and surprising answer to this question; and the fact that so many have said the same surprising thing without previous acquaintance with each other lends weight to the testimony. They say that it is hard to classify the blessed as either clothed or naked. [60] If clothed, it is as if the clothing were a part of the body, an organic growth, rather than an accidental, foreign covering: it reveals rather than conceals,

[58] C. S. Lewis, *Till We Have Faces* (New York: Harcourt, Brace, 1957), p. 279.

[59] C. S. Lewis, *God in the Dock* (Grand Rapids, Mich.: Eerdmans, 1970), p. 216.

[60] C. S. Lewis, *The Great Divorce*, p. 107. Cf. Martin Ebon, *The Evidence for Life after Death* (New York: New American Library, 1971), p. 112.

and it is natural and necessary rather than artificial and accidental.[61] If naked, it is shameless and not arousing erotic desires. It is not the result of "naking",[62] the process of taking off the clothes that in our present state are natural, thus attaining a state of nudity that is (in our present state) *un*natural. (Nudist camps are *not* "natural".)

The principle behind the naturalness of Heavenly clothing is the overcoming of the distinction between appearance and reality. In Heaven, light reigns; we know and are known.[63] On earth, shadows reign, reality hides behind appearances as a mercy to fallen and weakened eyes.[64] We need the double-lensed sunglasses of reason and faith to know truth now; in Heaven we shall see the truth naked and direct. When reality appears and no longer hides, so will we.

The clothing of Heaven is described in Scripture as "white garments".[65] White is the color of light. Light reveals. On earth, clothes partly conceal and partly reveal, just as language does.[66] In Heaven all is revealed. "Nothing is hid that shall not be made manifest."[67]

Here, truth is *aletheia*, overcoming of *Lethe*: forgetfulness, appearance, concealment. So clothing hides the body, and the truth about the body is reached by unveiling, naking. In Heaven, the truth will be *in* the appearances (fully revealed, fully apparent), so the truth of the resurrection body will be revealed *in* its clothes. As the Son perfectly expresses the Father, clothes will express the body.

Our heavenly clothes may express our earthly story and success. Socrates will have his philosopher's robe. Heroes will

---

[61] C. S. Lewis, *That Hideous Strength*, pp. 360–64; *The Great Divorce*, p. 107.

[62] C. S. Lewis, *The Four Loves* (New York: Harcourt, Brace, 1957), p. 147.

[63] 1 Corinthians 13:12.

[64] St. Thomas Aquinas, *Summa Theologiae*, I, 1, 5 ad 1.

[65] Matthew 17:2; Revelation 3:5, 18; 7:9; 19:8.

[66] Martin Heidegger, *On the Way to Language*, trans. Hertz (New York: Harper & Row, 1971), p. 81.

[67] Luke 8:17.

wear the clothes associated with their heroism.[68] Jesus will wear His crown of thorns. Each thorn will be a diamond.

10. *Are There Animals in Heaven?*

The simplest answer is: Why not? How irrational is the prejudice that would allow plants (green fields and flowers) but not animals into Heaven![69] Much more reasonable is C. S. Lewis' speculation that we will be "between the angels who are our elder brothers and the beasts who are our jesters, servants, and playfellows".[70] Scripture seems to confirm this: "thy judgments are like the great deep; man and beast thou savest, O Lord".[71] Animals belong in the "new earth"[72] as much as trees.

C. S. Lewis supposes that animals are saved "in" their masters, as part of their extended family.[73] Only tamed animals would be saved in this way. It would seem more likely that wild animals are in Heaven too, since wildness, otherness, not-mine-ness, is a proper pleasure for us.[74] The very fact that the seagull takes no notice of me when it utters its remote, lonely call is part of its glory.

Would the same animals be in Heaven as on earth? "Is my dead cat in Heaven?" Again, why not? God can raise up the very grass;[75] why not cats? Though the blessed have better things to do than play with pets, the better does not exclude the lesser. We were meant from the beginning to have stewardship over the animals;[76] we have not fulfilled that

[68] Bruce Palmer, *Of Orc-Rags, Phials, and a Far Shore: Visions of Paradise in The Lord of the Rings* (Kansas City, Mo.: T-K Graphics, 1976), p. 25.

[69] St. Thomas Aquinas, *Summa Theologiae*, III (Supplement), 91, 5.

[70] C. S. Lewis, *That Hideous Strength*, p. 3/8.

[71] Psalm 36:6.

[72] Revelation 21:1.

[73] C. S. Lewis, *The Problem of Pain*, pp. 138–39.

[74] C. S. Lewis, *Miracles*, p. 78.

[75] Psalm 90:5–6. If we are "like grass", and we are raised, grass can be raised too.

[76] Genesis 1:28.

divine plan yet on earth; therefore it seems likely that the right relationship with animals will be part of Heaven: proper "pet-ship". And what better place to begin than with already petted pets?

11. *Is There Music in Heaven?*

First of all, the Bible says so.[77]

Secondly, great earthly music is particularly Heavenly, a sign or pointer beyond itself to Heaven. What was dimly suggested in all earthly music that moved us so much that the ancients necessarily ascribed it not to men but to gods[78]— goddesses, the nine Muses—is precisely Heavenly music. That is why we were moved here; it reminded us of There, which is our home.

Third, it may well be *in* music that the world was created,[79] and that music is the original language. Spoken poetry is to music what prose is to poetry.[80] Poetry is not ornamented prose, and music is not accompanied poetry. Prose is ossified poetry,[81] and poetry is half of music.

It is not that music is in Heaven; Heaven is in music. Heaven is "the region where there is only life, and therefore all that is not music is silence".[82] Heaven is both silent, like the contemplative mystic, and full of sound, like a dance or a symphony.

---

[77] Revelation 14:3.

[78] Plato, *Ion*, 533c–35c; Isadore of Seville, *Etymologiae*, bk. III, chap. 15.

[79] J. R. R. Tolkien, *The Silmarillion* (Boston: Houghton Mifflin, 1977), p. 25; C. S. Lewis, *The Magician's Nephew* (New York: Macmillan, 1955), chap. 9.

[80] Martin Heidegger, "Hölderlin and the Essence of Poetry" in *Existence and Being*, trans. Ralph Manheim (Chicago: Regnery, 1967), pp. 281, 283–84; "The Nature of Language", *On the Way to Language*.

[81] George MacDonald in C. S. Lewis, ed., *George MacDonald: An Anthology* (New York: Macmillan, 1978), p. 113.

[82] Ibid., p. 19.

12. *How Big Is Heaven?*

The very nature of space, and therefore of size, changes in Heaven. Meaning determines size, rather than size, meaning. The New Jerusalem's measures are symbolic, not physical.[83] Heaven is big enough so that billions of races of billions of saved people are never crowded, yet small enough so that no one gets lost or feels lonely. And we can travel anywhere in Heaven simply by will.[84]

13. *Is Heaven Serious or Funny?*

The very distinction is too funny to take seriously. The distinction between humor and seriousness is strictly earthly. Here on earth, much humor is "comic relief" from the grim business of "real" life. But in Heaven, humor is high seriousness. It is the inner secret of God and the blessed.[85]

Even on earth, saints play with their lives in the most outrageous way. Saint Thomas More ended his life with a bad joke, telling the axman "please do not chop my beard in two; *it* has not committed treason."[86]

Jesus has the most perfect sense of humor of all.[87] We do not often see it, because we think of humor as *jokes*. But the most perfect humor is in the very situation itself, especially irony,[88] the contrast between appearance and reality. "Let him

[83] Revelation 11:1.

[84] Plotinus, *Enneads*, I, 6, 8; Raymond Moody, *Life after Life* (New York: Bantam, 1976), p. 52.

[85] G. K. Chesterton, *Orthodoxy* (New York: Dodd, Mead, 1957), pp. 298–99.

[86] E. E. Reynolds, *The Field Is Won: The Life and Death of St. Thomas More* (Milwaukee, Wisc.: Bruce, 1968), pp. 265–66.

[87] Henri Cormier, *The Humor of Jesus*, trans. David Heiman (New York: Alba, 1977).

[88] Søren Kierkegaard, *The Concept of Irony*, trans. M. C. Lee (New York: Harper & Row, 1966).

who is without sin among you be the first to throw a stone at her"[89] is irony. It could be more clumsily and directly rendered, "You judgmental fools are worse than that adulteress—taking out splinters with logs in your eyes."[90] There is great irony in the Sermon on the Mount: "Consider the lilies of the field. . . . they toil not, neither do they spin: And yet I say unto you, That even Solomon in all his glory was not arrayed like one of these."[91] In other words, "You're sillier than the lilies. Who do you think you are anyway? God?[92] He'll take as good care of you as the lilies, won't he?" There is irony in "You search the scriptures, because you think that in them you have eternal life; and it is they that bear witness to me."[93] That is, "You're trying to read the sign as if it pointed to itself." It is the same irony as Pilate's "What is truth?"[94] as Truth stands in front of him. Finally, there is Jesus' ironic remark to Nicodemus, who cannot understand being "born again" and asks whether he must return to his mother's womb: "Are you a teacher of Israel and yet you do not understand this?"[95] You experts know everything except what it's all about.

Jesus is our best indicator of Heaven, and if there is humor in Jesus, there is humor in Heaven. Jesus is the manifestation of the Father, and if there is humor in the personality of the Son, there is humor in the personality of the Father. For some reason, people think of the Persons of the Trinity as *lacking* personality, as nebbishes. In fact, the three fullest personalities in all reality are the Father, the Son, and the Spirit. They are *characters*! They designed ostriches, for goodness' sake (literally). And—supreme joke—us.

[89] John 8:7.
[90] Matthew 7:3.
[91] Matthew 6:29 (KJV).
[92] Matthew 6:27.
[93] John 5:39.
[94] John 18:38.
[95] John 3:10.

Many of the resuscitated perceive and share Heavenly humor, even God's laughter at repented and forgiven sins.[96] We can laugh only when we are free, detached. The saint can laugh at life in his martyrdom, and once freed from sin (but not till then) we can laugh even at sin in Heaven. Detachment is necessary for humor. And in Heaven there is perfect detachment, even from self (*ek-stasis*, "standing-outside-oneself"). Therefore in Heaven there is perfect humor.

The saint and the clown share the secret of levity, the union between the two meanings of "light": truth (opposite of falsehood and darkness) and levity (opposite of gravity and heaviness). Saints *levitate*! Body follows spirit.

But Heavenly humor is not the opposite of seriousness, only of joyless seriousness. Saints, mystics, and the resuscitated take life *more* seriously than others do. Everything gains an infinite importance, an "eternal weight of glory".[97] Joy is a serious matter—too good to be wasted on jokes. The saint does not usually tell jokes,[98] because he does not need to, to relieve the joylessness, to relieve sadness, to distract from the heavy, practical world. "Joy is the serious business of Heaven."[99]

14. *Why Won't We Be Bored in Heaven?*

Because we are with God, and God is infinite. We never come to the end of exploring Him. He is new every day.

Because we are with God, and God is eternal. Time does

---

[96] Raymond Moody, *Life after Life* (New York: Bantam, 1976), pp. 64–73, 156; *Reflections on Life after Life* (New York: Bantam, 1977), pp. 29–40; Philip Swihart, *At the Edge of Death* (Downers Grove, Ill.: InterVarsity Press, 1978), pp. 60–63.

[97] 2 Corinthians 4:17.

[98] Like Alyosha in Dostoyevski's *The Brothers Karamazov*, trans. Constance Garnett (New York: Vintage Books, 1955), part I, bk. 1, chap. 4, p. 18.

[99] C. S. Lewis, *Letters to Malcolm* (New York: Harcourt, Brace & World, 1964), p. 93.

not pass (a condition for boredom); it just *is*. All time is present in eternity, as all the events of the plot are present in an author's mind. There is no waiting.

Because we are with God, and God is love. Even on earth, the only people who are never bored are lovers.

Chapter Three

What Will We Do in Heaven?

This is probably the first question most people ask about Heaven. But it shouldn't be. What we do is not as important as what we are. Our functionalistic[1] modern society tends to reduce our being to our function. What is the first question we ask about someone? "What does he *do*?" But love never asks that question first. The first question for love is always "Who are you?" rather than "What do you do?" Being is prior to doing, and love's realism refuses to reverse that real order. This is primordially true of Primordial Love:

> We are apt to think that God only wants *actions* of a particular kind, whereas He is most interested in *people* of a particular sort.[2]

Nevertheless, though the question "What do you do?" is not primary, it is important: first, because what we do flows from and reveals what we are; second, because what we do also flows *into* what we are, helps construct our selves. Third, creative work is a primary human need, and our conventional pictures of Heaven are boring partly because they do not fulfill this need. Playing harps and polishing halos is an obviously bad answer to a good question. A second answer, the more philosophical alternative of an eternity of abstract contem-

[1] Gabriel Marcel, *The Philosophy of Existentialism*, trans. Manya Harari (New York: Citadel Press, 1966), pp. 10–12.
[2] C. S. Lewis, *Mere Christianity* (New York: Macmillan, 1960), p. 77.

plation of changeless truth, moves only philosophers (and even among them only the minority). The third, biblical answer, the enjoyment of God,[3] is true but must be fleshed out by the imagination. The mere words "the enjoyment of God" make sense only to those who already enjoy God; the vast majority of us seem to enjoy the vast majority of things vastly more than we enjoy God. (In fact, it is only God *in* these things that we enjoy, but we do not recognize that.)

We may even fear Heaven, consciously or unconsciously, because we fear boredom. Then death is truly terrible, for it offers only the two hellish alternatives of boredom or agony. Earth seems much more interesting than Heaven because there seems to be nothing to do in Heaven. What work needs to be done in a world of eternal perfection? Yet how can we be happy without creative work?

The basic idea for my answer to that question comes from Richard Purtill's book *Thinking about Religion*.[4] In chapter 10—"Life after Death: What Might It Be Like?"—he postulates three human tasks in Heaven, in this order: (1) understanding our earthly life "by Godlight", (2) sharing all other human lives, and (3) exploration into God. First we review our past life with divine understanding and appreciation of every single experience, good and evil: we milk all our meaning dry. Then we do the same to others' lives from within. We know them more intimately and completely than we could ever know our most intimate friend on earth because we share God's knowledge of each one. When these two preliminary lessons are complete—when we know, love, understand, and appreciate completely by inner experience everything we and everyone else have ever experienced—only then we are spiritually mature enough to begin the endless and endlessly

[3] Psalm 27:4.
[4] Richard Purtill, *Thinking about Religion* (Englewood Cliffs, N.J.: Prentice Hall, 1978), pp. 136–52.

fascinating task of exploring, learning, and loving the facets of infinity, the inexhaustible nature of God.

The idea is not new, for it corresponds to three traditional doctrines: Purgatory, the Communion of Saints, and the Beatific Vision. But each is given new life by being related to the others in this sequence. Purgatory turns out to be part of Heaven rather than a distinct place, and consists of moral reeducation rather than mere punishment, rehabilitation rather than retribution. The Communion of Saints is rescued from a vague, philanthropic goodwill and made as interesting as human love and communion on earth; getting to know people is in one way or another the only thing we find inexhaustible here as well as there. Finally, the contemplation of God is not boring because it is done with souls matured by the first two tasks. The difference this maturing makes is as great as the difference between a dying saint and a newborn baby. The Beatific Vision is also not boring because it is dynamic rather than static, exploring rather than staring at God, endless beginnings rather than merely the end.

The more we think about it, the more inevitable and proper the idea seems to be. Yet I have not seen it explicitly anywhere else in print; nor has Purtill.[5] This chapter explores some of its details:

1. the psychology of Heaven,
2. the physics of Heaven,
3. the history of Heaven,
4. the epistemology of Heaven,
5. the ethics of Heaven.

The Psychology of Heaven: The Need for the Three Stages

The reason we need Heaven in the first place is to complete ourselves and the task we began on earth. No one dies finished.

[5] In a personal letter to the author.

There is never enough time to do and to be all that we can, even all that we should. Our lives are incomplete in all three of their essential relationships: (1) to ourselves, (2) to others, and (3) to God.

It seems necessary to take them in this order. For we must first know ourselves before we can even know who it is that knows others; and only after purgatorial purification of our attitudes are we mature enough to understand others adequately. And we must learn to love the human images in ourselves and others before we can love their divine Model: "for he who does not love his brother whom he has seen, cannot love God whom he has not seen."[6]

But we cannot complete task one without task two: only in relationship to others can we truly love ourselves, because only in relationship to others do we *become* human selves, that is, lovers.[7] Also, we cannot complete either task one or two without three, because only in the God Who holds the secret of our identities can we know ourselves and others.

The order, then, must be musical rather than mathematical. Musical themes, unlike numbers, interpenetrate. The three stages cannot be simply sequential; all three must begin as soon as we die. We cannot wait until Purgatory is ended to begin the Communion of Saints, and we cannot wait until the Communion of Saints is over to begin the Beatific Vision. We need the Communion of Saints for Purgatory because we need teachers there, saintly fathers in the faith, examples. This is the best, perhaps the only, way to teach goodness here; it is probably so there, too. And we need the Beatific Vision for the Communion of Saints because only in the Author's mind do we fully understand all His characters.

Yet our original sequence seems necessary, since we need a Purgatorially perfected instrument to participate in the Communion of Saints, and only the whole of redeemed and

---

[6] 1 John 4:20.
[7] Martin Buber, *I and Thou* (New York: Scribners, 1958), pp. 4, 13.

perfected humanity in communion is the adequate instrument for the Beatific Vision.

The solution to the dilemma is simply that the *perfection* of stage one is necessary before the perfection of stage two, and so with two and three; but the *beginning* of one and two cannot be independent of three. All begins at once at death, as all begins at once at birth.

The Physics of Heaven: Different Bodies for Different Stages

If we take seriously the "out-of-the-body-experiences" of resuscitated patients, the traditional beliefs and stories of many premodern cultures, and Saint Paul's own words in 2 Corinthians 12:1–5, we shall have to conclude that immediately after death we find ourselves out of our old body and in another kind of body, and that this experience occasionally happens to people *before* death. Some of these people are saints and mystics, like Saint Paul, but many are not. The body experienced in this state seems to be an ethereal one, a mere shadow or prophetic hint of the more solid resurrection body we shall receive later, the Artist's preliminary sketch of His later masterpiece.

This first after-death body is really an "out-of-the-body" body, hardly distinguishable from a disembodied soul.[8] Thus Platonism, which teaches the immortality of the soul distinct from the body but not the resurrection of the body, is right as far as it goes; it just does not go far enough. As C. S. Lewis says, "Mystics have got as far in the contemplation of God as the point at which the senses are banished; the further point, at which they will be put back again, has (to the best of my knowledge) been reached by no one."[9]

---

[8] C. S. Lewis, *A Grief Observed* (New York: Bantam, 1976), pp. 85–88; *Letters to Malcolm* (New York: Harcourt, Brace & World, 1964), pp. 123–24; Heraldsson and Osis, *At the Hour of Death* (New York: Avon, 1977), chap. 13.

[9] C. S. Lewis, *Miracles* (New York: Macmillan, 1955), p. 190.

The resurrection body Saint Paul speaks of in 1 Corinthians 15 and which Jesus assumed for forty days on earth between His Resurrection and His Ascension is a different kind of body: it is solid. Perhaps this kind of body is to be our instrument for the second stage, the Communion of Saints, the tool for expressive arts "of which earthly art and philosophy are but clumsy imitations".[10]

Finally, the third stage would have a body that "eye has not seen, nor ear heard, nor has it entered into the heart of man". At each stage we find a change and a surprise, and the greatest surprise comes last. We know our present bodies best, by experience; the out-of-the-body body we know next best, by manifold testimony and philosophers' guesses; the resurrection body we know only through Christ and through Revelation; and the finally glorified body we know only by a few suggestive hints in Scripture:

> As we have borne the image of the earthy, we shall also bear the image of the heavenly.[11]

> Behold, what manner of love the Father hath bestowed upon us, that we should be called the sons of God. . . . Beloved, now are we the sons of God, and it doth not yet appear what we shall be: but we know that, when he shall appear, we shall be like him; for we shall see him as he is.[12]

> I will give him a white stone, with a new name written on the stone which no one knows except him who receives it.[13]

The History of Heaven: Different Kinds of Time for Different Stages

Although the stages are in a sense sequential, there is not a single common time measure to date them, for the nature of

[10] C. S. Lewis, *The Problem of Pain* (New York: Macmillan, 1962), p. 150.
[11] 1 Corinthians 15:49 (KJV).
[12] 1 John 3:1–2 (KJV).
[13] Revelation 2:17.

time itself changes as we move from one stage to another. None of the stages is measurable in clock time. Clocks are one of the things "you can't take with you" when you die. If there are "years" in Purgatory, they are only symbolic.

But clock time (*chronos* in Greek) is not the only kind of time. We live in *kairos*: lived time, or life-time. *Kairos* is time *for* something, time relative to human purpose. There is never enough time for anything, enough *kairos*, because *kairos* is bounded by *chronos* here on earth. But not in Heaven. After death there will be all the time in the world—more than all the time in the world—to learn, to savor, to sink totally into the meaning of everything.

At the moment of death, according to very widespread testimony, your whole lifetime often flashes before you in vivid detail, in perfect order, and in a single instant. All your *kairos* does not take a single minute of *chronos*, for the boundary, the *chronos*-limit, is removed. An infinitely small unit of *chronos* (the instant in which your lifetime flashes by) is in fact enormous. For it is *kairos* measured not by *chronos* but by eternity. Here is unlimited presence: no waiting, no boredom, no not-yet future or no-longer past. It is Vanauken's "David Copperfield effect",[14] the wholeness of the person (yourself) experienced only at the point of completion, the point of death: the book is finished and "goes home to the Printer".[15]

The Epistemology of Heaven: Light in All Three Stages

Time has something to do with knowing. Time is a mind-shielding device for us on earth. Without it, we could not endure the plenitude of naked, eternal truth. Aristotle and Aquinas say that our minds are related to the truth as bats' or

[14] Sheldon Vanauken, *A Severe Mercy* (San Francisco: Harper & Row, 1977), p. 185.
[15] Ibid., p. 184.

owls' eyes are to the sun: proportioned to shadows.[16] James and Huxley say that the brain is an organ of forgetting rather than remembering, a "reducing valve" to let through to our temporal lives only that trickle of truth that we now need and can endure.[17] Stage one removes the reducing valve of the brain and its body. Stage two removes the separations between individual egos, allowing us to get inside other lives. Stage three removes time itself.

Light, or truth, is the point of all three stages. "Nothing is covered that will not be revealed."[18] Even Hell is truth, known too late. Truth must win in the long run; it can be covered up only in the short run, in time. Everything that has ever happened, every thought and deed of every person, must be known, open, available to everyone in Heaven. There are no closed doors in Heaven: "I looked, and lo, in heaven an open door!"[19]

No one will feel threatened by the fact that all knowledge is open and public in Heaven because (1) no one will misunderstand anyone, since all will be known through God's totally accurate knowledge; (2) thus there will be no prejudice or put-downs, no rejections; (3) therefore there will be no fear of rejection, and thus no walls, no hiding. We *want* to be known—even our sins:

> It may be that salvation consists not in the cancelling of those eternal moments—the times we sinned which are before God always—but in the perfected humility that bears the shame forever, rejoicing in the occasion which is furnished to God's compassion and glad that it should be common knowledge to the universe. Perhaps in that eternal moment St. Peter—he

[16] Aristotle, *Metaphysics*, I, 993b, 10–12; St. Thomas Aquinas, *Summa Theologiae*, I, 1, 5 ad 1.

[17] William James, *The Varieties of Religious Experience* (New York: New American Library, 1959), p. 324; Aldous Huxley, *The Doors of Perception* (New York: Harper & Row, 1963), pp. 22–24.

[18] Matthew 10:26.

[19] Revelation 4:1.

will forgive me if I am wrong—forever denies his Master. If so, it would indeed be true that the joys of Heaven are, for the most of us in our present condition, "an acquired taste"— and certain ways of life may render the taste impossible of acquisition. Perhaps the lost are those who dare not go to such a *public* place.[20]

The Ethics of Heaven as Following from the Epistemology of Heaven

The morality of truth-telling, the absolute value of honesty, comes clear in the light of Heaven. Because there is Heaven and because Heaven is absolute truth, therefore no lie can ever work in the long run. All lies are self-defeating, not only (as Kant says) because if everyone lied your lie would lose its effectiveness,[21] but (more realistically) because "truth will come to light".[22] The necessity of honesty is based not on the unreal hypothesis "if everyone lied" but on the actuality that we *will* be in the presence of light forever.

Every little lie, every deception, every half-truth and pretense and mixed motive will be unveiled. Then we will clearly see that it was never any advantage to lie, that it was a foolish short-range investment toward a long-range bankruptcy.

However, we should not exaggerate the connection between ethics and Heaven, as Dostoyevski does when he has Ivan Karamazov claim that "if there is no immortality then everything is permissible".[23] That is simply not true. Immortality is not the root of ethics, only its flower. Even if there were no immortality, ethical obligation would still bind absolutely. God is to be loved and good is to be done for their own sakes, not for the sake of reward (though reward is

[20] C. S. Lewis, *The Problem of Pain*, p. 61.

[21] Kant, *Groundwork of the Metaphysics of Morals*, VI, 18–19, 89.

[22] Shakespeare, *The Merchant of Venice*, act II, scene 2, line 86.

[23] Dostoyevski, *The Brothers Karamazov*, trans. Constance Garnett (New York: Modern Library, 1955), part I, bk. 2, chap. 6.

indeed promised). That is the lesson God taught His chosen people for many centuries before clearly revealing immortality. Only after lesson one is learned, only after we learn to love God for God and not for His gifts, can He safely reveal His gifts. If they come too soon, they are bribes, and we are religious hedonists, loving the gifts more than the Giver, our enjoyment more than God's goodness. We must not be spoiled children; we must "be holy for I the Lord your God am holy":[24] that is the ethics of Heaven.

[24]Leviticus 11:44; 19:2; 20:26.

Chapter Four

Is There a Purgatory?

Can Protestants Believe in Purgatory?

Protestants and Catholics seem irreconcilably split on the simple issue of whether Purgatory exists or not. Protestants argue persuasively, from Scriptures like "today you shall be with me in Paradise",[1] and from the whole pervasive tone of triumph in death that is clearly and strongly taught in the New Testament,[2] that the Catholic notion of Purgatory is a pagan, not a Christian one, and that having to suffer temporal (though not eternal) punishment for sins there detracts from the finished work of Christ[3] and the completeness of joy announced by the Gospel. Catholics argue, also persuasively, that at the moment of death we are still imperfect, and in Heaven we are perfect in sanctity; therefore there must be an intermediate state between earthly imperfection and Heavenly perfection during which we are perfected and purified. They also point to a few Scripture texts, such as being "saved by fire".[4] They can even point to C. S. Lewis, that Protestant "mere Christian"[5] who did more for Christian unity than all

---

[1] Luke 23:43.
[2] E.g., 1 Corinthians 15:55; Romans 8:35–39; Philippians 1:21–23.
[3] John 19:30.
[4] 1 Corinthians 3:15.
[5] Cf. the Introduction to his *Mere Christianity* (New York: Macmillan, 1943, 1977), pp. 5–12.

the theologians put together and without compromises or obfuscations. Lewis wrote:

> Our souls *demand* Purgatory, don't they? Would it not break the heart if God said to us, "It is true, my son, that your breath smells and your rags drip with mud and slime, but we are charitable here and no one will upbraid you with these things, nor draw away from you. Enter into the joy"? Should we not reply, "With submission, Sir, and if there is no objection, I'd *rather* be cleansed first." "It may hurt, you know."— "Even so, Sir."[6]

The dispute seems irresolvable without compromise. Yet it *is* resolvable if we only look at Purgatory as the saints do. Purgatory is

1. part of Heaven, not a distinct, third place between Heaven and Hell—thus the absolute antithesis between Heaven and Hell, and its infinite spiritual seriousness, is preserved;

2. joyful, not gloomy—thus not detracting from the joy and triumph of Christian death (in fact, one of the saints even says that the pains of Purgatory are incomparably more desirable than the most ecstatic pleasures on earth!)[7]

3. a place of sanctification, not justification, where sin is not paid for (that was completed on Calvary) but surgically removed. As George MacDonald says, He was called Jesus not because He was to save us from punishment merely, but because He was to save us from our *sins*.[8] (Thus Purgatory is not part of "a different gospel",[9] not salvation by works.)

4. Purgatory is also a place of spiritual education rather than deeds; thus it is not a "second chance" to pay for sin or

[6] C. S. Lewis, *Letters to Malcolm* (New York: Harcourt, Brace, Jovanovich, 1973), pp. 108–9.

[7] St. Catherine of Genoa, *Purgatory, The Spiritual Dialog* (New York: Paulist Press, 1979), p. 84.

[8] C. S. Lewis, ed., *George MacDonald: An Anthology* (London: Geoffrey Bles, 1946), p. 18.

[9] Galatians 1:6.

merit salvation, but a full understanding of deeds already done during our first and only chance, and a full disposal of all that needs to be disposed.

Purgatory as Truth: Completion

Purgatory is necessary not only from our point of view but from God's point of view. God wastes nothing. Everything must be completed, must "come true". The Scriptural meaning of Truth is historical: promises "come true"[10] or "stand true".[11] The divine masterpieces that are human selves must ring true; the story that is my life must have its perfect consummation. Our earthly lives are fallow fields, unread books, unmilked cows. All their seeds must flower, all their lessons be learned, all their meanings milked. God's word uttered immediately after Creation must be uttered also at the end: "very good". For God's word is eternal Truth, both Alpha and Omega. The First Word is also the Last Word, the Last Judgment, the eternal pronouncement about creation.

The completion we need is internal, not external—not to *do* all the things in Purgatory that we should have done on earth, but to become the persons God longs for and in our heart of hearts we longed to become. Love either will not or cannot impose this by force, against the beloved's will. There is no reason to think His heart's desire changes when we die. Therefore after death He must make us perfect, through our free cooperation, in Purgatory.

Purgatory is like an incubator. A premature baby is put into an incubator because he needs to finish outside the womb the growing he should have done in the womb. Our fetal souls also are born at death into Heaven in an immature state. Before they are strong enough to survive the Heavenly light, they need a "thickening process".[12] We now have a baby spirit

---

[10] Matthew 5:17–18; Ezekiel 12:25.   [11] Psalm 12:6; Isaiah 40:8.
[12] C. S. Lewis, *The Great Divorce* (New York: Macmillan, 1946), p. 69.

in an adult body; the spiritual maturity that so lags behind our physical maturity needs a "physic", a vitamin, a course in Remedial Spirituality before it can assume the resurrection body, as a child needs lessons in horsemanship using ponies before being able to ride a great and powerful stallion.[13]

Purgatory as Truth: Light

We have seen that all three stages are stages of initiation into the light of truth, since "truth is the ultimate end of the whole universe".[14] No thinker was ever more single-mindedly devoted to Truth than Socrates, the pure and model philosopher. But Socrates' confidence in Truth led him to teach the apparently non-Christian and non-Biblical thesis that evil is only ignorance, that no one willingly and knowingly does evil,[15] and that consequently the cure for all evil and the prescription for Utopia is moral education.[16] Is this a foolish naïveté or a profound insight into the power of Truth?

Both. It is naïveté if applied to practical life now. It ignores "the mystery of iniquity"[17] and the power of free will. It is true insight if applied to our ultimate destiny, the Beatific Vision, and also to Purgatory, where our joy is in the truth, even the truth of our sins. Since in Purgatory we do not make different choices but only see and understand clearly all our past choices, the only virtue there *is* knowledge, and education there does cure all moral ills. Like most Utopian ideas, this one is profoundly true except for the timing; it is too soon. It has not the *patience* to wait for God.

---

[13] C. S. Lewis, *Miracles* (New York: Macmillan, 1947), chap. 16; cf. *The Great Divorce*, chap. 11.

[14] St. Thomas Aquinas, *Summa contra Gentiles*, I, 1, 2.

[15] See *Apology*, 25c–26a, and *Protagoras*.

[16] This is the practical presupposition of *The Republic*.

[17] 2 Thessalonians 2:7.

Purgatory as Reading

Purgatory is reading the already-written book of your life with total understanding and acceptance—the total understanding that comes only *from* total acceptance.

There is thus a deep connection between literature and purgation, as Aristotle saw.[18] Speaking of drama as purgative sounds terribly demeaning, like comparing Hamlet with an enema. But it is really the opposite: it sees literary art as a foretaste of Heaven—and *not* because Heaven is an enema. Purging doesn't mean *eliminating* but *purifying*. Fear becomes respect. Pity becomes understanding. *Thus* fear and pity are purged.

In Purgatory the reading of our lives is done without passion, as in a theater. The word "theater" comes from *theoria*, to look or contemplate. In Purgatory you are outside your life looking in, like Emily in Thornton Wilder's play *Our Town*, and without passion and fear you understand everything for the first time. No one can fully understand life only from within or only from without, by blind involvement or by uncaring detachment. We must first be in the picture, then out; we must have passion to understand, but the understanding must transcend passion.

The latter point needs proving to the modern mind, as the former point needed proving to the mind of the ancient philosopher. We know the need for involvement, but not (usually) the need for detachment. But look at literature to see it. A story about an unappreciative old grouch, like "I Never Sang for My Father",[19] makes you pity him as you failed to do when you were involved in living with him. Look at Nathan's story of the poor man's lamb, which he told to King David to convict him of his theft of Bathsheba:[20] David got

---

[18] Aristotle, *Poetics*, chap. 6, 1449b, 27–28.

[19] *"I Never Sang for My Father"* by Robert Woodruff Anderson (1917) (New York: Random House, 1968).

[20] 1 Kings 11 and 12.

the point of the story only because he thought it was about someone else. Detachment is necessary for the lesson to sink in.

Purgatory as Detachment

We can learn from this detachment now. Purgatory can work backwards and cast new light on our present earthly lives. For we should be working out some of our Purgatory now— not in the sense of paying for our sins but in the sense of a God's-eye view of our lives even as we live them. The Hindu teaching of jnana-yoga[21] teaches that lesson too: even as you live, look at yourself living from a standpoint outside.

This is possible only because we are not merely our life. As Marcel puts it,

> I carry with me that which I am and which perhaps my life is not. This brings out the gap between my being and my life. I am not my life. . . . I can judge my life. . . . My life may appear to me as for ever inadequate to something which I carry with me, which in a sense I am.[22]

We take this contemplative attitude towards others' lives when they are written up in stories; we can do it to our own life because it too is being written up as a story. God is even now writing the story of our lives, and we can begin reading it even as it is being written. We not only can, we should and we must detach ourselves from ourselves if we are not to be totally swamped by life. It is not passive, Stoic hardness of heart; it is the most active attitude we can take. Being swamped is passive; it is the sun, transcending the earth yet illuminating it, that is supremely active, though silently.

---

[21] See Huston Smith, *The Religions of Man* (New York: Harper and Row, 1965), chap. 2.

[22] Gabriel Marcel, *The Philosophy of Existentialism* (Secaucus, N.J.: Citadel Press, 1956, 1984), p. 24.

Its quietness is that of supreme life, not death: we moderns believe that only a restless spirit is really alive, but the saints and mystics know that only a quiet spirit is truly alive. The result of the silent contemplation of the saint is not apathy but joy.

"Wasted Lives"

All lives are more or less wasted lives. But Purgatory "redeems the time":

> The reading analogy may be useful. On the first reading of some book we may appreciate only a little of its significance and richness, but subsequent rereading will enable us to appreciate the book more and more. And as we might write a commentary on a book that has meant much to us, so part of our afterlife could be an appreciation and correction of our present lives. Even if our present lives have been almost a failure—even if we are barely saved after a life of folly and waste—we could still make these wasted lives the foundation of something glorious—a "commentary" much better than the book.[23]

For the rereading and commenting is (1) in the clear light of God and (2) unhurried eternity; we are no longer victims of (1) ignorance or (2) time. The time of earthly life makes for ignorance because we are unfreely driven along its span like hearing a tape or a movie. In Purgatorial rereading, we step off the tyrant Time's treadmill and enter God's Sabbath where all time comes home. Living is like painting a picture, a picture that is also the painter—a self-portrait; after death, we step off the finished canvas. Only then is our time free from the frame of *chronos*.

---

[23] Richard Purtill, *Thinking about Religion* (Englewood Cliffs, N.J.: Prentice-Hall, 1978), p. 150.

Paradoxically, this detached rereading is a greater involvement than our lives in time could ever be. We do not merely remember but re-live, not re-present but present, for all times are present, not past, in eternity.

I think this Purgatorial appreciation would have to include not only our lives but also the whole created world: seeing each leaf, each star, as it is: a triumph of glory, a Hymn of the Universe. For the universe is to be our own greater body, so its life is part of ours. Of the universe too it will be true to say that only by death and detachment from it, can we be so fully involved in it as to appreciate it adequately.

What Happens to Sin in Purgatory?

Sin is purged by sharing in our destiny as light. We see the meaning and the effects of all our sins in Purgatory—their effects on others as well as ourselves, both directly and indirectly, through chains of influence presently invisible, chains so long and effectual that we would be overwhelmed with responsibility if we saw them now. Only a few can endure the saint's insight that "we are each responsible for all".[24] But the vision is true. The web of human causality is at least as brimming with articulated efficacy as the web of physical causality, where every event in the universe occurs within a common field and makes some difference, however tiny, to every other event.[25] The universe is a vast body in which each cell both physical and spiritual lives in interdependence and interchange with every other cell.

In this body we sometimes see the effects of sin "unto the

---

[24] Fyodor Dostoyevski, *The Brothers Karamazov*, trans. Constance Garnett (New York: Vintage Books, 1955), pp. 344, 362.

[25] See Ray Bradbury, *A Sound of Thunder* (New York: Random House, 1980). See also Pascal, *Pensées*, trans. Krailsheimer (New York: Penguin Books, 1966, 1985), p. 148: "Cleopatra's nose: if it had been shorter, the whole face of the earth would have been different" (no. 413).

third and fourth generation of those that hate Me",[26] those spatio-temporally juxtaposed in the same family. We also sometimes see the effects of sanctity "to thousands of generations of those that love Me and keep My commandments"[27] down through the centuries.

All sin harms someone else in the Body of Christ who needs the health of the spiritual organ that is myself just as the kidney needs an artery. In Purgatory I will experience all the harm I have done, with sensitized and mature conscience. This is a suffering both more intense and more useful than fire or merely physical pain. But I will experience it also with the compassion and forgiveness of God, forgiving myself as God forgives me. If we are to believe the resuscitated, we even align ourselves with God's laughter at our past, repented, and forgiven sins. After we remember sin, we can forget it; after we take it seriously, we can laugh at it: after we share in the sufferings of the God Who experienced Hell for us ("My God, My God, why hast Thou forsaken Me?"),[28] we can share in His "Father, forgive them, for they know not what they do."[29] Our experience *and* forgiveness will be perfect in Purgatory because there we will know.

The Joy of Purgatory

Our joy in Purgatory will come from the same source as our suffering: seeing. We will see the double meaning of our sins: the Hellish effects and the Heavenly effects, all things working together for good. Purgatory is the beginning of Heaven, and Heaven is the fulfillment of all God's promises, including the astonishing, all-comprehensive one just quoted.

We do not yet see this happening (though it is beginning, and we *sometimes* see it beginning), this "all things working

[26] Exodus 20:5.   [27] Exodus 20:6.
[28] Matthew 27:46.   [29] Luke 23:34.

together for good":[30] We do not yet see everything subject to Him (though it is, for "Thou hast put all things in subjection under His feet").[31] But we see Jesus.[32] "We live by faith, not by sight."[33] For if we saw now how everything works together for good, we would probably become indifferent to right choosing. We must first learn, through trusting and obeying, to create the drama that we afterwards read, to fight the fight we later detachedly contemplate, to accept the good and reject the evil so that afterwards we may accept the whole.

When Heaven's definitive solution to the problem of earth appears, when we are able to see how "all things work together for good" and are invited to "enter into the joy of the Lord",[34] then the only reason for refusal will be not ignorance but willful rebellion, like the rebellion of Ivan Karamazov:

> I believe in the underlying order and the meaning of life; I believe in the eternal harmony in which they say we shall one day be blended. . . . Yet would you believe it, in the final result I don't accept this world of God's, and although I know it exists, I don't accept it at all. . . . Let me make it plain. I believe like a child that suffering will be healed and made up for, that all the humiliating absurdity of human contradictions will vanish like a pitiful mirage, like the despicable fabrication of the impotent and infinitely small Euclidean mind of man, that in the world's finale, at the moment of eternal harmony, something so precious will come to pass that it will suffice for all hearts, for the comforting of all resentments, for the atonement of all the crimes of humanity, of all the blood they've shed; that it will make it not only possible to forgive but to justify all that has happened with men—but though all that may come to pass, I don't accept it. I won't accept it.[35]

[30] Romans 8:28.
[31] 1 Corinthians 15:27; Ephesians 1:22.
[32] Hebrews 2:8–9.
[33] 2 Corinthians 5:7.
[34] Matthew 25:21.
[35] Dostoyevski, *The Brothers Karamazov*, p. 279.

Purgatory, like Heaven, is joy and truth. Heaven is the perfection of joy and truth. Hell is the refusal to accept truth and therefore the refusal of joy.

Chapter Five

What Is the Communion of Saints?

The Relation between Purgatory and the Communion of Saints

Purgatory must be completed before the Communion of Saints can be completed because it takes a self fully grown to become one with billions of other selves, as it takes a complete foundation to ground a multi-storied building. Each of us acquires billions of new stories (in both senses of that equivocal word), new facets to our identity by knowing and by being known by the others in the Communion.

Each of us is indispensable to the completion of the others. John's understanding of Elizabeth, though true to Elizabeth's Elizabethness, is also true to John's Johnness; Mary's understanding of Elizabeth is Mary's, not John's. There is more to Elizabeth than meets any one set of eyes. One reason I must develop my unique personality is to add my unique angle of vision to each other. We are not only members of the same Body but also, St. Paul insists, "members of one another".[1]

But although Purgatory must be *completed* before the Communion of Saints is completed, it may require the Communion of Saints to *begin* Purgatory. For there is no more effective method of religious education than the presence of saints. Perhaps there is no other effective method at all. If we had

[1] Ephesians 4:25.

72

been around the Apostles, would we not have become an Apostle? Quite likely. Sanctity is an extremely contagious infection. Saints spring up around saints on earth and in Purgatory too, because their goodness is like light, "naturally diffusive of itself".[2] We often forget this dynamic, propagating aspect of sanctity. We think of it as merely "following Christ", or "imitating Christ". But "imitating" is monkey business; we are to *be* Christ, incorporated into His living, growing Body, haunted by His Spirit, the most powerful force on earth, more dynamic than dynamite, more nuclear and more energetic than nuclear energy.

It is in this second stage of Heaven, the Communion of Saints, that we receive our resurrection body, it seems—the body that is the new instrument for the new communication "whereof earthly art and philosophy are but clumsy imitations".[3] Having been purged of the sins and illusions of our earthly body, we can take up a living body again. As C. S. Lewis supposes,

> I don't say the resurrection of this body will happen at once. It may well be that this part of us sleeps in death, and the intellectual soul is sent to Lenten lands where she fasts in naked spirituality—a ghost-like and imperfectly human condition. . . . Yet from that fast my hope is that we shall return and re-assume the wealth we have laid down.
>
> Then the new earth and sky, the same yet not the same as these, will rise in us as we have risen in Christ. And once again, after who knows what aeons of the silence and the dark, the birds will sing and the waters flow, and lights and shadows move across the hills, and the faces of our friends laugh upon us with amazed recognition.
>
> Guesses, of course, only guesses. If they are not true, something better will be.[4]

[2] St. Thomas Aquinas, *Summa Theologiae*, I, 5, 4.

[3] C. S. Lewis, *The Problem of Pain* (New York: Macmillan, 1962), p. 150.

[4] C. S. Lewis, *Letters to Malcolm* (New York: Harcourt, Brace and World, 1963), pp. 123–24.

He now knows this "something better". Those are almost his last words.

The Communal Nature of Heaven

Heaven is more than the fulfillment of the Eastern mystic's quest for private ecstasy. Perhaps that is why God has not planned for most of us to be that kind of mystic. He gave us communal vocations on earth, in families, in schools, in congregations, to prepare us for Heaven. Scripture always describes Heavenly worship (and thus true mysticism) as loving, as communal, not private.[5]

But Heaven's community, unlike earth's, is never collectivistic. It is love, and love unifies by individuating and individuates by unifying. At what moment do lovers come into the most perfect possession of themselves as individuals if not when they are most lost in each other? Self is given up, but "he who loses his self will find it."[6] The reason for this deepest of all truths about the human image of God is that God Himself is this kind of society of self-giving:

> For in self-giving, if anywhere, we touch a rhythm not only of all creation but of all being. For the Eternal Word also gives Himself in sacrifice; and that not only on Calvary. For when He was crucified He "did that in the wild weather of His outlying provinces which He had done at home in glory and gladness." From before the foundation of the world He surrenders begotten Deity back to begetting Deity in obedience. . . . From the highest to the lowest, self exists to be abdicated and, by that abdication, becomes the more truly self, to be thereupon yet the more abdicated, and so forever.[7]

That's why God's will for us is that we learn to love: God's will is necessary, not contingent, it follows from His nature.[8]

[5] Revelation 4.   [6] Matthew 16:25.
[7] C. S. Lewis, *The Problem of Pain*, p. 152.
[8] St. Thomas Aquinas, *Summa Theologiae*, I, 19, 1.

We must learn to love in order to conform to Reality, to learn to live in the only world there is, to play the only game in town. "If we will not learn to eat the only food the universe grows—the only food any possible universe can grow—we must starve eternally."[9]

Understanding and love are the two absolute values, according to the insights of the philosophers, the revelations of the prophets, and the experiences of the resuscitated and the mystics. Both are required for true society, Heavenly or earthly. We cannot understand persons without loving them, and we cannot love them without understanding them. The traditional controversy between voluntarism and intellectualism, between the priority of will and love and the priority of intellect and understanding, the controversy over whether the Beatific Vision is primarily the love of God or the knowledge of God, is "probably one of those nonsense questions".[10]

"We Are Each Responsible for All"

Dostoyevski teaches two startling ideas through his mouthpiece Father Zossima, the spiritual master in *The Brothers Karamazov*: that we are all in Paradise right now, though we don't see it, and that we are each responsible for all.[11] The two are parts of a single vision, and the first is a function of the second: we are in Paradise *because* of the web of universal responsibility. What could this possibly mean, and how does it cast light on our Heavenly future in the Communion of Saints?

When expressed in abstract, philosophical terms the doctrine of universal responsibility usually seems unconvincing. Yet in the context of the novel, the lived experience, it often

[9] C. S. Lewis, *The Problem of Pain*, p. 54.

[10] C. S. Lewis, *A Grief Observed* (New York: Bantam, 1961, 1976), p. 89.

[11] Fyodor Dostoyevski, *The Brothers Karamazov*, trans. Constance Garnett (New York: Vintage Books, 1955), pp. 343–44, 362.

convinces the reader's imagination even if his intelligence rejects it, much as Tolkien's *Lord of the Rings* baptizes the imagination of many typically modern readers long before their minds are within a thousand miles of the traditional Christian world and life view that is implicitly but strongly present as the skeleton of that great epic.[12]

The web of universal responsibility is also a basic vision of the novels of Charles Williams.[13] He calls it "The City" (an Augustinian image) and contrasts the "coherence" of "Zion" (Augustine's "City of God") with the "incoherence" of "Gomorrah" (Augustine's "City of the World").[14] The principles by which these two invisible cities live—the real, spiritual life-blood of each—are as different as organic and inorganic compounds. The "City of God" lives by grace and by the divine providence of all things working together for good. The "City of the World" lives by chance, heredity and environment, and the natural principles of egotism (*or* collectivism) and self-preservation. The relationships among the members of the City of God are organic, like the relationships among the cells in a single body. Brothers in a single real family, their love is founded on their being. We must "love the brotherhood"[15] because we *are* the brotherhood. And far from impairing individuality, this relationship fulfills it, as in an animal body two organs are more individuated than two stones or two copies of a book.[16]

[12] See Willis B. Glover, "The Christian Character of Tolkien's Invented World" in *Criticism: A Quarterly for Literature and the Arts*, vol. 13, no. 1 (Winter, 1971), pp. 39–53.

[13] See Thomas Howard, *The Novels of Charles Williams* (Oxford: Oxford University Press, 1981). Cf. Robert Farrar Capon, *An Offering of Uncles* (New York: Crossroad, 1982).

[14] Charles Williams, *Descent into Hell* (Grand Rapids, Mich.: Eerdmans, 1937), pp. 174–75.

[15] 1 Peter 2:17.

[16] See C. S. Lewis, *The Problem of Pain*, p. 150.

We see this web now only "through a glass, darkly",[17] as we see the figures in a stained glass window that is blocked from our direct view but that reflects a fuzzy but suggestive pattern of interanimated color on the opposite wall. When one of us catches an unusually strong glimpse of this net of diamonds, this universal web, like St. Francis or Father Zossima, he seems almost like a lunatic:

> My brother asked the birds to forgive him; that sounds sense-less, but it is right; for all is like an ocean, all is flowing and blending; a touch in one place sets up movement at the other end of the earth. It may be senseless to beg forgiveness of the birds, but birds would be happier at your side—a little happier, anyway—and children and all animals, if you yourself were nobler than you are now.[18]

In this respect as in others, there is more connection and less difference between Heaven and earth than we think.

How Does It Work? Heavenly Empathy

The Communion of Saints works as God works. We know and love others in the Body *as God does*. "From now on, therefore, we regard no one from a human point of view . . . if anyone is in Christ, he is a new creation."[19] So how does God know us?

Not from without but from within, not by observing us but by designing us. So we will also fully understand others' lives not by looking at them but by living them, not by sympathy but by empathy. Perhaps we will be able to do this even with people who are still on earth, through a kind of spiritual bilocation; or perhaps only through the coming alive of the other person's memories in Heaven. But since Heaven

---

[17] 1 Corinthians 13:12 (KJV).
[18] Dostoyevski, *The Brothers Karamazov*, pp. 383–84.
[19] 2 Corinthians 5:17.

does not move by earthly time and since all of time is present at eternity, there is no waiting, and the question really makes no practical difference.

Suppose we could travel via an earthly time-machine to, say, sixteenth-century England. We would still be observers looking at Elizabeth or Henry from the outside. Heavenly time-travel may also be an ego-travel, an out-of-the-body experience, which would let us look *out* on Elizabethan England from within Elizabeth's consciousness (without losing our own), as subject, not object, feeling *with* the soul of Elizabeth rather than merely feeling it as an other.

If this is so, it is probably a consequence of the Incarnation. In Christ we too become all men and women, as He did—not just vaguely and abstractly but concretely and individually. That is why in Him we are not only "members of Christ" but also "members of each other".[20] We are in Christ, Christ is in neighbor, therefore we are in neighbor. (There's that word "in" again!)

We could be in all our neighbors, no longer separated by time or place. We could enter into the whole world that each of the blessed brings to Heaven. Nothing is lost to anyone. Christ's Incarnation made earth full of Heaven, and His Ascension made Heaven full of earth: our bodies and worlds are resurrected too. The divine fisherman does not merely hook Heavenly fish out of the earthly pond, but brings the whole pond to Heaven.

How big is the pond? How much of the worlds we share in earthly communion will enter our Heavenly communion? The best answer is a counter-question: why set any limits on God's generosity or imagination? Whatever the truth about Heaven, it will be more, not less, than these speculations; more than our wildest dreams. "Eye has not seen, ear has not heard . . . ."[21] It seems likely, therefore, that we shall enter without limit fully into all the lives that ever were, are, or

[20] Ephesians 4:25.   [21] 1 Corinthians 2:9.

will be, not only on earth but also of non-earthly creatures on other planets. Christ is not a merely *local* deity. Perhaps after all the individuals of the human race perfect *our* Communion of Saints, we will begin to share our racial experience with billions of other similarly perfected extraterrestrial races. Perhaps we will also descend into the consciousness of animals and plants, and even be initiated into the higher mysteries of angelic experience. If it is possible and if it is good, it will be made actual by Infinite Goodness.

Some Earthly Problems Solved by Heavenly Communion

One problem this view solves is the problem of injustice—not "the sufferings of the innocent", because none of us is innocent, but the unjust *distribution* of pleasures and pains, opportunities and rewards on earth. In Heaven, each of us will experience everything through the Communion of Saints. Heaven thus preserves both radical equality—kings and slaves enter into each other's lives—and individual differences.

Radical equality on earth, like most Utopian ideas, is a true vision but premature: an attempt to bring Heaven to earth. That is why Utopians tend to ignore the body, the foundation of individual differences and of apparent injustices (Why was I born lame? Why is my country so poor?). The fruit they desire—spiritual equality—is indeed Heavenly fruit, but it must ripen on the Heavenly tree of the Communion of Saints. The righteous are "like a tree planted by rivers of water, that yields its fruit in due season".[22]

The sharing of lives in Heaven would also deal with the injustice of premature deaths, especially those of children—an infinitely harder problem than death in general. Those children could receive in Heaven all the earthly experiences of growing in love and learning that they were denied on earth, through the sharing of lives in the Communion of Saints. God is an

[22] Psalm 1:3.

equal opportunity employer, and He outfoxes the Devil's invention of death; no one is denied earthly learning, but some postpone it until Heaven. Perhaps the children's Heavenly tutors would be their own parents,[23] whose deprivation of children would be compensated for by the same Heavenly device that compensates the children for their deprivation of their parents. It would be quite in the divine style.

Something similar may be true of all individuals, groups, or races who had been unjustly deprived of good things on earth.[24] Not only will they be given compensation in Heaven, but those very earthly goods denied them will be given to them in Heaven, perhaps from the very hands of their earthly persecutors (this would be part of their Purgatorial re-education). That too sounds like the divine style. Nothing is wasted.

Communion of persons entails personal recognition, thus immediately answering the oft-asked question: Will we recognize our friends in Heaven? In George MacDonald's words, "Shall we be greater fools in Paradise than we are here?"[25] In fact, *only* in Heaven will we really know our friends, from within.

Language in Heaven

The Communion of Saints requires a better instrument for communication than any earthly language. Scripture hints at this when it promises that we will receive a new name in Heaven,[26] and when it prophesies that all earthly tongues will cease,[27] even those charismatic gifts which are only fore-

[23] See Richard Purtill, *Thinking about Religion* (Englewood Cliffs, N.J.: Prentice-Hall, 1978), p. 145.

[24] Ibid., p. 149.

[25] C. S. Lewis, ed., *George MacDonald: An Anthology* (London: Geoffrey Bles, 1946), p. 98.

[26] Revelation 2:17.

[27] 1 Corinthians 13:8.

shadowings of Heaven's undoing of the babble of Babel, begun at Pentecost. The fragmentation of language since Babel has produced problems of communication between languages and between individuals. In Heaven the fragments of the broken mirror will be melted into a great, multifaceted lens to reflect prismatically the white light of the single eternal Word into the many-colored words of our Heavenly language.

This is the language spoken before the Fall (or even a better one), the single language of which all others are dim reflections, memories, and anticipations. The myth of a universal language is nearly universal. The traditional form is that of the original, primal language; the new myth of progress transforms it to a hoped-for Utopian language of the future. The myth explains the sense that a given writer (especially a poet) has found "just the right word", the word closest to the word in the Heavenly language.

Though "tongues will cease", perhaps we will fondly preserve our earthly languages in some form, even though they are clumsy and crude attempts to do what only Heavenly language can do with suppleness and quicksilver brilliance, much as we preserve a child's first crude drawings. In that case, we could read Shakespeare in Heaven as we read "Mary Had a Little Lamb" now.

The old language was for the old world; a new world, with new horizons of meaning, requires new language, since language is not merely a part of a world but shapes a world, constitutes its horizons. The world is in the word, not the word in the world. "It is *in* words and language that things first come into being and are."[28]

That is why mystics and resuscitated patients all say that their glimpses of the next world are ineffable. These experiences won't fit into our languages any more than Vergil can be

<hr />

[28] Martin Heidegger, *Introduction to Metaphysics*, trans. Ralph Manheim (New York: Doubleday Anchor Books, 1961), p. 11.

translated into the language of a three-year-old. To speak of Heaven is to try to contain new wine in old wineskins. They burst.

Transition to the Final Stage: The Beatific Vision

Perhaps in each of the three stages we learn a new, more mature language, just as we receive new, more perfect bodies. In any case, the wineskins of our present language burst most quickly and spectacularly when trying to talk about the final stage, the Beatific Vision. Nevertheless, since fools walk in where angels fear to tread, I will venture a few suggestions about this ultimate consummation of human existence.

Although the first two stages of Heaven may seem to demand an infinite length of time when compared to earthly life, they have an end. Even the complete sharing of billions of other lives, however unthinkably enormous, is finite and therefore has an end. Only God is infinite; therefore only stage three has no end.

When the dead appear to the living (as often happens), they sometimes reveal their transition from stage two, where they are still in touch with earth and earthly lives, to stage three, where they "turn to the eternal Fountain".[29] Sheldon Vanauken calls this "the Second Death". In *A Severe Mercy* he chronicles his wife's death, his experience of her continued presence, and then the removal of this presence, not by annihilation but by this turning, this transition. He found that his deep grief suddenly ceased, for grief was a response not just to her absence but to her presence (her presence as absent). We cease grieving, he supposes, not because something changes only within us but because something changes between ourselves and our beloved dead.[30]

[29] Dante, *Divine Comedy*, Paradiso, canto 31, line 93. Cf. C. S. Lewis, *A Grief Observed* (New York: Bantam, 1963, 1976), p. 89.

[30] See Sheldon Vanauken, *A Severe Mercy* (New York: Bantam, 1975, 1981), Epilogue.

What is the Eternal Fountain? What is the Beatific Vision? I dare not add specks to the mountains: go to the saints and mystics and find out. All I can say is to repeat and interpret Revelation, not add to it by any experience of mine.

One of the overlooked features of this vision that Scripture tells us is that there is no religion in Heaven. There is no temple in the New Jerusalem.[31] For religion was the ladder; God is the roof. Religion was the diving board; God is the pool. Religion was the raft (to use Buddha's image); God is the other shore.

Religion can become an idol, a substitute for God. There is a famous story of a preacher who died and was given a choice to go to Heaven or to a sermon on Heaven. He chose the latter. The greater things have the greatest built-in danger of becoming idols. Therefore the last Apostle warns us in the very last sentence of his Epistle, "Little children, keep yourselves from idols."[32] Thus the mystics prefer apophatic, dark, negative images: the light of the Beatific Vision is the divine darkness. Its *todo* (everything) is also *nada* (nothing), according to St. John of the Cross.[33] Saying is caught up in being; nothing more can be said. Nothing more needs to be said.

[31] Revelation 21:22.

[32] 1 John 5:21.

[33] See St. John of the Cross, *The Dark Night of the Soul* in *Collected Works* (Washington, D.C.: Institute of Carmelite Studies, 1983), pp. 295–389.

Chapter Six

Will We Have Bodies
in Heaven?

What Will We Be after We Die? Six Answers

The human race has come up with five basic answers to the
question, and God has come up with a sixth. (He is always
coming up with odd things, like planets and people and
platypuses; He is "the Great Iconoclast".[1])

1. Annihilation. Nothing. Death ends it all, except our
reputation, our works, and our children, which live on after
us—but we know and enjoy nothing of them if we are annihilated forever.

2. We survive death, but only as ghosts. We become pale
shadows of the living selves we once were.

3. Reincarnation. We come back to earth in another mortal
body.

4. The natural immortality of the soul. Each individual's
disembodied spirit, liberated by death, survives as a pure spirit,
like an angel. This spirit had been imprisoned in an alien thing,
a body, until released forever by death.

5. The only thing that survives death is the only thing that
was real before death: cosmic consciousness, the One, Atman,
the Buddha-mind, perfect, eternal, transindividual spirit.

---

[1] C. S. Lewis, *A Grief Observed* (New York: Bantam, 1976), p. 76.

Number one is materialism. It is typically modern, though a few ancient Greek and Roman philosophers, such as Democritus and Lucretius, held it.

Two is the mythic view of shades in Hades. It is the belief of most ancient tribes and cultures, even the early Jews and Greeks.

Three, reincarnation, is popular in many times and places. It usually exists together with four or five. Reincarnation serves then as a temporary means to one of these two eternal destinies.

Four is Platonism, but is often confused with Christianity, which teaches supernatural resurrection rather than natural immortality, and of the whole person, not just of the soul.

Five, the cosmic consciousness view, is Hinduism and Buddhism.

For materialism, death is everything, because in it we become nothing.

For Hinduism and Buddhism, death is nothing, because we already are everything, and death does not change that. It simply occurs *within* the all-encompassing Everything we are.

For Platonism, death is also nothing, as can be seen in the way Socrates faces death: as indifferently as Buddha. Whether the spirit is a universal impersonal spirit, as in Buddhism, or an individual human spirit, as in Platonism, death does not affect it, since it is radically different from the body. In Buddhism the individual body is illusion (so is the individual soul); in Platonism it is a mere prison (*soma*, "body", equals *sēma*, "tomb").

In the mythic view (number two), we become less than we were before death.

In reincarnation, we become the same sort of thing we were before death.

Only in Christianity do we become more than we were before death. It is the startling, surprising idea of a new, greater resurrected body:

The records represent Christ as passing after death (as no one had passed before) neither into a purely . . . "spiritual" mode of existence nor into a "natural" life such as we know, but into a life which has its own, new Nature. . . . The picture is not what we expected. . . . It is not the picture of an escape from any and every kind of Nature into some unconditional and utterly transcendent life. It is the picture of a new human nature, and a new Nature in general, being brought into existence. . . . That is the picture—not of unmaking but of remaking. The old field of space, time, matter, and the senses is to be weeded, dug, and sown for a new crop. We may be tired of that old field; God is not.[2]

The Fallacy of a Spiritual Heaven

The origin of the popular heresy that Heaven is purely spiritual is, paradoxically, materialism. The medievals were under no such illusion. Ages that believed in spirit did not believe Heaven was purely spiritual. What is the unraveling of this riddle?

"Spiritual" to premodern cultures did not mean "immaterial". Pre-Cartesian cultures did not divide reality into the two mutually exclusive categories of purely immaterial spirit and purely nonspiritual matter. Rather, they saw all matter as in-formed, in-breathed by spirit,[3] intelligibility manifesting intelligence, artistry manifesting an artist. This vision applied especially to that particularly intricately designed piece of spirit-haunted matter we call the human body, nature's masterpiece and microcosm.[4] We manifest the materiality of spirit as well as the spirituality of matter; in us, spirit is made

[2] C. S. Lewis, *Miracles* (New York: Macmillan, 1955), pp. 178–79.

[3] The progression (regression?) from pantheism to animism to hylozoism to hylomorphism to Cartesian dualism is a progression in the separation of spirit from matter. For a prognosis of the possible next step, cf. D. E. Harding, *The Hierarchy of Heaven and Earth* (London: Faber & Faber, n.d.).

[4] E. F. Schumacher, *A Guide for the Perplexed* (New York: Harper & Row, 1977); Huston Smith, *Forgotten Truth: The Primordial Tradition* (New York: Harper & Row, 1976).

incarnate. The human spirit is the soul *of the body*;[5] it is not just temporarily juxtaposed with it, like a ghost in a machine, a sardine in a can, or a prisoner in a cell (though this Platonic view persisted as an influential heresy alongside Christian orthodoxy and is perennially confused with it). Medieval philosophers were usually quite clear that humanity was a different species, of a different essence, from angels.[6]

Descartes initiates "angelism" when he says, "My whole essence is in thought alone."[7] Matter and spirit now become two "clear and distinct ideas";[8] for "matter" means something extended in space, and "spirit" means something not extended in space. "Matter" means something not conscious, and "spirit" means something conscious. This is *our* common sense; we have inherited these categories, like nonremovable contact lenses, from Descartes, and it is impossible for us to understand pre-Cartesian thinkers while we wear them. Thus we are constantly reading our modern categories anachronistically into the authors of the Bible—for instance, when we insist that a given story must be either mere myth (i.e., subjective, made up, not objectively real) or literal history (i.e., a scientific account).[9] We do not understand that history itself can have mythic dimensions.

After the Cartesian revolution comes the Kantian, the "Copernican revolution in philosophy". Spirit, having been dematerialized, is now subjectivized. "Consciousness" now replaces "knowledge" as the term referring to the distinctively human act. The difference between "knowledge" and

[5] St. Thomas Aquinas, *Summa contra Gentiles*, II, 71, 2; *Summa Theologiae*, I, 76, 1.

[6] St. Thomas Aquinas, *Summa Theologiae*, I, 75, 7; *Summa contra Gentiles*, III, 91, 5.

[7] Descartes, *Meditations*, II; *Discourse on Method*, IV.

[8] Descartes, *Discourse on Method*, IV, par. 3.

[9] C. S. Lewis, "Myth Become Fact" in *God in the Dock* (Grand Rapids, Mich.: Eerdmans, 1970), pp. 63–67; "Transposition" in *The Weight of Glory and Other Addresses* (New York: Macmillan, 1949), pp. 16–29.

"consciousness" is that "knowledge" necessarily refers to an object, while "consciousness" does not. Consciousness can be a world unto itself. Kant's "Copernican revolution" is intended to make the subject and the object exchange places, as Copernicus made sun and earth exchange places: consciousness (subjectivity) is no longer determined by its real object; but objects are structured and determined by consciousness. According to Kant, we unconsciously project our innate a-priori forms of consciousness onto the object, thus shaping a world. We do not discover a ready-made world of forms but make this world in the very act of knowing it. In other words, what Christian theology ascribes to God, Kant ascribes to us, except that we do not create the very existence of the world, only its form.[10] Formless matter is objectively given; form is subjectively created or imposed on it. In still other words, even our science is art.

Kant claims thus to free the human spirit from determinism[11] and from bondage to the objective world. This assumes the Platonic notion of the spirit as being imprisoned in an alien world; one speaks of liberating slaves from their chains but one does not speak of "liberating" water from its hydrogen.

It is after Kant thus "liberates" spirit from the objective world that the idea of a subjective Heaven becomes popular. The reason is not far to seek: once spirit is subjectivized, it follows that if Heaven is spiritual (Descartes' legacy), it must be subjective (the Kantian conclusion). Once objective reality is reduced to spiritless matter, subjectivity is the only place left for spirit, for Heaven, and ultimately even for God, in Kant's successors, notably Schleiermacher.[12]

[10] Fichte takes this next step, denying the objective "thing in itself" altogether and virtually identifying the human and the divine ego: *The Science of Knowledge*, trans. A. E. Kroeger (London: Trubner & Co., 1889), pp. 63–78.

[11] Kant, *Critique of Pure Reason*, Preface to the second edition.

[12] Schleiermacher, *The Christian Faith* (Philadelphia: Fortress Press), I, 4 (pp. 16–17).

Thus the origin of the modern idea of a purely spiritual and subjective Heaven is the materialistic view of the world.

This materialistic view of the world is often mistakenly believed to be a scientific necessity.[13] It is true that a brain chemist cannot worry about the soul in his chemistry, nor an astronomer about God in his astronomy. But the mistake is to forget that all science is selective, like photography. It always abstracts a part or aspect from a more complete, complex, concrete whole. It is science that is abstract and philosophy that is concrete, not vice versa.

One index of how typically modern our common-sense assumptions are is the degree of surprise we feel when we read that statement. Another such index is our puzzlement at Saint Paul's "spiritual body"[14]—a pure contradiction in terms, Cartesianly speaking. One more index of our modern assumptions is our misunderstanding of Plato's statement that "*Ouranos* [Heaven] rightly received its name from *nous* [mind]."[15] We immediately think that he means that Heaven is a state of mind, or subjective, forgetting that mind itself was objective for Plato, not just subjective. There is a cosmic Mind, objective Reason, or eternal Intelligence[16] that contains all the laws, principles, and structures of the universe. This is the divine *Logos*, the region of the Platonic Forms. This was Plato's Heaven, and it was resoundingly objective. As his greatest disciple put it, when our mind knows any truth, it is only by participating in this Mind, by "divine illumination".[17] (Yes, Augustine, not Aristotle, was Plato's greatest disciple, for Augustine expanded Plato and Aristotle contracted

[13] Huston Smith, *Forgotten Truth: The Primordial Tradition*, chap. 5.

[14] 1 Corinthians 15:44.

[15] *Theaetetus*, 202b.

[16] Whether this is Intelligence or just Intelligibility, subject of thought or just object of thought, is debated among Platonists. But the three greatest ancient Platonists, Aristotle, Plotinus, and Augustine, all chose the first alternative, in very different ways.

[17] St. Augustine, *De libero arbitrio*, 11; *De genesi ad litteram*, XII.

him. Augustine's God is the source and ground of Plato's Forms, while Aristotle reduces them to the forms of natural objects.)

Thus, Plato would not advise us to "keep Heaven in mind" so much as to "keep mind in Heaven". For Heaven is not a state of mind; mind is a state in the country of Heaven.

The Need for a Body in Heaven

Philosophical reasoning confirms Scripture's promise of a resurrected body in Heaven rather than a purely spiritual soul in six ways:

First, it is irrational to suppose we change our species. God does not rip up his handiwork as a mistake. We are created to fill one of the possible levels of reality, one of the unique rungs on the cosmic ladder, between animals and angels. This is our essence, our destiny, and our glory. We would lose that by becoming angels just as much as by becoming apes.

To put it in Saint Thomas' technical language, the human soul has an essential potency or tendency to in-form a body.[18] That natural tendency is actualized before death and after resurrection, when the soul *does* inform a body. But it is unactualized between those two states, between death and the resurrection of the body. Yet even then the tendency is there, just as the potency to become an adult oak is still there in a frozen acorn but not in a frozen tulip bulb, or as the potency to speak is there in a newborn baby but not in a newborn cat. Unfreeze the acorn and the tulip bulb, and only one becomes a tree. Unfreeze a disembodied soul and it fits a body, as an angel does not. The forms under which angels appear are not their true bodies, but assumed clothing or appearances for our sake.[19]

---

[18] *Summa Theologiae*, III (Supplement), 70, 1.
[19] St. Augustine, *The City of God*, XIII, 22–23.

As the form of the body, the soul retains the body's memories and personality, which have been conditioned by heredity and environment. If disembodied souls have any experience of time, they remember while awaiting their resurrected bodies how ice cream tasted on the Fourth of July. No angel can make that claim.

And this brings us to a second reason for the resurrection of the body: through our bodies we can do things that no mere spirit can do. We are better than angels at many things, and those things would be missing from us and those perfections missing from the universe if our souls were simply disembodied. Angels are much better than we at intelligence, will, and power; but they cannot smell flowers or weep over a Chopin nocturne.[20]

Only Christianity truly glorifies the senses. Plato thinks they are the prison-house and obstacle to consciousness.[21] Aristotle thinks they are only feeders, raw material for consciousness.[22] Buddha thinks they are distractions and illusions.[23] William James[24] and Aldous Huxley[25] think they and the reason are "reducing valves" to stop down cosmic consciousness. All of them are wrong; all miss the glory. God invented the senses to reveal the unique and irreplaceable tang of the particular to consciousness—the "inscape", as Gerard Manley Hopkins calls it,[26] the "thisness" (*hecceitas*), as his

[20] C. S. Lewis, "On Being Human" in *Poems* (New York: Harcourt, Brace & World, 1965), pp. 34–35.

[21] Plato, *Phaedo*, 64–68.

[22] Aristotle, *Metaphysics*, I, 1 (980a ff.).

[23] Mahaparinibbana Suttanta, "Buddha's Farewell Address" in E. Burtt, *The Teaching of the Compassionate Buddha* (New York: Mentor Books, 1955), p. 47.

[24] William James, *The Varieties of Religious Experience* (New York: New American Library, 1959), p. 324.

[25] Aldous Huxley, *The Doors of Perception* (New York: Harper & Row, 1963), pp. 22–24.

[26] *Notes on Parmenides*, Feb. 9, 1868, in *Journals and Notebooks of G. M. Hopkins*, ed. Humphrey House and Graham Storey (London, 1959), pp. 127, 228.

master Duns Scotus calls it,[27] of each thing in the universe. They are pluses, not minuses.

Therefore, something like them must be in God. Rather (we have it backwards again) they must be like something in God. For God is the source and model of all pluses, all perfections, all that it is better to be than not to be.[28] We usually think of God in Cartesian rather than biblical terms, as the model only of spiritual things, and as Himself spiritual in the Cartesian sense, that is, negatively spiritual, spiritual not only because of something He has (mind) but also because of something He lacks (body and senses). God does *not* have a physical body or senses, but He does not *lack* them either.

Just *how* God "sees", "hears", "feels", "tastes", and "smells" is not clear. It is an analogy, but of what? At least this: that He knows particulars, not just universals—this stone, this person, not just the species.[29] We know universals by the mind and particulars by the senses. What in us is separated is in God together. God knows the particular in the same act and by the same means by which He knows the universal. Perhaps the very distinction between "universal" and "particular" is necessary only on a human level. That seems to be what Duns Scotus meant when he said that essences (like humanness, redness, liverness, twoness, justice) were of themselves and as known by God neither universal nor particular.[30] For us, universals are abstract and particulars are concrete, but in God's mind there may be "concrete universals", as Hegel thought there were even to the human mind.[31] German Idealism is theology masked as anthropology; it is profoundly true, but confuses the human with the divine.

A third reason for the resurrection of the body is that the body is in the soul, not the soul in the body, as we will see in

[27] Duns Scotus, *Opus Oxoniense*, II, d. 3, q. 6, nn. 11–13.
[28] St. Anselm, *Monologium*, II.
[29] St. Thomas Aquinas, *Summa Theologiae*, I, 14, 11.
[30] Duns Scotus, *Metaphysics*, 5, 11.
[31] Hegel, *Phenomenology*, chap. VI, section A.

Chapter 7. The body is the content or material of the soul; the soul is the form of the body. We think it is a harmless platitude to say that we are one, not two; yet it entails the startling consequence that the answer to the question "What is the soul made of?" is "flesh and bones", just as the answer to the question "*What is* this bunch of flesh and bones?" is "a human soul". The body is the matter of the soul, and the soul is the form of the body. That is why the resurrection of the body is internal to the immortality of the soul, not a dispensable extra. The soul carries its body with it. When death separates the two, we have a freak, a monster, an obscenity. That is why we are terrified of ghosts and corpses, though both are harmless: they are the obscenely separated aspects of what belongs together as one. That is why Jesus wept at Lazarus' grave: not merely for His bereavement but for this cosmic obscenity.[32] A soul without its body is not liberated, any more than a body without its blood. It is empty.

A fourth reason for a body in Heaven is for the fulfillment of our soul's primary need, the need for love, for I-Thou relationship, for meeting. "All real living is meeting."[33] Spirits are the meeters, but matter is the street corner where they meet. It is difficult to conceive—perhaps it is impossible to create—a common field in which souls can meet without something that is matter to them; and if they are to inhabit this common world they must have material vehicles, or bodies.[34]

Fifth, our spirit needs a body for freedom, for free expression. A soul without a body is exactly the opposite of what Plato thought it is. It is not free but bound. It is in an extreme form of paralysis, like a person paralyzed in all five senses at once. God gave us senses to help us, not to hinder us. Insofar

[32] John 11:33–35.

[33] Martin Buber, *I and Thou*, trans. Ronald Gregor Smith (New York: Scribner's, 1958), p. 11.

[34] C. S. Lewis, *The Problem of Pain* (New York: Macmillan, 1962), pp. 29–32.

as they hinder or bind us, that is a result of the Fall, not of Creation, and the binding will be removed in Heaven.

Sixth, and finally, it is fitting that just as bodily death was the effect of spiritual death at the Fall,[35] so bodily immortality will be the effect of spiritual immortality in the redeemed. The divine life, the *zoë* that is in us even now as a seed, will in its mature form "flow over" into the glorified body in a "voluptuous torrent", according to Saint Augustine.[36] When the soul fell from God, its life-source, its body as a consequence fell from the soul, *its* life-source; and when the soul is reunited with God, it follows that its body is reunited with it forever.

But What in the World (or out of It) Is a "Spiritual Body"?

The concept of a "spiritual body" comes from Saint Paul. He insists that "if there is a physical body, there is also a spiritual body".[37] But what does he mean?

Not an angel, a ghost, or a disembodied soul, as we have seen. "Spiritual" means "living by the Holy Spirit". Saint Augustine puts it thus:

> And so they will be spiritual, not because they shall cease to be bodies, but because they shall subsist by the life-giving spirit. For as those bodies of ours that have a living soul, though not as yet a life-giving spirit [*zoë*], are called soul-informed bodies, and yet are not souls but bodies, so also those bodies are called spiritual—yet God forbid we should therefore suppose them to be spirits and not bodies—which, being quickened by the Spirit have the substance, but not the unwieldiness and corruption, of flesh.[38]

[35] Genesis 3:3, 4, 19; 5:5.
[36] C. S. Lewis, *The Weight of Glory*, p. 14.
[37] 1 Corinthians 15:44.
[38] St. Augustine, *The City of God*, XIII, 22–23.

The surprising but logically necessary consequences include such scripturally confirmed facts as the ability to eat, just as Jesus did after His Resurrection:[39]

> They shall not eat save when they choose, nor be under the necessity of eating, while they enjoy the power of doing so. For so also was it with the angels who presented themselves to the eye and touch of man, not because they could not do otherwise, but because they were able and desirous to suit themselves to men.[40]

Not that we shall *be* angels, but we shall be *like* angels in this respect: not dependent on the world, yet able to touch it if we please. The way we will do this is not the same as the angels' way. They put on and take off bodies as we do clothes; we exercise the bodies we have at will, for example, by eating only if we please. The common principle is freedom from need.

If we still have difficulty escaping Cartesian dualism and conceiving a "spiritual body", let me suggest three ways of thinking of "body" that will free us from the materialism of body that is the other half of the Cartesian angelism of soul: body is form, body is movement, and body is sensation.

First, body is form. Even now what makes our bodies our bodies is not atoms but structure. The atoms change every seven years; yet it is the same body because of its continuity of form. ("Continuity" does not mean "unchangingness", of course.) It is like a river. A river is not its water, which is always moving on, but its riverbed, which forms the formless water into this river.

As the river is its bed, not its water, my body is its form, not its atoms. This form is not just outer shape but life, animating principle. The Greek word often translated "form", *logos*, comes from *legein*, which means to collect, gather, or

---

[39] Luke 24; 41–43.
[40] St. Augustine, *The City of God*, XIII, 22–23.

make one.[41] Once the form (soul) departs, this unity departs: the atoms, molecules, tissues, and organs of the body begin to disintegrate and scatter.

The atoms of my soul come and go like a river, just like the atoms of my body. These soul-atoms are experiences, actions, thoughts, feelings, and choices. My spirit is to my soul what my soul is to my body: the unifying riverbed of *I*-ness that makes its waters all *mine*.

In Heaven we are given new body atoms, probably a new *kind* of body-atoms, or even a matter that is not composed of atoms at all but is continuous (therefore unbreakable and immortal). It is not the old atoms of our earthly body that are resurrected; they decompose in the grave and are eaten by worms, fish, and fishermen.[42] We all have someone else's secondhand atoms.

Perhaps we are also given new soul-atoms in Heaven. Certainly we have new, Heavenly experiences. And it is our spirit that makes them one, makes them all ours. The spirit is the form of the soul as the soul is the form of the body.

A second way to think of the body is as *movement*:

> Body is movement. If it is at one speed, you smell something; if at another, you hear a sound; if at another you see a sight; if at another you neither see nor hear nor smell, nor know the body in any way. But . . . the two ends meet. . . . If movement is faster, then that which moves is more nearly in two places at once. . . . But if the movement were faster still . . . in the end the moving thing would be in all places at once . . . that is the thing at the top of all bodies, so fast that it is at rest, so truly body that it has ceased being body at all.[43]

[41] Martin Heidegger, *Introduction to Metaphysics*, trans. Ralph Manheim (New York: Doubleday, Anchor Books, 1961), pp. 108–109, 145.

[42] Shakespeare, *Hamlet*, act III, scene 7, lines 17–39. Also, St. Thomas Aquinas, *Summa Theologiae*, III (Supplement), 80, 5 *sed contra*.

[43] C. S. Lewis, *Out of the Silent Planet* (New York: Macmillan, 1938), p. 91.

In this sense God, "the thing at the top of all bodies, so fast that it is at rest", is a body. Our bodies, not just our souls, are the image of God.

Finally, from the same author—in fact, from the last chapter of his last book—a third way of seeing the body and its resurrection:

About the resurrection of the body . . . we are not, in this doctrine, concerned with matter as such at all; with waves and atoms and all that. What the soul cries out for is the resurrection of the senses. Even in this life matter would be nothing to us if it were not the source of sensations.

Now we already have some feeble and intermittent power of raising dead sensations from their graves. I mean, of course, memory . . . memory as we now know it is a dim foretaste, a mirage even, of a power which the soul . . . will exercise hereafter . . . I can now communicate to you the fields of my boyhood—they are building-estates today—only imperfectly, by words. Perhaps the day is coming when I can take you for a walk through them. [44]

[44] C. S. Lewis, *Letters to Malcolm* (New York: Harcourt, Brace & World, 1964), pp. 121–22.

Chapter Seven

What Will Our Bodies Be Like?

THE RESURRECTION OF THE BODY

> He's a terror, that one—
>   Turns water into wine,
>   Turns wine into blood—
> What on earth does he turn blood into?[1]

The only sure way to proceed in exploring this extremely speculative question is to examine the only case of a resurrection body that we know to be authentic: Jesus. The Christian has two good reasons for identifying the resurrection body he or she will get with Christ's resurrection body. First, Christ is the New Man, New Adam; not a freak but the first fruits of *our* body-tree. Second, His resurrection body was not just a resuscitated body, like Lazarus', but a new *kind* of body. He could (and did) take it to Heaven with Him, when He ascended. And so can we.

Identity in the Resurrection Body

How did Jesus' disciples recognize Him in His resurrection body? There is a fascinating puzzle here in the New Testament

---

[1] Christopher Derrick in *New Oxford Review*, October 1981, p. 23.

records; for on three occasions Jesus' disciples, who knew Him intimately for three years, did not at first recognize Him. This happened with Mary Magdalene (John 20:11–18), the Emmaeus disciples (Luke 24:13–35), and the Twelve (John 21:1–7). *Something* was different about Him. What? On the other hand, it was *He*. They eventually did recognize Him without doubt. How?

The answer to the last question that is suggested by the texts is that they recognized Him by what He *did* and *said*—for example, His opening the meaning of the Scriptures and breaking bread at Emmaeus. This seems to indicate a reversal of our present way of knowing persons: we now recognize character through body. But Jesus' disciples recognized His body through His acts-in-character.

The Fall turned things upside down between soul and body. Before the Fall, the body was a transparent window, a totally malleable instrument, a perfectly obedient servant of the soul. The Resurrection restores this relationship. Once the perfected soul is perfectly subject to God, the perfected body can be perfectly subject to the soul, for the soul's authority over the body is a delegated and dependent authority.

This principle of a new soul-body relationship in the Resurrection has important consequences for both soul and body. Soul will no longer be frustrated by a semi-independent, recalcitrant body ("Brother Ass", Saint Francis of Assisi called it); and body will be a bright ray of light from soul, not an opaque object; it will be more subject, less object, more truly mine, truly me. No more will I crave ec-static out-of-the-body experiences, for the highest flights of mystic ecstasy will be *in* this new body. My present drive to self-forgetful, ecstatic joy is like a balloon held under water longing to rise into its native air. But its native air is a body. We long to be re-clothed, not un-clothed.[2]

Our present bodies are neither evil things, like demons, to

[2] 2 Corinthians 5:4.

be hated, nor perfect things, like gods, to be worshiped, but useful and humble things, like donkeys, to be used.[3] There is one part of the body that even now retains something of its pre-Fall transparency to spirit; and this foreshadows its resurrection perfection. It is the face.

The Resurrection Body as "All Face"

The face is me.[4] It is where the body comes to a point, comes to its expression. Perhaps you have noticed the amazing change in the face of a friend who has suddenly fallen in love (with a human being or with God), or who has fallen out of love, or into depression or despair or dishonesty. The change did not consist in anything physically catastrophic. The eyes did not grow farther apart. No Pinocchio nose appeared on the liar. Yet a far more catastrophic change took place, and our eyes can see it if they are wise. See Plain Jane suddenly become radiant; see the dissipated playboy suddenly become self-aware and self-possessed; see the self-satisfied millionaire suddenly recognize his life is spiritually bankrupt. The face is a window.

We are *responsible* for our face, as we are not responsible for our legs, or our height.[5] The physical contours of Miss America's body and even of her face are merely a gift of nature and God; but the personality shining through your loved one's face is him or her; it is character. It is loved not impersonally, like Miss America's "perfect" features, but personally. As the soul is the image of God in the world, the face is the image of the soul in the body.

Contrast the face of a saint with that of a gross sinner. Notice especially the eyes. Contrast eyes tempered with love

---

[3] *The Life of St. Francis* in *The Little Flowers of St. Francis, The Mirror of Perfection,* and *The Life of St. Francis* (New York: Dutton; London: Dent, Everyman's Library, 1934), p. 331; C. S. Lewis, *The Four Loves* (London: Collins Fontana Books, 1965), p. 93.

[4] John Liggett, *The Human Face* (London: Constable, 1974).

[5] W. H. Auden, *The Protestant Mystics* (New York: New American Library, 1964), pp. 27–28.

and suffering with eyes that have refused these lessons. Environmental tools providentially wielded by the divine sculptor have chiseled fine lines on His masterpieces, the saints. Yet it is impossible to put it into a verbal formula. You just *see* it.

Medieval art is wonderfully sensitive to the magical power of faces. The Middle Ages is the great age of the Incarnation, of the spiritualization of matter, of the sacraments, and of the body. Its bodies are more like resurrection bodies—especially the faces, and most especially the eyes. The presence of God gives them depth, light, energy, harmony, and inexhaustible significance.

The rest of the body shares this significance to a lesser degree, especially its posture, its carriage, its "body language". Sanctity brings not only a quiet glow to the face but purposive movement, confidence, and health to the whole body. The hand of God is made visible in the hands of men. Zen masters are often called "holy to their fingertips", like Buddha.[6] They do not "wobble". Jesus was "full of grace and truth".[7] Not the *soul* of Jesus, but *Jesus*. Extend these visible beginnings to totality and you have the spiritual body: *all face!* In fact, all eyes, like Ezekiel's unearthly, arresting vision.[8] All subject, not object, not *thing*.

This is how Jesus' friends recognized Him spiritually after the Resurrection. Spirit is act, activity. It is not material activity, but it manifests itself in material activity. In the music, in the poem, in the architecture, it makes matter live, and move, and have spiritual being.

Spirit is also free; free choice is essential to spirit. It seems reasonable, therefore, to think that we will get to choose our bodies in Heaven freely, rather than having them imposed on us.[9] But such choice, like such freedom, would not be

---

[6] Hermann Hesse, *Siddhartha* (New York: New Directions, 1957), p. 30.
[7] John 1:14.
[8] Ezekiel 1:18.
[9] Plato, *Republic*, X, 617e–21a.

arbitrary, not subject to the caprice of a hereditary quirk or
the whim of environmental conditioning. It would be a fitting,
predictable, and even necessary choice, like a saint's choice to
love. For at their apex, freedom and necessity converge,[10] for
God is the apex of both freedom and necessity. The closer
we are to God, the more a choice is fully free because fully
ours, not alien to but expressive of our true nature and destiny,
which are hidden in God.[11] He has the white stone with our
new name on it,[12] in Him is the secret of our identity, which
is both our freedom and our destiny.[13] Our bodies would
express both the freedom and the necessary destiny of the soul.

Freedom in the Resurrection Body

During our life on earth, many things are forced on us: birth,
race, temperament, parents, and so forth. When we mature,
we can freely reconquer much of the territory that conquered
us. We can choose to be born, to affirm life, to prefer life to
death. We can affirm our temperament, accepting our hot-
headedness, or analytical bent, or activism. We can relate freely
to our parents, especially after we become parents ourselves.

All these things are foreshadowings of Heavenly freedom.
We are destined to conquer completely all the unfree things
imposed on us here. And all these things come to us through
our body. The body receives; the soul acts.

When we choose our resurrection bodies, we reconquer all
our unfreedom, because it all comes through the body. In
fact, we may be doing that right now: shaping the atoms of
our spiritual bodies by every choice we make. For our choices

---

[10] C. S. Lewis, *Surprised by Joy* (New York: Harcourt, Brace & World,
1955), p. 237; *A Grief Observed* (New York: Bantam, 1976), p. 89.

[11] Thomas Merton, *Seeds of Contemplation* (New York: Dell, 1949), chap. 3.

[12] Revelation 2:17.

[13] Peter Kreeft, "The Wonder of the *Silmarillion*" in *Shadows of Imagination*,
ed. Mark Hillegas (Carbondale, Ill.: Southern Illinois University Press, 1979),
p. 177.

shape our souls, and these are the forms of our bodies, as the hand is the form of the glove.

But is not the resurrection body a gift of God, a divine miracle rather than a human achievement? Yes, but God likes to work even miracles via human intermediaries, to associate creatures with Himself in creating. He gave us free will so that we could be co-creators of our selves, our souls, the forms of our bodies.

Wounds and Imperfections in the Resurrected Body

One of the most intriguing features of Christ's post-Resurrection appearances is the fact that His new, glorified body still had its crucifixion wounds, its stigmata. He showed them to "doubting Thomas", remember, as proof that it was really He.[14] And He gave them to Saint Francis of Assisi as a badge of glory, not scars of ugliness.[15] The dead who appear to the living also sometimes manifest their marks of suffering. Sheldon Vanauken's wife had dark shadows under her eyes when she appeared to her husband after her death. She had acquired them through suffering in the hospital.

> Then I couldn't resist asking her how she, in heaven, could have dark shadows under her eyes. She grinned, knowing me, and then said seriously, "I can't tell you that. I can't tell you very much at all."[16]

On the other hand, many of the resuscitated patients Moody interviewed reported their wounds were healed and broken limbs mended.[17]

[14] John 20:24–29.
[15] St. Bonaventura, *The Life of St. Francis*, trans. E. Gurney Salter (London: J. M. Dent, 1934).
[16] Sheldon Vanauken, *A Severe Mercy* (New York: Bantam, 1975, 1981), p. 222.
[17] Raymond Moody, *Life after Life* (New York: Bantam, 1976), pp. 47–54; Maurice Rawlings, M.D., *Beyond Death's Door* (New York: Bantam, 1979), chap. 6.

The explanation of the apparent contradiction seems to be this: many cosmetic features of the body that are imperfections when judged by human standards, especially the wounds of Christ and of the Christian, freely accepted and offered to God, are in fact badges of beauty. The eyes of love see truly; where they see beauty, beauty is, even if the world sees ugliness.[18] Love sees such wounds as augmenting the body's beauty by expressing the beauty of soul or character. Who has not marveled at the deep inner beauty of a careworn face full of wrinkles, tempered by suffering? How beautiful are the wise and gentle eyes of a very old woman at peace with God!

> Like a white candle in a holy place
> Such is the beauty of an aged face.[19]

How fatuous and empty by comparison are the eyes of some childish, spoiled movie star. The heavenly body is made beautiful by its soul, not its shape; by its inscape, not its landscape. So are our earthly bodies, if only we had eyes to see, if only we applied our Heavenly wisdom.

On the other hand, a wound or deformity is of its own nature a work of Satan, not of God. God is the author of healing, not of disease. Few things are more certain in Scripture than that the popular attitude "God wants me to suffer" is profoundly false. Christ is our surest word about the Father, the complete revelation of the Father,[20] and Christ healed all who came to Him, though sometimes after a time of testing, short ("Go, wash in the pool of Siloam"[21]) or long (Saint Paul's lifelong "thorn in the flesh"[22]). Healing is a sign

[18] Charles Williams, *The Figure of Beatrice: A Study in Dante* (London: Faber & Faber, 1943), pp. 47–48.

[19] Joseph Campbell, "The Old Woman" in *The Garden of Bees and Other Poems* (Dublin: H. Gill & Sons, 1905).

[20] Colossians 2:9.

[21] John 9:7.

[22] 2 Corinthians 12:7.

(*sēmeion*, "miracle") of the Kingdom of Heaven. Heaven is complete healing.

All prayers for healing are answered. The puzzle of how to understand Christ's oft-repeated promises in the New Testament, such as "Whatever you ask Me, I will do it for you",[23] is easily solved. He means exactly what He says—no watering down, no evasion, no "nuancing". But He has not yet fulfilled all His promises. Many prayers for good things like healings have not been answered—yet. The only understanding of these passages that does not make nonsense of the two facts of promises and nonfulfillments is that it is only a matter of time, and the timing is God's, not ours. Not even the Son knows when the ultimate prophecy, His own Second Coming, will come true.[24]

He has not told us how soon He will keep His promises, but He *has* promised us an astounding basket of goodies, and it is certain that He will keep His promises. Heaven will be the answer to every prayer, every desire for healing, physical, emotional, mental, and spiritual. All healings on earth are previews of coming attractions.[25]

What Age Will Our Heavenly Bodies Be?

As heavenly bodies do not die, they do not age. So what age will we be in Heaven?

Resuscitated patients report their out-of-the-body body as not having any particular age.[26] Naturally; it is measured not by *chronos* but only by *kairos*, not by physical time but by soul time. And since time is differently related to the soul and the soul differently related to the body in Heaven,[27] therefore

[23] Matthew 7:7; 21:22; Luke 11:9; John 14:13; 15:7; 16:24.
[24] Matthew 24:36.
[25] Luke 11:20.
[26] Ralph Wilkerson, *Beyond and Back* (New York: Bantam, 1978); E. Haraldsson and K. Osis, *At the Hour of Death*.
[27] Cf. chap. 5.

time is differently related to the body in Heaven. The measure of matter moving through space does not measure Heavenly bodies; "the heavenly bodies" do not measure our Heavenly bodies.

We see traces of Heavenly agelessness on earth occasionally: in the timeless wisdom of the infant or in the womblike stillness of the wise who approach death in perfect peace. This agelessness is like the perfect age that includes all ages, as all ages of one's life pass in instant review before the dying.[28] The Heavenly age is no age and all ages.

Saint Thomas Aquinas taught that the perfect age was thirty-three, since it was the age Christ had attained when He died; therefore, he thought everyone would have a body like a thirty-three-year-old body in Heaven.[29] Like the numbering of days in Purgatory, this is to be taken only symbolically, not literally, because in Heaven there is neither birth nor death, the measuring sticks of age.

Oneness with Nature in the Resurrection Body

When our bodies and nature are both resurrected, as Scripture promises,[30] we will no longer be under the dominion of nature. We will not need to breathe, or eat; yet we will be able to, like Christ after His Resurrection.[31] We will not be dependent on "incessant subsidies" of food, air, and water from nature, but we will still be *with* "our old enemy, friend, playfellow and foster-mother".[32]

It is a tempting thought to which many philosophers, beginning with Plato, have succumbed, to think that the more spiritual we are, the less material, the less concerned with

[28] Moody, *Life after Life*, pp. 64–72; Vanauken, *A Severe Mercy*, pp. 185–86.

[29] St. Thomas Aquinas, *Summa Theologiae*, III (Supplement), 81, 1.

[30] Romans 8:21–22; Revelation 21:1.

[31] Luke 24:41–43.

[32] C. S. Lewis, *Miracles* (New York: Macmillan, 1955), p. 81.

matter, the more indifferent and absentminded we are. It is not so. Even now, when we are most mindful, we are most mindful of matter; when we are the most spiritual and conscious, the most alive and awake and alert and aware, we are most present to the world—just as God is.

To quote Moody's resuscitated patients again, some said about their bodies' presence to the world: "It was like I was *just there*."[33] Usually we are not "just there"; we are half present and half absent. The spiritual body is more *there*, more present to its world, than the physical body is to its world. One patient said, "It seemed to me at the time that if something happened any place in the world that I could just be there."[34] Space will exist but it will not separate. We will have what Saint Thomas calls "agility".[35]

There is still more. More than *presence* to the world, the resurrection body will give us *union* with the world. The mystics and the romantic poets foresee this, perhaps foretaste it, this overcoming of alienation between ourselves and nature, subject and object. It is a half-truth that the body (*soma*) is a prison (*sēma*); as a hyphen both joins and separates two parts of a word, the body both joins us to nature and separates us from it. It identifies us with this part of nature but separates us from the rest. We long to "put on" the rest, the whole of nature, as our greater body:

> We do not want merely to *see* beauty, though, God knows, even that is bounty enough. We want something else which can hardly be put into words—to be united with the beauty we see, to pass into it, to receive it into ourselves, to bathe in it, to become part of it. That is why we have peopled air and earth and water with gods and goddesses and nymphs and elves—that, though we cannot, yet these projections can, enjoy in themselves that beauty, grace and power of which Nature

---

[33] Moody, *Life after Life*, p. 50.
[34] Ibid, p. 52.
[35] St. Thomas Aquinas, *Summa Theologiae*, III (Supplement), 84.

is the image. That is why the poets tell us such lovely false-hoods. They talk as if the west wind could really sweep into a human soul; but it can't. They tell us that "beauty born of murmuring sound" will pass into a human face; but it won't. Or not yet. For if we take the imagery of Scripture seriously, if we believe that God will one day *give* us the Morning Star and cause us to *put on* the splendour of the sun, then we may surmise that both the ancient myths and the modern poetry, so false as history, may be very near the truth as prophecy. At present we are on the outside of the world, the wrong side of the door. We discern the freshness and purity of morning, but they do not make us fresh and pure. We cannot mingle with the splendours we see. But all the leaves of the New Testament are rustling with the rumour that it will not always be so. Some day, God willing, we shall get *in*.[36]

Our foretaste of this union is our present bodies. For the body is me and is nature, subject and object at once without diminution. It is a thing "out there" and a thing "in here", object of consciousness, yet conscious of objects. It transcends the subject-object dualism but not by dissolving it or by seeing through it as an illusion or by some strange third kind of reality that is neither the one nor the other but a kind of infinite indefiniteness. Rather, it is wholly subject and wholly object, as Christ is wholly God and wholly Man at the same time: a hypostatic union rather than a mystical transcendence.[37]

If this hypostatic union with nature is one of our natural desires, and if "no natural desire is in vain",[38] then this desire is not in vain but destined for fulfillment. The pagan dream is fulfilled in the Christian reality. For pagans dimly saw in their gods what we foresee in our selves: persons who could

---

[36] C. S. Lewis, *The Weight of Glory* (New York: Macmillan, 1949), pp. 12–13.
[37] St. Thomas Aquinas, *Summa Theologiae*, III, 2, 3–6.
[38] Aristotle, *Ethics*, I, 2 (1094a20).

put on and take off the powers of nature as clothing.[39] We will put on nature as our body when God puts us on as *His* body.

How much of nature will rise with us? How great will our resurrection body be? As big as the soul wills. All that we "identify with" is part of our identity. We are not even now just an ego in a bag of skin. We are outside our epidermis; we are everything we love. Materially, the world and the epidermis enclose us; spiritually, we enclose the world. "By space the universe swallows me; by thought, I contain the universe."[40] Spirit is a rubber band. Love stretches it. It is our rehearsal for Heaven's infinite stretching.

Another reason for this total stretching of the spirit is our task of thoroughly understanding every other soul that God created.[41] Since every soul assimilates a different part and aspect of nature as part of its earthly experience, we would have to assimilate all experienced nature to fulfill this "Communion of Saints." All that has been "tamed" (in the sense of *The Little Prince*)[42] by others will be tamed by us, without thereby losing its wildness, its glorious independence.[43]

Power over Nature: Magic and Miracles

Our heavenly power over nature will be as great as our present power over our own bodies, because nature will then be our greater body. Since our present body magic is our empirical clue to our future Heavenly powers, let us explore this clue.

We do not usually realize that we have great magical powers

---

[39] J. R. R. Tolkien, *The Silmarillion* (Boston: Houghton Mifflin, 1977), p. 21.

[40] Pascal, *Pensées*, trans. Krailsheimer (New York: Penguin Books, 1985), 113.

[41] Cf. chap. 20.

[42] Antoine de Saint-Exupery, *The Little Prince*, trans. Katherine Woods (New York: Harcourt, Brace & World, 1943).

[43] C. S. Lewis, *Miracles*, chap. 9.

right now. For instance, we can levitate. By sheer force of
spiritual willpower we can force our bodies to defy the physical
law of gravity and rise into the air. It is called jumping. The
only reason we think of it as nonmiraculous is its frequency,
not its nature. It is as miraculous as walking on water. More
miraculous, in fact; since the difference between a bunch of
molecules and a soul-enlivened body is far greater than the
difference between walking on land and walking on water.

We can also perform magic on nature as well as on our
body when we use our body as our magic wand to touch
other parts of nature. Gravity says to the stone, "Down!"
Our will says to the stone, "Up!" and the will's magic wand,
the arm, enforces the magic.

Even technology participates in magic, for it is the extension
of our magic wands. But direct soul-body magic is more
powerful than technology, because it needs no instrument.
The soul does not move the body in the same way as the
body moves a stone; it needs no crowbar. The greatest power
comes from union. The closer you are to a thing or to a
person, the more power you have over it or him. You have
more influence with your close friends than with strangers,
and most of all with yourself.

True magic is not the popular, Faustian kind.[44] It is not the
power of the magician but of the *Tao*, the cosmic root from
which both we and nature flow. The true magician works
from the *Tao*, as its instrument; he unites will and nature at
their common Source.

(Yes, magic does occasionally really happen, especially in
the East. Only the prejudice of dogmatic skepticism blinds
the modern mind to many well-attested cases of it.[45])

---

[44] J. R. R. Tolkien, "On Fairy Stories" in *Tree and Leaf* (Boston: Houghton
Mifflin, 1965), p. 10; C. S. Lewis, *The Abolition of Man* (New York: Macmillan, 1965), pp. 67–91; *Letters to Malcolm* (New York: Harcourt, Brace &
World, 1964), pp. 103–4.

[45] Cf. *Proceedings of the Society for Psychical Research*, London, 1882–present
(published irregularly).

The *Tao*, like the *Logos*, is no other than God, of course. "In the beginning was the *Tao*", as John may well have written had he written Chinese instead of Greek. The equation of *Tao* with *Logos* reminds us that the Source of Life (the *Tao*) is the Word (*Logos*), that there is living magic in the Word. When Adam named the animals, he shared God's word-magic. For this was not labeling, this was making: "whatever the man called every living creature, that was its name."[46] God had created the universe simply by naming it: Let there be *X* . . . and there was *X*.[47] As Heidegger says, "It is in words and language that things first come into being and are."[48]

Human creative artists dimly reflect this divine power, and our love of artistic creation is both a shadow of the Creator in whose image we are created and a foreshadowing of our creative task to come in Heaven. For our power over nature in Heaven may well extend to co-creating, in union with God, new natures, new worlds in fact as we now make them in fantasy, as Tolkien supposes:

> The Evangelium has not abrogated legends; it has hallowed them, especially the "happy ending". The Christian . . . may now, perhaps, fairly dare to guess that in Fantasy he may actually assist in the effoliation and multiple enrichment of creation. All tales may come true; and yet, at the last, redeemed, they may be as like and as unlike the forms that we give them as Man, finally redeemed, will be like and unlike the fallen that we know.[49]

This may also explain our fear of getting too deeply into fantasizing, our fear that we cannot get back into reality, our fear that our dreams will come true. Thus the child often feels as guilty for his desires and dreams of evil deeds as if he had

[46] Genesis 2:19.

[47] Genesis 1:3, 6, 9, 14, 20, 24, 26.

[48] Martin Heidegger, *Introduction to Metaphysics*, trans. Ralph Manheim (New York: Doubleday, Anchor Books, 1961), p. 11.

[49] J. R. R. Tolkien, "On Fairy Stories" in *Tree and Leaf*, p. 73.

actually done them: "Grandma died because I hated her." This
is not mere foolishness, as we usually think, and we can feel
it in ourselves as well as children if we let ourselves enter into
it. Try it. Really imagine you are a cat, or a piece of music.
Are you unable to do it or afraid to do it? Isn't there something
in you that is afraid because it fears you might really become
the thing you imagine? I think there is, though most of us
have "succeeded" in burying it. It is not an unintelligible
illusion, but only an illusion of time. It is a foreshadowing of
heavenly creative magic.

Our present powers over nature have been severely limited.
We are spoiled children whose Father has taken away their
dangerous toys. Imagine the chaos the world would be if it
were inhabited by a billion evil magicians, each trying to be
its own God. God could not allow nature to be our greater
body once we had fallen, because billions of warring spirits
would fight for control over the same body—which is exactly
what human history has in fact been, except that the spirits
are mercifully exiled from that body of nature and can control
it only indirectly and in part. If nature had not been emptied
of the human spirit, it would have had a horribly schizoid,
multiple personality, like the Gadarene demoniac: "My name
is Legion; for we are many."[50] Before the power of union
with nature can be restored, union with God must be restored;
we become truly a "we" by obeying one "I AM". The Greek
philosopher Plotinus says:

> We are like a chorus grouped around a conductor who allow
> their attention to be distracted by the audience. If, however,
> they were to turn toward their conductor, they would sing as
> they should and would really be one with him. We are always
> around The One. If we were not, we would dissolve and cease
> to exist. Yet our gaze does not remain fixed upon The One.
> When we look at it, we then attain the end of our desires and

[50] Mark 5:9.

find rest. Then it is that, all discord past, we dance an inspired dance around it.[51]

Christianity adds that the "it" is a "Him", and the song is a hymn.

God will let nature obey our authority only when we obey His as perfectly as the Son obeys the Father.[52] The natural hierarchy of authority and obedience was so upset by the rebellion of the Fall that we rebel against the very *words* "authority", "obedience", and "hierarchy" today. As long as we are not content with our weakness, we cannot be given power. We are given power only when we have no enemies to conquer—indeed, having no enemies gives us unconquerable power, as both Lao Tzu's *Tao Te Ching* and Jesus' Sermon on the Mount reveal.[53] When we succumb to the serpent's temptation to "be like God" in power but not in virtue, we reenact Adam's Fall. Modern technology has enormously increased our ability to fulfill that promise. Though of course not intrinsically evil, it has become a great selling point in the serpent's advertising campaign. The crucial turn would come with the discovery of artificial immortality. That would be the conquest of the supreme power, the power of life. It would be our invasion into Eden past God's forbidding seraphim to eat the fruit of the second tree, the tree of life.

The serpent, as every reader of Scripture knows, is "the father of lies".[54] The Heaven-on-earth he promises would become a Hell-on-earth. The tourniquet of impotence that minimized the bleeding of our disease of sin would be loosened; the quarantine that confined that disease by death would be broken, and our "nightmare civilizations" would

---

[51] Plotinus, *Enneads*, VI, 9, 8.

[52] C. S. Lewis, *The Weight of Glory*, p. 13; *The Problem of Pain* (New York: Macmillan, 1966), chap. 5, especially pp. 81–83; *George MacDonald: An Anthology* (New York: Macmillan, 1978), p. 54 (122).

[53] Lao Tzu, *Tao Te Ching*, 30, 50, 64.

[54] John 8:44.

the greatest thing, now or then, and we should not over-emphasize it, as our idolatrous civilization has done for four centuries. Specifically, the powers of the resurrection body are not as wonderful as we tend to think, for three reasons.

First, they are only an extension of the power we already have. The augmentation of our body power in Heaven will no more bring us meaning or happiness than its augmentation by technology on earth has done. As Freud so puzzledly but honestly observes, we have become like gods but our godlike condition has not brought us any increase in happiness, as it promised.[57]

A second reason heavenly magic should not overawe us is that we take our present magic powers for granted. We therefore would probably take for granted even heavenly wizardry if we did not also acquire wisdom. Unless Heaven gives us an enlightened spirit and sense of appreciation for the powers we have even now—unless Heaven encloses its power in wisdom—it is not Heavenly. A Heavenly appreciation of earthly powers is more Heavenly than an earthly appreciation of the most Heavenly powers.

In the third place, even Heavenly magic is not the most wonderful thing. To see this, notice that we use *wonder* in three different ways: (1) anything that strikes us as unusual or surprising; (2) wonder*ing*, questioning, curiosity; and (3) awe and appreciation. The third, not the first, is the deepest and truest kind of wonder. The intrinsically wonderful things are the already widespread goodness and truth and beauty we find in our lives, not spectacular powers, which are wonderful not in themselves but only by a subjective standard of what is wonderful, that is, their newness to us. The supremely wonderful reality is God, and the true standard of wonderfulness is proximity to God. Truth, goodness, and beauty are closer to the essence of God than power; "God is not in

[57] Sigmund Freud, *Civilization and Its Discontents* (New York: Norton, 1961), pp. 38–39.

strength but in truth." [58] Therefore Heaven's greatest wonder is not miracles but goodness. The same was true of Heaven-on-earth, Christ. And the same is true right now of the Christian. Our Heavenly power, both now and then, is only in the third place our power over nature. It is in the second place our power over ourselves, our power over our power (the thing our age of atomic toys so crucially lacks), [59] and in the first place God's power over us.

[58] Dostoyevski, *The Brothers Karamazov*, trans. Constance Garnett (New York: Vintage Books, 1955), p. 369.

[59] Gabriel Marcel, *The Philosophy of Existentialism*, trans. Manya Harari (New York: Citadel, 1966), p. 31.

Chapter Eight

Is There Sex in Heaven?

We cannot know what X-in-Heaven is unless we know what X is. We cannot know what sex in Heaven is unless we know what sex is. We cannot know what in Heaven's name sex is unless we know what on earth sex is.

But don't we know? Haven't we been thinking about almost nothing else for years and years? What else dominates our fantasies, waking and sleeping, twenty-four nose-to-the-grindstone hours a day? What else fills our TV shows, novels, plays, gossip columns, self-help books, and psychologies *but* sex?

No, we do not think too much about sex; we think hardly at all about sex. Dreaming, fantasizing, feeling, experimenting—yes. But honest, look-it-in-the-face *thinking*?—hardly ever. There is no subject in the world about which there is more heat and less light.[1]

Therefore I want to begin with four abstract philosophical principles about the nature of sex. They are absolutely necessary not only for sanity about sex in Heaven but also for sanity about sex on earth, a goal at least as distant as Heaven

---

[1] For some light, see Stephen Clark, *Man and Woman in Christ* (Ann Arbor, Mich.: Servant, 1980); Frank Sheed, *Society and Sanity* (New York: Sheed & Ward, 1953), chap. 8; C. S. Lewis, *The Four Loves* (New York: Harcourt, Brace Jovanovich, 1960); Jerry Exel, *Sex and the Spirit* (Berkeley, Calif.: Genesis Publications, 1973); Robert Farrar Capon, *Bed and Board* (New York: Simon & Schuster, 1965).

to our sexually suicidal society.[2] The fact that sex is public does not mean it is mature and healthy. The fact that there are thousands of "how to do it" books on the subject does not mean that we know how; in fact, it means the opposite. It is when everybody's pipes are leaking that people buy books on plumbing.[3]

My four philosophical principles will seem strange or even shocking to many people today. Yet they are far from radical, or even original; they are simply the primeval platitudes known to all premodern societies; the sane, sunny country of sexual common sense by the vote of "the democracy of the dead".[4] Yet in another way they are "radical", in the etymological sense of the word: they are our sexual *roots*, and our uprooted society is rooting around looking for sexual substitute-roots like a pig rooting for truffles. It has not found them. That fact should at least make us pause and look back at our "wise blood",[5] our roots. Here are four of them.

First Principle: Sex Is Something You Are, Not Something You Do

Suppose you saw a book with the title "The Sexual Life of a Nun".[6] You would probably assume it was a scurrilous, gossipy sort of story about tunnels connecting convents and monasteries, clandestine rendezvous behind the high altar, and masking a pregnancy as a tumor. But it is a perfectly proper title: all nuns have a sexual life. They are women, not men. When a nun prays or acts charitably, *she* prays or acts, not he. Her celibacy forbids intercourse, but it cannot forbid her to be a woman. In everything she does her essence plays

---

[2] George Gilder, *Sexual Suicide* (New York: Quadrangle, 1973).

[3] Exel, *Sex and the Spirit*, p. 6.

[4] G. K. Chesterton, *Orthodoxy* (New York: Dodd, Mead, 1946), p. 85.

[5] Flannery O'Connor, *Wise Blood* (New York: Harcourt, Brace, 1962).

[6] Capon, *Bed and Board*, p. 12.

a part, and her sex is as much a part of her essence as her age, her race, and her sense of humor.

The counterfeit phrase "having sex" (meaning "intercourse") was minted only recently. Of course a nun "has sex": she is female. Draftees often fill in the box on their induction forms labeled "sex" not with the word "male" but "occasionally" or "please!" The joke would have been unintelligible to previous generations. The significance of the linguistic change is that we have trivialized sex into a thing to do rather than a quality of our inner being. It has become a thing of surfaces and external feeling rather than of personality and internal feeling.[7] Thus even masturbation is called "having sex", though it is exactly the opposite: a denial of real relationship with the other sex.

The words "masculinity" and "femininity", meaning something more than merely biological maleness and femaleness, have been reduced from archetypes to stereotypes. Traditional expectations that men be men and women be women are confused because we no longer know what to expect men and women to be. Yet, though confused, the expectations remain. Our hearts desire, even while our minds reject, the old "stereotypes". The reason is that the old stereotypes were closer to our innate sexual instincts than are the new stereotypes. We have sexist hearts even while we have unisex heads. Evidence for this claim? More people are attracted to the old stereotypes than to the new ones. Romeo still wants to marry Juliet.

The main fault in the old stereotypes was their too-tight connection between sexual being and social doing, their tying of sexual identity to social roles, especially for women: the feeling that it was somehow unfeminine to be a doctor, lawyer, or politician. But the antidote to this illness is not confusing sexual identities but locating them in our being rather than in our doing. Thus we can soften up social roles without softening

[7] Exel, *Sex and the Spirit*, p. 8.

up sexual identities. In fact, a man who is confident of his inner masculinity is much more likely to share in traditionally female activities like housework and baby care than one who ties his sexuality to his social roles.

If our first principle is accepted, if sexuality is part of our inner essence, then it follows that there is sexuality in Heaven, whether or not we "have sex" and whether or not we have sexually distinct social roles in Heaven.

Second Principle: The Alternative to Chauvinism Is Not Egalitarianism

The two most popular philosophies of sexuality today seem totally opposed to each other; yet at a most basic level they are in agreement and are equally mistaken. The two philosophies are the old chauvinism and the new egalitarianism; and they seem totally opposed. For chauvinism (a) sees one sex as superior to the other, "second", sex.[8] This is usually the male, but there are increasingly many strident female chauvinist voices in the current cacophony.[9] This presupposes (b) that the sexes are intrinsically different, different by nature not social convention. Egalitarianism tries to disagree with (a) totally; it thinks that to do so it has to disagree with (b) as well. But this means that it *agrees* with chauvinism on (c), the unstated but assumed premise *that all differences must be differences in value*, or, correlatively, that the only way for two things to be equal in value is for them to be equal in nature. Both philosophies see sameness or superiority as the only options. It is from this assumption (that differences are differences in value) that the chauvinist argues that the sexes

[8] Simone de Beauvoir, *The Second Sex* (New York: Knopf, 1953).

[9] E.g., Mary Daly, *Gyn-Ecology: The Metaethics of Radical Feminism* (Boston: Beacon Press, 1979); Una Stannard, *Mrs. Man* (San Francisco: Germain Books, 1977); Kathy Ferguson, *Self, Society and Womankind: The Dialectic of Liberation* (Westport, Conn.: Greenwood Press, 1980); Zillah Eisenstein, *The Radical Future of Liberal Feminism* (New York: Longmans, 1981).

are different in nature, therefore they are different in value. And it is from the same assumption that the egalitarian argues that the sexes are *not* different in value, therefore they are not different in nature.

Chauvinism:	*Egalitarianism:*
(c)	(c)
and (b)	and not (a)
therefore (a)	therefore not (b)

Once this premise is smoked out, it is easy to see how foolish both arguments are. Of course not all differences are differences in value. Are dogs better than cats, or cats than dogs? Or are they different only by convention, not by nature? Chauvinist and egalitarian should both read the poets, songwriters, and mythmakers to find a third philosophy of sexuality that is both more sane and infinitely more interesting. It denies neither the obvious rational truth that the sexes are equal in value (as the chauvinist does) nor the equally obvious instinctive truth that they are innately different (as the egalitarian does). It revels in both, and in their difference: *vive la différence!*

If sexual differences are natural, they are preserved in Heaven, for "grace does not destroy nature but perfects it".[10] If sexual differences are only humanly and socially conventional, Heaven will remove them as it will remove economics and penology and politics. (Not many of us have job security after death. That is one advantage of being a philosopher.) All these things came after and because of the Fall, but sexuality came as part of God's original package: "be fruitful and multiply".[11] God may unmake what *we* make, but He does not unmake what *He* makes. God made sex, and God makes no mistakes.

[10] St. Thomas Aquinas, *Summa Theologiae*, I, 1, 8 ad 2.
[11] Genesis 1:28.

Saint Paul's frequently quoted statement that "in Christ . . . there is neither male nor female"[12] does not mean there is no sex in Heaven. For it refers not just to Heaven but also to earth: we are "in Christ" *now*.[13] (In fact, if we are not "in Christ" now there is no hope of Heaven for us!) But we *are* male or female now. His point is that our sex does not determine our "in-Christness"; God is an equal opportunity employer. But He employs the men and women He created, not the neuters of our imagination.

Third Principle: Sex Is Spiritual

That does not mean "vaguely pious, ethereal, and idealistic". "Spiritual" means "a matter of the spirit", or soul, or psyche, not just the body. Sex is between the ears before it's between the legs. We have sexual *souls*.[14]

For some strange reason people are shocked at the notion of sexual souls. They not only disagree; the idea seems utterly crude, superstitious, repugnant, and incredible to them. Why? We can answer this question only by first answering the opposite one: why is the idea reasonable, enlightened, and even necessary?

The idea is the only alternative to either materialism or dualism. If you are a materialist, there is simply no soul for sex to be a quality of. If you are a dualist, if you split body and soul completely, if you see a person as a ghost in a machine,[15] then one half of the person can be totally different from the other: the body can be sexual without the soul being sexual. The machine is sexed, the ghost is not. (This is almost the exact opposite of the truth: ghosts, having once been persons, have sexual identity from their personalities, their souls. Machines do not.)

[12] Galatians 3:28.   [13] Galatians 2:20.

[14] Exel, *Sex and the Spirit*, chap. 1.

[15] Gilbert Ryle, *The Concept of Mind* (New York, London: Hutchinson's University Library, 1949).

No empirical psychologist can be a dualist; the evidence for psychosomatic unity is overwhelming.[16] No pervasive feature of either body or soul is insulated from the other; every sound in the soul echoes in the body, and every sound in the body echoes in the soul. Let the rejection of dualism be Premise One of our argument.

Premise Two is the even more obvious fact that biological sexuality is innate, natural, and in fact pervasive to every cell in the body. It is *not* socially conditioned, or conventional, or environmental; it is hereditary.

The inevitable conclusion from these two premises is that sexuality is innate, natural, and pervasive to the whole person, soul as well as body. The only way to avoid the conclusion is to deny one of the two premises that logically necessitate it—to deny psychosomatic unity or to deny innate somatic sexuality.

In the light of this simple and overwhelming argument, why is the conclusion not only unfamiliar but shocking to so many people in our society? I can think of only two reasons. The first is a mere misunderstanding, the second a serious and substantial mistake.

The first reason would be a reaction against what is wrongly seen as monosexual soul-stereotyping. A wholly male soul, whatever maleness means, or a wholly female soul, sounds unreal and oversimplified. But that is not what sexual souls implies. Rather, in every soul there is—to use Jungian terms— *anima* and *animus*, femaleness and maleness; just as in the body, one predominates but the other is also present.[17] If the dominant sex of soul is not the same as that of the body, we have a sexual misfit, a candidate for a sex change operation of body or of soul, earthly or Heavenly. Perhaps Heaven supplies such changes just as it supplies all other needed forms of healing.

---

[16] Gilbert Ryle, *The Concept of Mind*.

[17] C. G. Jung, *The Structure and Dynamics of the Psyche* (New York: Pantheon Books, 1960), p. 345.

In any case, the resurrection body perfectly expresses its soul, and since souls are innately sexual, that body will perfectly express its soul's true sexual identity.

A second reason why the notion of sexual souls sounds strange to many people may be that they really hold a pantheistic rather than a theistic view of spirit as undifferentiated, or even infinite. They think of spirit as simply overwhelming, or leaving behind, all the distinctions known to the body and the senses. But this is not the Christian notion of spirit, nor of infinity. Infinity itself is not undifferentiated in God. To call God infinite is not to say He is everything in general and nothing in particular: that is confusing God with The Blob! God's infinity means that each of His positive and definite attributes, such as love, wisdom, power, justice, and fidelity, is unlimited.

Spirit is no less differentiated, articulated, structured, or formed than matter.[18] The fact that our own spirit can suffer and rejoice far more, more delicately and exquisitely, and in a far greater variety of ways, than can the body—this fact should be evidence of spirit's complexity. So should the fact that psychology is nowhere near an exact science, as anatomy is.

Differences in general, and sexual differences in particular, increase rather than decrease as you move up the cosmic hierarchy. (Yes, there is a cosmic hierarchy, unless you can honestly believe that oysters have as much right to eat you as you have to eat them.) Angels are as superior to us in differentiation as we are to animals. God is infinitely differentiated, for He is the Author of all differences, all forms.

Each act of creation in Genesis is an act of differentiation— light from darkness, land from sea, animals from plants, and so on.[19] Creating is forming, and forming is differentiating. Materialism believes differences in form are ultimately illusory

---

[18] C. S. Lewis, *Miracles* (New York: Macmillan, 1955), pp. 108–12.
[19] Genesis 1:4, 7, 10, 18, 21, 25, 27.

appearance; the only root reality is matter. Pantheism also believes differences in form are ultimately illusory; the only root reality is one universal Spirit. But theism believes form is real because God created it. And whatever positive reality is in the creation must have its model in the Creator. We shall ultimately have to predicate sexuality of God Himself, as we shall see next.

Fourth Principle: Sex Is Cosmic

Have you ever wondered why almost all languages except English attribute sexuality to things? Trees, rocks, ships, stars, horns, kettles, circles, accidents, trips, ideas, feelings—these, and not just men and women, are masculine or feminine. Did you always assume unthinkingly that this was *of course* a mere projection and personification, a reading of our sexuality into nature rather than reading nature's own sexuality out of it (or rather, out of *her*)? Did it ever occur to you that it just might be the other way round, that human sexuality is derived from cosmic sexuality rather than vice versa, that we are a local application of a universal principle?[20] If not, please seriously consider the idea now, for it is one of the oldest and most widely held ideas in our history, and one of the happiest.

It is a happy idea because it puts humanity into a more human universe. We fit; we are not freaks. What we are, everything else also is, though in different ways and different degrees. We are, to use the medieval image, a microcosm, a little cosmos; the universe is the macrocosm, the same pattern written large. We are more like little fish inside bigger fish than like sardines in a can. It is the machine-universe that is our projection, not the human universe.

We do not have time here to apply this idea, so pregnant with consequences, to other aspects of our being, to talk about

[20] C. S. Lewis, *That Hideous Strength* (New York: Macmillan, 1969), p. 315; *Perelandra* (New York: Macmillan, 1965), pp. 200–1.

the cosmic extension of consciousness and volition, but many philosophers have argued for this conclusion,[21] and a deeper eye than reason's seems to insist on it. But we can apply it to sexuality here. It means that sexuality goes all the way up and all the way down the cosmic ladder.

At the "down" end there is "love among the particles": gravitational and electromagnetic attraction. That little electron just "knows" the difference between the proton, which she "loves", and another electron, which is her rival. If she did not know the difference, she would not behave so knowingly, orbiting around her proton and repelling other electrons, never vice versa.

But, you say, I thought that was because of the balanced resultant of the two merely physical forces of angular momentum, which tends to zoom her straight out of orbit, and bipolar electromagnetic attraction, which tends to zap her down into her proton: too much zoom for a zap and too much zap for a zoom. Quite right. But what right do you have to call physical forces "mere"? And how do you account for the second of those two forces? *Why* is there attraction between positive and negative charges? It is exactly as mysterious as love. In fact, it *is* love. The scientist can tell you *how* it works, but only the lover knows *why*.

Sex at the Top

Sex "goes all the way up" as well as "all the way down". Spirit is no less sexual than matter; on the contrary, all qualities and all contrasts are richer, sharper, more real as we rise closer and closer to the archetype of realness, God. The God of the Bible is not a monistic pudding in which differences are reduced to lumps, or a light that out-dazzles all finite lights

---

[21] For an ancient version, see Plato, *Timaeus*, 30b ff., 34b ff. For a modern version, see Teilhard de Chardin, *The Phenomenon of Man* (New York: Harper & Row, 1961), bk. I, chap. 2 (pp. 53–65).

and colors. God is a sexual being, the most sexual of all beings.

This sounds shocking to people only if they see sex only as physical and not spiritual, or if they are Unitarians rather than Trinitarians. The love relationship between the Father and the Son within the Trinity, the relationship from which the Holy Spirit eternally proceeds, is a sexual relationship. It is like the human sexual relationship from which a child proceeds in time; or rather, that relationship is like the divine one. Sexuality is "the image of God" according to Scripture (see Genesis 1:27), and for B to be an image of A, A must in some way have all the qualities imaged by B. God therefore is a sexual being.

There is therefore sex in Heaven because in Heaven we are close to the source of all sex. As we climb Jacob's ladder the angels look less like neutered, greeting-card cherubs and more like Mars and Venus.

Another reason we are more, not less, sexual in Heaven is that all earthly perversions of true sexuality are overcome, especially the master perversion, selfishness. To make self God, to desire selfish pleasure as the *summum bonum*, is not only to miss God but to miss pleasure and self as well, and to miss the glory and joy of sex. Jesus did not merely say, "Seek ye first the kingdom of God", but also added that "all these things shall be added" when we put first things first.[22] Each story fits better when the foundation is put first.

C. S. Lewis calls this the principle of "first and second things".[23] In any area of life, putting second things first loses not only the first things but also the second things, and putting first things first gains not only the first things but the second things as well. So to treat sexual pleasure as God is to miss not only God but sexual pleasure too.

---

[22] Matthew 6:33 (KJV).
[23] C. S. Lewis, "First and Second Things" in *God in the Dock* (Grand Rapids, Mich.: Eerdmans, 1970), pp. 278–81.

The highest pleasure always comes in self-forgetfulness. Self always spoils its own pleasure. Pleasure is like light; if you grab at it, you miss it; if you try to bottle it, you get only darkness; if you let it pass, you catch the glory. The self has a built-in, God-imaging design of self-fulfillment by self-forgetfulness, pleasure through unselfishness, ecstasy by *ekstasis*, "standing-outside-the-self". This is not the self-conscious self-sacrifice of the do-gooder but the spontaneous, unconscious generosity of the lover.

This principle, that the greatest pleasure is self-giving, is graphically illustrated by sexual intercourse and by the very structure of the sexual organs, which must give themselves to each other in order to be fulfilled. In Heaven, when egotistic perversions are totally eliminated, all pleasure is increased, including sexual pleasure. Whether this includes *physical* sexual pleasure or not, remains to be seen.

Application of the Principles: Sex in Heaven

In the most important and obvious sense there is certainly sex in Heaven simply because there are human beings in Heaven. As we have seen, sexuality, like race and unlike clothes, is an essential aspect of our identity, spiritual as well as physical. Even if sex were *not* spiritual, there would be sex in Heaven because of the resurrection of the body. The body is not a mistake to be unmade or a prison cell to be freed from, but a divine work of art designed to show forth the soul as the soul is to show forth God, in splendor and glory and overflow of generous superfluity.

But is there sexual intercourse in Heaven? If we have bodily sex organs, what do we use them for there?

Not baby-making. Earth is the breeding colony; Heaven is the homeland.

Not marriage. Christ's words to the Sadducees are quite clear about that.[24] It is in regard to marriage that we are "like

[24] Matthew 22:30.

the angels". (Note that it is *not* said that we are like the angels in any other ways, such as lacking physical bodies.)

Might there be another function in which baby-making and marriage are swallowed up and transformed, *aufgehoben*? Everything on earth is analogous to something in Heaven. Heaven neither simply removes nor simply continues earthly things. If we apply this principle to sexual intercourse, we get the conclusion that intercourse on earth is a shadow or symbol of intercourse in Heaven. Could we speculate about what that could be?

It could certainly be spiritual intercourse—and, remember, that includes sexual intercourse because sex is spiritual. This spiritual intercourse would mean something more specific than universal charity. It would be special communion with the sexually complementary; something a man can have only with a woman and a woman only with a man. We are made complete by such union: "It is not good that the man should be alone."[25] And God does not simply rip up His design for human fulfillment.

The relationship need not be confined to one in Heaven. Monogamy is for earth. On earth, our bodies are private.[26] In Heaven, we share each other's secrets without shame, and voluntarily.[27] In the Communion of Saints, promiscuity of spirit is a virtue.

The relationship may not extend to *all* persons of the opposite sex, at least not in the same way or degree. If it did extend to all, it would treat each differently simply because each *is* different—sexually as well as in other ways. I think there must be some special "kindred souls" in Heaven that we are designed to feel a special sexual love for. That would be the Heavenly solution to the earthly riddle of why in the world John falls for Mary, of all people, and not for Jane, and why romantic

[25] Genesis 2:18.

[26] This is the bane of Plato's *Republic*; e.g., at 464e.

[27] C. S. Lewis, *The Problem of Pain* (New York: Macmillan, 1962), p. 61.

lovers feel their love is fated, "in the stars", "made in Heaven".[28]

But this would differ from romantic love on earth in that it would be free, not driven; from soul to body, not from body to soul. Nor would it feel apart from or opposed to the God-relationship, but a part of it or a consequence of it: His design, the wave of His baton. It would also be totally unselfconscious and unselfish: the ethical goodness of *agape* joined to the passion of *eros*;[29] *agape* without external, abstract law and duty, and *eros* without selfishness or animal drives.

But would it ever take the form of physical sexual intercourse? We should explore this question, not to kowtow to modernity's sexual monomania but because it is an honest question about something of great significance to us now, and because we simply want to know all we can about Heaven.

Since there are bodies in Heaven, able to eat and be touched, like Christ's resurrection body,[30] there is the *possibility* of physical intercourse. But why might the possibility be actualized? What are its possible purposes and meanings?

We know Heaven by earthly clues. Let us try to read all the clues in earthly intercourse. It has three levels of meaning: the subhuman, or animal; the superhuman, or divine; and the specifically human. (All three levels exist *in* us humans.)

Animal reasons for intercourse include (1) the conscious drive for pleasure and (2) the unconscious drive to perpetuate the species. Both would be absent in Heaven. For although there are unimaginably great pleasures in Heaven,[31] we are not *driven* by them. And the species is complete in eternity: no need for breeding.

Transhuman reasons for intercourse include (1) idolatrous

---

[28] Peter Kreeft, *Heaven: The Heart's Deepest Longing* (San Francisco: Ignatius Press, 1989), pp. 107–8.

[29] Anders Nygren, *Agape and Eros* (London: S.P.C.K., 1953).

[30] John 20:27.

[31] Psalm 16:11.

love of the beloved as a substitute for God and (2) the Dante–Beatrice love of the beloved as an image of God. As to the first, there is, of course, no idolatry in Heaven. No substitutes for God are even tempting when God Himself is present. As to the second, the earthly beloved was a window to God, a mirror reflecting the divine beauty. That is why the lover was so smitten. Now that the reality is present, why stare at the mirror? The impulse to adore has found its perfect object. Furthermore, even on earth this love leads not to intercourse but to infatuation. Dante neither desired nor enacted intercourse with Beatrice.

Specifically human reasons for intercourse include (1) consummating a monogamous marriage and (2) the desire to express personal love. As to the first, there is no marriage in Heaven. But what of the second?

I think there will probably be millions of more adequate ways to express love than the clumsy ecstasy of fitting two bodies together like pieces of a jigsaw puzzle. Even the most satisfying earthly intercourse between spouses cannot perfectly express *all* their love. If the possibility of intercourse in Heaven is not actualized, it is only for the same reason earthly lovers do not eat candy during intercourse: there is something much better to do.[32] The question of intercourse in Heaven is like the child's question whether you can eat candy during intercourse: a funny question only from the adult's point of view. Candy is one of children's greatest pleasures; how can they conceive a pleasure so intense that it renders candy irrelevant? Only if you know both can you compare two things, and all those who have tasted both the delights of physical intercourse with the earthly beloved and the delights of spiritual intercourse with God testify that there is simply no comparison.

[32] C. S. Lewis, *Miracles*, p. 160.

A Heavenly Reading of the Earthly Riddle of Sex

This spiritual intercourse with God is the ecstasy hinted at in all earthly intercourse, physical or spiritual. It is the ultimate reason why sexual passion is so strong, so different from other passions, so heavy with suggestions of profound meanings that just elude our grasp. No mere practical needs account for it. No mere animal drive explains it. No animal falls in love, writes profound romantic poetry, or sees sex as a symbol of the ultimate meaning of life because no animal is made in the image of God. *Human* sexuality is that image, and human sexuality is a foretaste of that self-giving, that losing and finding the self, that oneness-in-manyness that is the heart of the life and joy of the Trinity. That is what we long for; that is why we tremble to stand outside ourselves in the other, to give our whole selves, body and soul: because we are images of God the sexual being. We love the other sex because God loves God.

And this earthly love is so passionate because Heaven is full of passion, of energy and dynamism. We correctly deny that God has passions in the passive sense, being moved, driven, or conditioned by them, as we are. But to think of the love that made the worlds, the love that became human, suffered alienation from itself and died to save us rebels, the love that gleams through the fanatic joy of Jesus' obedience to the will of His Father and that shines in the eyes and lives of the saints—to think of this love as any less passionate than our temporary and conditioned passions "is a most disastrous fantasy".[33] And *that* consuming fire of love is our destined Husband, according to His own promise.[34] Sex in Heaven? Indeed, and no pale, abstract, merely mental shadow of it either. *Earthly* sex is the shadow, and our lives are a process of thickening so that we can share in the substance, becoming Heavenly fire so that we can endure and rejoice in the Heavenly fire.

[33] C. S. Lewis, *Miracles*, pp. 92–93.
[34] Hosea 2:16–20; Isaiah 54:5.

Part II

Heavenly Space and Time

whirl around themselves in never-ending circles of gyrating egotism and despair.[55] Instead of only spoiled children playing with dangerous toys like atom bombs, we would become devils eating our own souls away.

There are only two safeguards against this Hell. One comes to us against our will, the other only with it. They are natural weakness and supernatural virtue, weakness against nature and weakness against God. The first is God's gift to us after the Fall, though we see it as a curse (death, pain, sickness, "thorns and thistles"). And we are learning more and more how to destroy that gift. More and more, our only hope is the second kind of weakness, the one Saint Paul speaks of in the mysterious words, "when I am weak, then I am strong."[56] But it seems to be becoming increasingly unlikely that we newly empowered gods, "Humanity come of age", "emancipated" from tradition, authority, hierarchy, and obedience, will yield the sovereignty, or bow the knee, or turn and repent. You may draw your own apocalyptic conclusions.

Yet we should not be doomsters—first, because of what we do not know (the future—unless we have the divine gift of prophecy), and second, because of what we do know: we have not just our own foolishness but God's providence. An example from recent history of God's providential brinkmanship that does not quite let us fall over the brink may be the timing and placing of the discovery of nuclear fission. Only when the world was a global village united in international defense against an obvious and terrible evil (Nazism) was the power discovered and unleashed. Suppose any one of a hundred "chances" had allowed Hitler to get the bomb! Even now, our power over nature is providentially supervised. At least, up to now.

We have spent more time discussing our power over nature than any other aspect of the Heavenly body; but power is not

[55] C. S. Lewis, *Miracles*, p. 156.
[56] 2 Corinthians 12:18.

Chapter Nine

Where Is Heaven?

Is Heaven in space? It seems so, because we know from Revelation that we get new bodies after death,[1] and we know from reason that bodies are by definition in space. Thus we conclude that Heaven is in space.

But if so, why can't you get there by rocket ship?

Let's re-examine our argument. The reason we concluded that Heaven was in space was that we have bodies in Heaven. But these "resurrected bodies" are called spiritual bodies. Saint Paul distinguishes them from our present physical bodies.[2] If physical bodies are in physical space, spiritual bodies would be in spiritual space. Now what in the world (or out of it) is "spiritual space"? Can the imagination flesh out this unfamiliar concept that has just been laid in our lap by Revelation and reason?

Let's begin with two things spiritual space is *not*: (1) physical space and (2) mental space. (1) Spiritual space is not physical space simply because spirit is not physical. (2) But spiritual space is also not mental space because "spiritual" does not mean "mental". "Mental" means "psychological", "subjective", "in the mind"; but Heaven is an objectively real place, independent of the mind. Whether I know it or not, think it or not, believe it or not, it exists. Heaven is a spiritual place but a real place.

---

[1] I Corinthians 15:35–53.   [2] I Corinthians 15:44.

When people ask whether Heaven is a real place, I wonder whether they are materialists, for they seem to be using "real" and "material" synonymously. They seem to mean by "a real place" simply "a material place"; they are really asking whether Heaven is another world "out there", another planet, or only a subjective, inner state of mind, whether Heaven is physical or mental.

The answer is: neither. The mistake is the division of reality into two and only two categories: objective matter and subjective spirit. It is the assumption that the only two possibilities are (1) an objective, material place like a planet and (2) a subjective, nonmaterial place, a state of mind; the assumption that if a place is objective it must be only material and if it is spiritual it must be only subjective. This is a combination of Descartes' dualism between matter and spirit with Kant's dualism between the subjective and the objective. But if we go back beyond these philosophers to premodern thinkers like Plato, Aristotle, Augustine, or Aquinas, we find a third possibility, a third category of reality, a third kind of place for Heaven to be. Heaven is an objective spiritual place. (See Diagram 1.)

An example of the modern dualism is the assumption that if moral values are spiritual, they must be subjective, and if they are objective they must be material (social mores, observable consequences of behavior, or positive laws—something visible). The traditional ethics of objective values depends on the traditional metaphysics of objective spirit. Objective spiritual values need an objective spiritual place.

But what does *that* mean? What is "an objective spiritual place"?

Matter and Spirit

Let's use the words *spirit* and *soul* interchangeably, as ordinary language usually does.[3] A soul is simply a spirit animating

[3] Scripture only occasionally distinguishes them: Hebrews 4:12; 1 Thessalonians 5:23.

Diagram 1

Descartes	Spirit	Matter

+

Kant	Subject	Object

↓

Modern Mind:	Subjective Spirit	Objective Matter

Premodern Alternative: (Plato, Aristotle, Augustine, Aquinas)	Subjective Spirit: Soul, Mind	Objective Spirit: Heaven
	Subjective Matter: Body, Senses	Objective Matter: Earth

a body, and a spirit is the *I* that thinks and wills. Spirit is the nonmaterial aspect of me, the more-than-bodily *me* that I refer to when I speak of myself *having* a body rather than *being* a body, or when I call it "my" body.

Matter and spirit are clearly distinct kinds of reality.[4]

---

[4] Descartes, *Discourse on Method*, part 4, par. 3; *Meditations*, 3, par. 3.

Matter can be measured and weighed; spirit cannot. My body is six feet high but my spirit is not. If I cut half an inch off my hair, I have not whittled down my spirit by half an inch. I lose no spirit when I reduce only fat. Spirits are not fat. Spirits are not extended in space.

Yet, on the other hand, matter and spirit are not distinct in my life, my activity.[5] When I move my body from Philadelphia to Boston, my spirit moves with it. It seems that souls (embodied human spirits) are in bodies, which are in space, therefore spirits *are* in space.

But the previous paragraph seemed to prove they are *not*. Are spirits in space or not?

To resolve this dilemma we must explore three very tricky words: first the word *in*, then the words *space* and *place*. We shall see first that spirits are not in bodies but bodies are in spirits, and that bodies are not in space but space is in bodies. Then we shall see that space and place are not the same, and that spirits are in places (like Boston) without being in spaces (like six feet of height). If you find these questions too abstract or difficult, you can skip to the next chapter without losing any prerequisites.

"In"

What do we mean when we say one thing is "in" another? Let us not begin at the top of the scale of in-ness by trying to understand the ultimate "in-ness", the Trinity ("the Father is in me and I am in the Father"),[6] or the Incarnation ("God was in Christ reconciling the world to himself"),[7] or the Mystical Body (we are "in Christ");[8] let us only consider the

[5] Karl Rahner, *Spirit in the World*, trans. William Dyck (New York: Herder & Herder, 1960).
[6] John 18:38; 14:11; 17:21.
[7] 2 Corinthians 5:19.
[8] 1 Corinthians 1:30.

four possible combinations of matter and spirit in our natural human experience:

1. matter in matter,
2. spirit in spirit,
3. spirit in matter,
4. matter in spirit.

1. One material body is "in" another in a material and spatial way. Sardines are "in" a can; a room is "in" a house. This is pretty clear. Matter is in matter materially.

2. Now, how is spirit in spirit? Obviously, spiritually, not materially. A thought is "in" a mind or a feeling is "in" the emotions not as in a physical container, not even the brain, which is the physical instrument of the mind. Thoughts are not in the brain any more than they are in the fingernails; thoughts are in the mind. Brains have size; thoughts and minds do not.

3. Spirit, then, is not *in* matter at all, for spirit is not spatially measurable and matter is. You can contain marbles in a box, but not souls. You can find chemicals confined in a test tube, but not spirits. The only "spirits" in bottles are alcohol. Souls are not "in" bodies at all.

We think they are because we think Platonically rather than biblically. We think of souls as trapped in bodies like animals trapped in cages, or prisons, or even tombs.[9] But tombs hold the dead, not the living; if the body is a tomb, the soul is a corpse! No, God created bodies not to imprison souls but to empower them, not for death but for life.

Why do we think of souls as contained in bodies? Because we are materialists. We think of spirit as less real than matter. and we use "heavier" to symbolize "more real", and "lighter" to symbolize "less real" because there is more matter in heavier things. That is why we think of spirit as lighter than matter. The final step is to think of spirits as contained in bodies

[9] Plato, *Phaedo*, 67b–d.

because light things are usually contained in heavy things rather than vice versa.

If we use "heavy" to symbolize "real", we should imagine spirits as heavier, not lighter, than bodies[10] and therefore as containing bodies rather than contained by them.

4. But *how* is matter in spirit? How do souls contain bodies?

Whatever is contained, is contained according to the container's mode of containing.[11] Whatever is contained in a body is contained in a bodily way, and whatever is contained in a spirit is contained in a spiritual way. Spirits cannot be contained in bodies because they cannot be contained in a bodily way. But bodies can be contained in spirits because they can be contained in a spiritual way.

Now what does that mean, that bodies are contained in spirits in a spiritual way? It means that bodies are part of spirit's identity, part of spirit's meaning, life, and destiny. Somewhat as physical settings (places and things) are *in* (aspects of, contained in) stories, my body and its places are contained in my personhood, my *me*. I give my body meaning as *my* body. It does not contain me and my meaning; I contain it and its meaning. It is not my body that makes my spirit mine, but my spirit that makes my body mine.

The next step is to see that bodies are not in space but space is in bodies; bodies are not aspects of space but space is an aspect of bodies. (See Diagram 2.)

This is true only of living, ensouled bodies, not dead bodies. Dead bodies, like stones, are in space, determined by space. Living bodies determine space, make a difference to space. (In another sense, even dead bodies determine space, for all matter curves space according to Einsteinian relativity. But our concern is for the special way in which the ensouled human body determines space.)

[10] C. S. Lewis, *The Great Divorce* (New York: Macmillan, 1975), chaps. 3, 4, 6.
[11] Boethius, *Consolation of Philosophy*, book 5, prose 4.

Diagram 2

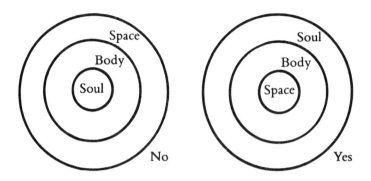

This is done by transforming *space* into *place*. And here are the other two tricky words. What is the difference between *space* and *place*?[12]

Place versus Space

Space is (1) abstract, not concrete, and (2) has no character.

1. Space never exists in itself, but is simply an aspect of some things (like oranges, rooms, doughnuts, holes in doughnuts, roads, and galaxies) but not others (like numbers, thoughts, minds, angels, virtues, and emotions). It is an aspect that we can abstract in thought and consider in itself, though it never exists in itself. It is not a thing but an aspect of things.

2. Space has no character, no "personality", no identity or individuality. One inch of space is always exactly the same as any other inch of space, no matter what is in it.

Place, on the other hand, (1) is concrete and (2) has character.

1. Place is not an abstracted aspect of a concrete reality, but is itself concrete (e.g., New York City, under the spreading

[12] Robert Farrar Capon, *An Offering of Uncles* (New York: Sheed & Ward, 1967), chaps. 1–2.

chestnut tree, on the corner of Main and Broadway, across the river, in this room).

2. Place has character, as in the previous examples. There may be the same number of cubic feet of space in this room as on the corner of Main and Broadway, but they are very different places, even though they have the same amount of space.

A parallel distinction, which we have already referred to, is the distinction between two meanings of *time*: *chronos* and *kairos*.[13] (Greek almost always has more useful distinctions than English.) *Chronos* is abstract, characterless time, the time measured with chronometers. One moment of *chronos* is always exactly the same as any other. But every moment of *kairos* is unique, like every place. For *kairos* is concrete time, lived time, human time, time full of meaningful content. What time is it? Chronologically, it is 2:00 A.M. Kairotically, it is time to go to bed, or the time Father comes home, or time to die. There is "a time to live and a time to die", "a time to plant, and a time to pluck up what is planted",[14] and they are very different *kairos*-times, though they may be the same *chronos*-times.

History—real, lived, meaningful human history—is a tapestry warped by place and woofed by *kairos*. Mere abstract calibrations that graph concrete history by space and *chronos* are like the "inchworm, inchworm, measuring the marigolds".[15] They use empty language like this: "In 1975, the borders were extended beyond the twelve-mile limit." But real history speaks words like these: "In the year that King Uzziah died I saw the Lord sitting upon a throne, high and lifted up; and his train filled the temple."[16]

[13] Wm. F. Arndt and F. Wilbur Gingrich, *A Greek-English Lexicon of the New Testament and other Early Christian Literature* (Chicago: University of Chicago Press, 1957), p. 395.

[14] Ecclesiastes 3:2.

[15] Frank Loesser, *The Frank Loesser Songbook* (New York: Simon & Schuster, 1971).

[16] Isaiah 6:1.

The scientific historian asks: *Which* temple? And the human being in him answers: Who cares? That is like asking: Which rose? when the poet says, "My love is like a red, red rose".[17]

Just to sound very professional, let's use technical terms. Let's call *kairos* and place together "place-time" and *chronos* and space "space-time".

Spirit and Matter in Space-Time and Place-Time

The relations between spirit and matter differ between space-time and place-time. In place-time, spirit determines matter; in space-time, matter determines spirit.

The creative artist lives in both worlds (and therefore we all live in both worlds, because we are all some sort of creative artists). As an artist, my spirit lives in place-time and determines it. But as an ingredient in the space-time world, my body is determined by it. It is six feet high and forty-four years long.

Here is Shakespeare writing Hamlet's "to be or not to be" soliloquy. As an artist, he is in the castle where Hamlet is soliloquizing. Shakespeare is having an out-of-the-body experience, as any writer or reader of fiction can have; he is not in Elizabethan England, he is in medieval Denmark. A second power of the creative consciousness is to interpenetrate and bring together various places and times at once: in this place and time where Hamlet soliloquizes, Shakespeare sees and brings together the meaning of the ghost's visit in Act I and the king's execution in Act V. *In* Hamlet's indecision "to be or not to be" there is the task given by his father's ghost to avenge his murder and also the execution of that task. This in-ness is possible in place-time but not in space-time. Place-time transcends the laws of space-time as spirit transcends the laws of matter. Different spaces and *chronos*-times exclude

[17] Robert Burns, "A Red, Red Rose" in *Johnson's Musical Museum* (1787–96) (New York: McGraw-Hill, 1967), vol. VII, p. 306.

each other; different places and *kairos*-times include each other. For space-time physically includes the author's and reader's bodies, while their spirits include place-time. The author transcends, and therefore can include, all his places and times.

A third power of spirit over place and time manifested by the creative artist is freedom. The author freely determines how much delay there shall be between Act I's task and Act V's execution during Act III's indecision. Then comes a knock at Shakespeare's door. It is the landlord: "First of the month. Rent's due." And there can be no delay or indecision in paying the rent, or Shakespeare is evicted. As creative artist he lives in the place-time of his spirit and freely determines it; as renter he lives in the space-time of his physical world and is unfreely determined by it. His body is in space-time for seventy years, dependent for its life upon continual gifts from the space-time world: air, food, water. Even as he writes, death's clock ticks inexorably in him. But his spirit breathes not space-time but place-time, for its life is not mortal. Even its time to die is determined not by matter but by spirit, destiny, meaning, divine art: predestination, not genetics. God *uses* genetics as Shakespeare uses pens.

Take a simpler, merely spatial image: Michelangelo is designing a large triptych. He is the creator and master of its space; he turns its space into place by his spirit. But he does not have enough room in his studio for it; he must move. As a material part of the material world, he is mastered, enclosed and determined by space; as spiritual master of his created world, he determines, encloses and masters its space, transforming it into place.

Insofar as we make of our lives a work of art, we similarly master and transform our lives.

Presence

How does spirit transform space into place? By presence.[18]
This is a mysterious and wonderful power, usually unappre-
ciated and unexplored. Let's explore and appreciate it.

Only persons, only spirits (with or without bodies) can be
present. Sardines are not present in cans, but I am present in
a meeting hall. My furniture is not present in my house, but
I am. The definition of "my home", in fact, is: "the place
where I am habitually present". Le Corbusier is wrong: a
house is not "a machine to live in".[19] It is my extended body.
I am present at home as I am present in the body. Little
children know that; "home" to them is like "mother", and
"going out" is like being born.

The word for presence is "here". The word for existence
without presence is "there". The furniture is "there". I am
always "here". I can never cease to be "here"; I can never be
"there" until I cease to be I. Corpses are "there"; living bodies
are "here". Once I die, I am no longer "here". Corpses are
not "here" because corpses are not I's.

I can treat others as corpses, as dead objects, as ingredients
in my world, as walk-ons in my play, as things. As such,
they are "there". This is what Buber calls the "I-it relationship".[20] Or I can treat them as living subjects, as "here" *with*
me.[21] This is what Buber calls the "I-thou relationship".[22] It
is only the living subject that is present, *here*, in this *place*.

---

[18] Kenneth Gallagher, *The Philosophy of Gabriel Marcel* (New York: Fordham University Press, 1966), pp. 22–28; Gabriel Marcel, *The Philosophy of
Existentialism*, trans. Manya Harari (New York: Citadel, 1966), pp. 36–39.

[19] Norma Evenson, *Le Corbusier: The Machine and the Grand Design* (New
York: Braziller, 1970).

[20] Martin Buber, *I and Thou*, trans. Ronald Gregor Smith (New York:
Scribner's, 1958), part I.

[21] Marcel, *The Philosophy of Existentialism*, p. 39; Gallagher, *The Philosophy
of Gabriel Marcel*, pp. 26–29.

[22] Buber, *I and Thou*, part II.

The dead object is *there*, in that *space*: "You there, sit down at that table. You there, stand on that line."[23]

Before we apply what we have found about space to the question of space in Heaven, let us summarize:

place	space
kairos	*chronos*
place-time	space-time
concrete	abstract
personal	impersonal
living	dead
qualitative	quantitative
subject	object
I-thou	I-it
here	there
present	absent

Place is made by the presence of a person, that is, a spiritual body. Already our bodies are somewhat spiritual: they are determiners of space and time, like artists. But they are also somewhat nonspiritual, determined by space and time. In Heaven our bodies will be perfectly spiritual; therefore they will be perfectly present to Heaven's places.

"Perfectly spiritual"—what does that mean? It means perfectly obedient to the soul, which in turn is perfectly obedient to God. A spiritual body is one that lives by the Spirit of God, the Holy Spirit. Since it is perfectly spiritual, it is perfectly present. It shares in God's omnipresence, His presence to all places and times. That is why their lives can pass before the dying in a single instant: it is a beginning of Heaven's omnipresence to earth. Eventually, all their lives, all the earth,

---

[23] C. S. Lewis, *A Grief Observed* (New York: Bantam, 1976), p. 14: "We both knew this. I had my miseries, not hers; she had hers, not mine. . . . We were setting out on different roads. This cold truth, this terrible traffic regulation ('You, Madam, to the right—you, Sir, to the left') is just the beginning of the separation which is death itself."

and even all other earthly lives will become fully present to them in Heaven (see Chapter 3).

Since the spiritual body is perfectly present, it has place. Heaven is its place. Heaven is indeed "a real place".

Heaven is not only a real place, Heaven is what "a real place" ultimately means. Real places on earth are more or less real places insofar as they resemble Heaven. That wonderful out-of-the-way spot that had such character, that landscape you saw long ago and have been haunted by ever since, that little village that almost spoke to you, it had such personality— these places on earth were images of the Place of all places, the model or archetype of place, Heaven.

Thus, paradoxically, the more we are present on earth, the more we are present in Heaven. God is supremely present, with total attention and total love. The more like God we are, the more "in Heaven" we are. The alternative to Heaven is not earth. Heaven and earth are not exclusive alternatives, not opposites. The alternative to Heaven is Hell. Hell is absence, the refusal of I-thou presence, of consciousness and love. These are our only two alternatives on *earth*. "All that seemed earth is hell or heaven." [24]

God and Space

God is the origin and giver of all places. By designing and creating everything, God gives it its metaphysical place, its place in relation to Him. This is its true place; God is everything's home.

In this light, let us ask again our original question: where is Heaven? The literalist answer is that Heaven is in the sky, or beyond the sky. (In that case, why can't you get there by space ship?) The modernist answer is that Heaven is in the heart, or in your life. (In that case, death is terrible, for it kills Heaven!) A better answer is that Heaven is where God is.

---

[24] C. S. Lewis, *Poems* (New York: Harcourt, Brace & World, 1965), p. 87.

The first answer made Heaven relative to earth; the second made it relative to us. Should it not be relative to God? *Everything* is relative to God.

God is not determined by space. (God is not determined by anything.) It is not true to say that God is in some space, as paganism does. It is also not true to say that God is in all space, as pantheism does. God is not in space at all, for He is pure spirit. He so transcends space that He can be present to all spaces at once and can manifest Himself in special ways in special places without thereby being limited spatially. "God is present in a great many different modes: not present in matter as He is present in man, not present in all men as in some, not present in any other man as in Jesus."[25] If Heaven is where God is, then Heaven, too, is more in some places than in others without thereby being enclosed or limited by space.

We too, like God, are more present in some places than in others, and more present at some times than at others. Our spirit is a rubber spirit; it stretches or contracts. Sometimes we are just "not here". The extreme case of such absent-mindedness would be amnesia, identity disorientation, and multiple personality: "My name is Legion; for we are many."[26] Hell is the consummation of these things, The rubber stretches from Hell to Heaven, from the dimensionless void to the omnipresent plenum, from Nowhere to Everywhere.

A Zen disciple asked his *roshi*: "What is the secret of Zen?" The master answered: "Have you eaten?" "Yes." "Then wash your dishes." "But what is the secret of Zen?" "I have just told you. Were you not listening?" "But I wash my dishes every day. Why have I not mastered the secret of Zen?" "You never wash your dishes." "What do I do?" "You wobble."[27]

---

[25] C. S. Lewis, *Miracles* (New York: Macmillan, 1955), p. 103.

[26] Mark 5:9.

[27] Paul Reps, *Zen Flesh, Zen Bones* (Rutland, Vt.: Charles E. Tuttle, 1957), p. 69.

"Wobbling" means not being here, and not being here-now. Wobbling means oscillating between presence and absence, hereness and thereness, consciousness and unconsciousness, Heaven and Hell. Not-wobbling means perfect presence, and this is Heaven.

Is Heaven in the Heart?

Is the modernist right, then? Is Heaven just the mental habit of presence? Is Heaven in us?

No, for presence is not in us; we are in it. It is not a subjective mental habit of alertness, but a real relation between subject and object. As Buber says of spirit, "it is not in the I but *between* I and thou." [28] It is like love: we are "in love" rather than love being in us. [29] It is like joy, as Aquinas explains:

> "It has not entered into the heart of man what God hath prepared for those that love him." . . . Nevertheless, because no creature is capable of joy such as God's, the text says, not that man grasps this joy, but that he enters into it: "Enter thou into the joy of the Lord." [30]

Heaven is not in us, we are in it. Heaven is not in the heart. The psalm says: "In the heart are the highways to Zion." [31] It does not say: "In the heart is Zion [Heaven]." A highway is like a sign, or a finger: it points. We are to look along it, not at it. "A finger is good for pointing at the moon, but woe to him who mistakes the finger for the moon." [32]

So Heaven is not in the heart; the modernist is wrong. But the literalist is also wrong: Heaven is not in space either, and

[28] Buber, *I and Thou*, pp. 15, 39.

[29] Peter Kreeft, *Heaven: The Heart's Deepest Longing* (San Francisco: Ignatius Press, 1989), pp. 61–66.

[30] St. Thomas Aquinas, *Summa Theologiae*, II-II, 28, 3. Cf. St. Anselm, *Proslogion*, 25–26.

[31] Psalm 84:5–6.

[32] Paul Reps, *Zen Flesh, Zen Bones*, p. 113.

the way to it is not a material way. As Plotinus put it,

> "Let us flee to the beloved Fatherland." Here is sound counsel.
> But what is this flight? How are we to "gain the open sea"?
> . . . Here is no journeying for the feet; feet bring us only from
> land to land. Nor is it for coach or ship to bear us off. We
> must close our eyes and invoke a new manner of seeing, a
> wakefulness that is the birthright of all of us, though few put
> it to use.[33]

Heaven is spiritual, and the way to it is spiritual. But "spiritual" does not mean "subjective". The spirit has roads as objective as the body and the mind, and they lead to places as objective and objectively different as two cities at the end of two bodily roads or two conclusions at the end of two different mental roads. Heaven is the place at the end of the spiritual road that begins with faith and becomes love and presence. Hell is the place at the end of the spiritual road that is refusal of God's presence. "And though a man may walk a thousand different paths through the world, there is not one of them that does not eventually lead either to the beatific or the miserific vision."[34]

The body has many destinations, not just two. A great number of material roads lead to a great number of material places for bodies to travel to. The mind's roads are fewer, and the places that mental and rational roads lead to are also fewer: logical possibilities are more limited than physical possibilities. The spirit has only two roads, and two places at their ends. "All that seems earth is Hell or Heaven."

---

[33] Plotinus, *Enneads*, I, 6, 8.
[34] C. S. Lewis, *Perelandra* (New York: Macmillan, 1974), p. 111.

Chapter Ten

Is There Time in Heaven?

We egalitarian, uniformist Americans have a strange, irrational prejudice against being different. And just as everyone must be the same, every chapter in a book must be the same in difficulty; authors are not expected to put in a more difficult chapter. I disagree with this prejudice, and I have dared to include this difficult chapter about that difficult subject, time. If you want to skip it, please do. If you do not understand everything in it, please don't despair of understanding the rest of the book.

This is the most difficult chapter because time is one of the most mysterious of realities. As Saint Augustine says, "When you don't ask me, I know what it is, but when you ask me, I don't know."[1]

Our first question is: Is there time in Heaven, in eternity? I think there must be, for the same reason there is space in Heaven: "to make the life of the blessed dead strictly timeless is inconsistent with the resurrection of the body."[2]

A second reason for this conclusion is the principle of analogy. Heaven is not wholly the same nor wholly different from earth, but analogous to earth. (Rather, earth is analogous to Heaven, earth is Heaven's image.) Therefore, Heaven is not

[1] St. Augustine, *Confessions*, XI, 14.
[2] C. S. Lewis, *Letters to Malcolm* (New York: Harcourt, Brace & World, 1964), p. 102.

the mere presence of earthly things, nor the mere absence of earthly things, but the transformation of earthly things. Earth is neither continued nor removed but *aufgehoben*,[3] taken up, perfected, and consummated.

There are many other examples of the same principle. God's Revelation neither merely extends nor merely removes human reason, but perfects it. Loving God does not detract or distract from loving neighbor, but perfects it. Emotional health perfects bodily health psychosomatically; moral health perfects emotional health, psychologically; spiritual health perfects moral health, supernaturally. Each level is for the level above it, and when the lower submits to the higher, the higher perfects the lower. So God perfects humanity, Heaven perfects earth, eternity perfects time. Just as Heaven's space is more truly a place than earth's, so Heaven's time is more truly time, more timely.

But what does that mean? How shall we imagine this conclusion that reason has deduced from Revelation? How is eternity more timely than time? What is eternity, anyway?

What Time Is Eternity?

It is usually easier to say what a thing is *not* than what it is. So let's begin with three popular misconceptions of eternity.

1. First, "eternal" often means simply a vague, unimaginably long time. Rome was called "the eternal city", and sentimental songs call romantic love "eternal". This, of course, is not eternity at all but merely a relatively long time whose future ending has been ignored or denied. In fact, Rome lasts only a few centuries and most romances a few years, months, or even days.

2. A second and profounder meaning of "eternity" is "unending time", a line with *no* last point. But this too is merely time, though time without end, *per omnia saecula saeculorum*, "through all ages of ages".

---

[3] Hegel, *Encyclopedia*, first part (*Logik*), introduction (vol. V, 2, 27–30).

The conception of eternity as unending time gives rise to the "boredom-or-frustration" dilemma about Heaven. If Heaven is a final arriving at the top of the mountain of changeless perfection, it sounds terribly boring—at least after a few centuries, perhaps even after a few days. It is not fit for us, creatures essentially geared to time and progress and purpose. In that most philosophical little ditty, "the bear went over the mountain" only to climb another mountain. But (the other horn of the dilemma) if Heaven is always climbing and never arriving, we are forever frustrated.

A popular cliché tries to solve this problem by taking the dilemma by one horn: "it is better to travel hopefully than to arrive." C. S. Lewis demolishes this bromide with one fatal stroke of his logical broadsword: "If that were true, and known to be true, how could anyone travel hopefully? There would be nothing to hope for."[4]

3. There is no solution to the boredom-or-frustration dilemma within time. But perhaps eternity is timeless. This leads us to a third conception of eternity, one much closer to the truth—in fact, a profound half-truth. Even now we experience "timeless moments", intimations of eternity as the pure present, like a point, rather than spread out into the future like a line. This would not be boring because it has no duration in time, no waiting. And it is apparently faithful to the meaning of the word *e-ternal*, "not-ternal", "not-temporal". It seems that eternity is a different dimension from time, as a point is a different *dimension* from a line—qualitatively not just quantitatively more, neither finitely more (popular misconception number one) nor infinitely more (number two).

But the "point" metaphor fails in one way: a point is *less* than a line, while eternity is more than time, not less. Eternity cannot have fewer dimensions than time. The picture of eternity as a mere point is connected with the other popular picture that we have already criticized in Chapter 7, that of spirit as

[4] C. S. Lewis, *The Great Divorce* (New York: Macmillan, 1975), p. 43.

lighter than matter. The common mistake is to picture what is more as if it were less.

The image of eternity as a point does, however, contain an essential truth: that eternity is not spread out like time. It is simultaneously present all at once, not piece by piece in passing. The answer to the question "What time is it in eternity?" is: Now. Thus Boethius' classic definition of eternity is "the simultaneous possession of all perfection in a single present".[5] Time is like a floor, and our lives in time are like buckets of water spilled out along that floor. Eternity is like all the water gathered together in a bucket. One of the reasons we need eternity is so that our lives can finally have that wholeness, that oneness, that all-together-ness.

Suppose we try to preserve the truth in the image of the point while amending its failing by saying that eternity's point includes all time's lines, as a tape measure includes all the tape rolled up, or as a spider includes its web, or an author his books.

This may be good philosophy but it is bad geometry. Geometrically, a point does not include lines, a line includes points. If we naturally think of time as a one-dimensional line, then the geometrical image that would symbolize eternity as more than time must be a two-dimensional surface with time as its one-dimensional linear boundary, or even as a three-dimensional solid with time as its two-dimensional surface. In fact, since time is the fourth dimension, we could even symbolize eternity as a four-dimensional process of change with time as a three-dimensional body included in that process. (Thus, paradoxically, time symbolizes eternity and space symbolizes time.)

But we need no dimensional *analogy*, for we can be literal about dimensions: if there are three dimensions of space and time is the fourth dimension, then eternity is the fifth dimension. Eternity includes time as time includes space.

[5] Boethius, *Consolation of Philosophy*, bk. 5, prose 6.

Eternity: The Sixth Dimension

Unfortunately, it is a bit more complicated than that. Eternity is the sixth dimension, not the fifth. *Chronos*-time is the fourth dimension, *kairos*-time[6] the fifth, and eternity the sixth. Thus there are three temporal dimensions, just as there are three spatial dimensions. *Chronos* is the first temporal dimension, like a line; *kairos* is the second, like a surface; and eternity is the third, like a solid: the concrete reality of which the others are only abstract aspects.

Chronos measures the quantity (but not the quality) of *kairos*; clocks measure how much life-time we live, as a surface boundary measures a surface by quantifying the area bounded by it. The lesser dimension is the boundary of the greater.

We need an image that will combine the truth symbolized by the point (viz., that in eternity all time is present at once, rather than dispersed into past and future) with the truth symbolized by the solid body (viz., that time is only the abstract boundary of a full eternity). We also need an image that will include all three temporal dimensions. Suppose we visualize *kairos* as a cone. All its radii come together at its point, eternity. The cone is bounded externally by *chronos* as an arc (p. 156).

At one end, the cone of our life-time touches the eternal center, the inner heart of time. At the other end, it is made finite and bounded by its amount of *chronos*, the outer skin of time. Our lived time has both an inside and an outside, a heart and a surface skin; our human time (*kairos*) touches both superhuman time (eternity) and subhuman time (*chronos*), both the divine and the material, just as our subjective spirit touches both objective spirit (God) and objective matter (the world).

There are three levels of reality: the human, the superhuman, and the subhuman: humanity, God, and the material world. Each has its own kind of duration that is natural to it: eternity for God, *kairos* for humanity, *chronos* for the world.

---

[6] See Appendix, Second Principle, p. 142.

Diagram 4

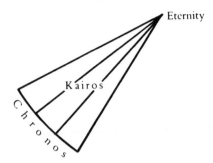

Our *kairos* includes as one of its dimensions the world's *chronos*, for time is part of our experience. And our *kairos* is included in God's eternity. God is not an ingredient in our experience; we are ingredients in God's experience. The meaning of our life's time is in God's eternity. The point of *kairos*, the point of our lives, what it all points to, is eternity. Eternity is "the point of it all", the alternative to Ecclesiastes' "vanity of vanities", the answer to the question "What's the point of living?"

Diagram 5

Superhuman	*Human*	*Sub-human*
God	Soul	World
Objective Spirit	Subjective Spirit	Objective Matter
Eternity	*Kairos*	*Chronos*
6th Dimension	5th Dimension	4th Dimension
Heart of Time	Body of Time	Skin of Time

Chronos gets nowhere; it is Ecclesiastes' and Buddha's cyclic time.[7] If you take your notion of time from your observations of the subhuman world, as those thinkers did, you will come

---

[7] Ecclesiastes 1:2–11; 3:1–9; cf. chap. 9, n. 23.

up with the cyclic notion of time, for everything in the visible world seems to move in cycles. If, on the other hand, you take your notion of time from the experience of human life, you will see time as linear, going somewhere, pointing to something, progressing from a real beginning (birth) through growth and maturity to a real ending (death).

Chronos, the circumference of time, circles round eternity, its center, as a hunter circles round his quarry. But he never captures it. *Chronos* never touches eternity, but *kairos* does.

Another difference between *chronos* and *kairos* that our image makes evident is that *chronos* has no *width*: the circumference is a line, not an area: it is one-dimensional. But *kairos*, the segment of the circle, has a second dimension, a dimension of width. Therefore, unlike *chronos*, it has internally differentiated areas, some nearer and some farther from eternity. (This applies to both the cone of my individual life-time and the whole circle of the life-time of history.) Each point on the arc of the cone or the circumference of the circle is equidistant from the center point; but areas in the cone or the circle can be nearer or farther from the center. Thus, our lifetime can approach eternity, but the world's clock-time cannot. You can get closer to Heaven by human living, but the

Diagram 6

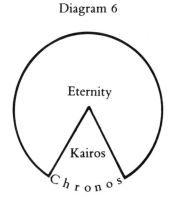

universe does not get closer to Heaven simply by chronological aging. Nor does the body, insofar as it is part of and subject to the laws of the material world. The only hope of eternity for the body and the universe is through the soul. Only the soul, which lives in *kairos*, touches eternity and can take the body and even the universe with it to eternity through the Resurrection.

This gives us a new outlook on the question of progress. There *is* no merely material progress. Only spirit can progress because only spirit can touch eternity, the goal. Progress is not merely change but change towards a goal. The goal of time is eternity, and only spirit's time, *kairos*, can touch it. However, matter can progress too, in and for spirit—but *only* in and for spirit. Spirit saves the world, as God saves our spirits.[8]

Note also the point that different sections of the cone can have different colors. Two-dimensional areas can have color; one-dimensional lines cannot. *Kairos* has color, character, quality. One moment of lived time is different from another, more or less meaningful, differently meaningful. *Chronos* has no character. A date is almost nothing.

This liberates us from the nagging desire to be "up to date", or modern, or contemporary. Nothing can ever really be "up to date". A date has no character.[9] The myth of up-to-dateness is one of our silliest and most wasteful myths.

No one of the images we can use for eternity is adequate even as an image. Whenever a higher truth is expressed on a lower level, opposite images are needed for balance, as both male and female sexes are needed for humanity to be the balanced and complete "image of God" according to Genesis.[10] So on the one hand, eternity is like a point: all time is simultaneously present in eternity, as all the events in the novel

---

[8] Teilhard de Chardin, *The Divine Milieu* (New York: Harper & Row, 1965), pp. 56–62.

[9] G. K. Chesterton, *Orthodoxy* (New York: Dodd, Mead, 1946), p. 101.

[10] Genesis 1:27.

are present in the mind of its author. But on the other hand, eternity is like a sphere: it is more, not less, than time. The eternal sphere is the home of all *kairos* circles bounded by *chronos* circumferences, and the life-time of each of us is a conic section of that sphere.

A medieval image for God was "a spiritual sphere whose center is everywhere and whose circumference is nowhere".[11] The universe images God in these two ways: its center is also everywhere, because there is no absolute center in relative space; and its circumference is nowhere because its boundaries (finitude) are everywhere *in* it, not outside it.

The Principle of In-ness

Our image of dimensions illustrates a universal law: the principle of in-ness, or co-inherence (as Charles Williams calls it).[12] If philosophers and theologians knew what they meant whenever they used the word "in", they would have solved nearly all their problems. Gabriel Marcel makes in-ness (he calls it "participation") the leitmotif of his entire philosophy because he sees it as the leitmotif of the whole of reality, from God on down.[13] The reason in-ness is the key principle of creation is that it is the inner nature of the Creator; the Trinity is an interpersonal, relational society of co-inherence. The Father is in the Son, the Son is in the Father, and both are in the Holy Spirit and He in Them. Since creation necessarily reflects its Creator (it has no other place to go to get anything!), in-ness is somehow reflected in all creatures. They are in each other in various ways: (1) spatially, (2) temporally, (3) dimen-

[11] Alan of Lille, *Regulae de Sacra Theologia*, I, 627. Cf. Etienne Gilson, *History of Christian Philosophy in the Middle Ages* (New York: Random House, 1955), p. 636, n. 130.

[12] Mary McDermott Shideler, *The Theology of Romantic Love: A Study in the Writings of Charles Williams* (Grand Rapids, Mich.: Eerdmans, 1966), p. 236.

[13] Kenneth Gallagher, *The Philosophy of Gabriel Marcel* (New York: Fordham University Press, 1966), pp. xi, 13–29.

sionally, (4) or spiritually. We have seen (1) spatial-in-ness in Chapter 9, and (2) temporal-in-ness and (3) dimensional-in-ness in this chapter. In-ness is also (4) the spiritual relationship between God and creatures: all creation is in God as in His mind, His eternal plan, and God is in all creatures by His presence of love and will, providence and power.

Within creation also, in-ness reigns: humanity is in nature and nature in humanity. Within a human being, soul is in body in one way and body in soul in another (cf. Chapter 9 again). Grace as well as nature works by in-ness: God is in humanity (Christ) so that humanity can be in God (Christians). Christ's Incarnation in Mary's womb and in the believer's soul are the same in-ness: eternity in time, the eternal truth of God come to us, made small so that we could fit into it. We enter into in-ness by in-ness entering into us. *In us*, Christ's Incarnation and life and death and Resurrection and Ascension are enacted; in us the gospels happen again.[14] Our spiritual womb is impregnated by the Holy Spirit, our blind see, our Lazarus is raised, our Thomas doubts, our Judas betrays, our Peter denies, is forgiven, and becomes a Rock.

And finally, life and death co-inhere: as we live, we meet death in life, for as soon as we are born we begin to die; and when we die, we meet life in death, for death becomes the door to eternal life. There is no way out of co-inherence except incoherence, no way out of Heaven except Hell. "All that seems earth is Hell or Heaven."

Eternity as "The Fullness of Time"

Eternity is the home of all time; it is so full of time that it is "the fullness of time". Eternity is full of time as an author's mind is full of plots. Yet all these times simultaneously present

---

[14] This is the familiar "moral sense" of medieval exegesis. Cf. St. Thomas Aquinas, *Summa Theologiae*, I, 1, 10.

in eternity are in order, as many ideas can be present simultaneously, yet in order, to a creative mind. Because of the simultaneity there is no waiting and no boredom; because of the order there is no confusion, no loss of form and structure and significance.

The phrase "the fullness of time" has traditionally been used to refer to the time providentially prepared in earth's history for Christ's first coming.[15] Just as Mary's small womb was prepared in its way, so the larger womb of the world was prepared in its way for the Incarnation: Jewish messianic prophecies, Roman peace and worldwide travel and communications for the spread of the Good News, Greek universal language and philosophical vocabulary, and a universal religious questing. But "the fullness of time" also means the time of Christ's second coming. And this is the consummation of all time. It is not just the last moment of time, the last point on time's line, "the end of the world", but it is the *fullness* of time. It is like an individual's death: it does not merely end, but consummates and makes whole, his lifetime. It is not just *finis* but *telos*, not just finish but purpose, destiny, completion. At death my lifetime is completely present to me so that I can present it complete to God.[16] Similarly, at the death of the world's time, all of history is present and presented to God, a completed story.

Death touches time to eternity, and all time rises from the dead at that point. Here, the three meanings of "present" come together: (1) all of time is living present, not dead past or unborn future; (2) it is all present, not absent; and (3) it is presented, not withheld, the gift given back at the end to the Giver of all time in the beginning. The Omega touches Alpha; the circle is completed.

[15] Teilhard de Chardin, "The Heart of the Problem" in *The Future of Man* (New York: Harper & Row, 1964), pp. 267–68.

[16] Karl Rahner, *On the Theology of Death*, trans. Charles H. Henkey (New York: Herder & Herder, 1961), pp. 30–31.

Time is (1) present rather than past in eternity because eternity is living, but the past is dead. (Cf. Christ's answer to the Sadducees in Matthew 22:31–32.) Time is (2) present rather than absent in eternity because (as we have seen in Chapter 9) the greater dimension includes rather than excludes the lesser. And time is (3) presented rather than withheld only if we will. We are time's priests; to offer up our life-time or to refuse it is our "fundamental option",[17] the choice between Heaven and Hell.

[17] Ladislaus Boros, *The Mystery of Death* (New York: Herder & Herder, 1965), I, 3 (pp. 8–9); III, 6 (especially p. 165).

Chapter Eleven

What Is Eternity?

In the last chapter, we found that there is time in eternity. In this chapter we explore seven consequences of this truth, seven differences it makes to our experience now.

The Death and Resurrection of Time

Time dies and rises again with the soul.

The only way for time to attain eternity is by dying. The only way for anything created to attain eternity is through the narrow gate of death.[1] Nothing can be ours forever by nature, for time and dying are built into the essence of nature.

But self (soul) and time (soul-time, *kairos*) are essentially connected. Therefore we can find the death and resurrection of time if we look at the death and resurrection of soul.

But isn't the soul immortal? No! The New Testament does *not* teach the natural immortality of the soul, as Platonism does.[2] Immortality is ascribed not to us but to God, in fact *only* to God.[3] In the Bible the soul is not aloof and unchanging, as in Plato; it is part of the human being who is born, changes,

---

[1] C. S. Lewis, *The Great Divorce* (New York: Macmillan, 1975), chap. 11. Cf. John 12:24.

[2] *Immortality and Resurrection*, ed. Pierre Benoit and Roland Murphy (New York: Herder & Herder, 1970); also *Immortality and Resurrection: Ingersoll Lectures*, ed. Krister Stendahl (New York: Macmillan, 1965).

[3] 1 Timothy 1:17.

lives, dies, and is resurrected. The body, too, is part of the whole person, and shares in all these stages. The soul shares in death and the body shares in resurrection. Body and soul do not have separate destinies; only for a while are they separated, and then unnaturally, by death.

But the way the soul dies is not the same as the way the body dies. There are two kinds of death available to the soul, and it can and must choose between them. The first is indicated by the words, "the soul that sinneth, it shall die".[4] The second is indicated by the words: "I live; yet not I, but Christ liveth in me;"[5] and by these: "You have died, and your life [soul] is hid with Christ in God."[6] The choice is between a living death and a dying life. "Whoever would save his life will lose it, and whoever loses his life for my sake will find it."[7] C. S. Lewis says exactly the same thing in other words: "There are only two kinds of people in the end: those who say to God, 'Thy will be done', and those to whom God says, in the end, '*Thy* will be done.'"[8]

The soul dies to itself and its life—and that means its lifetime, its *kairos*—when it accepts itself, its identity and its lifetime, from God's hand rather than its own, when it stops trying to be its own God. "Thy will be done" is its food, as it was Jesus' ("My food is to do the will of him who sent me")[9]; "*My* will be done" is its poison.

Just as our lives are saved, not lost, by this blessed death, so all our time, all *kairos*, is saved. This follows the principle that everything becomes truly itself by death and resurrection: body, place, soul, and time. We have seen in Chapter 7 that the resurrection body is more truly body (because it is perfectly obedient to the soul). We have seen in Chapter 9 that place

---

[4] Ezekiel 18:4, 20 (KJV).
[5] Galatians 2:20 (KJV).
[6] Colossians 3:3.
[7] Matthew 16:25.
[8] C. S. Lewis, *The Great Divorce*, p. 72.
[9] John 4:34.

is more truly place in Heaven. And soul is most perfectly soul by being obedient to God rather than to itself. Time, too, is most perfectly time in eternity. Eternity is not timelessness; all time is perfected in it. Eternity is thicker, solider, heavier, realer time. The reason time seems to thin out and die in eternity is that there is no *chronos*. But *chronos* is not the essence of time, only its boundary, as death is not the essence of life, only its boundary.

How all *kairos* is saved in eternity, we cannot imagine. But we can believe. For with God all things are possible.

> Behold I make all things new. Behold I do what cannot be done. I restore the years that the locusts and worms have eaten. I restore the years which you have drooped away upon your crutches and in your wheelchair. I restore the symphonies and operas which your deaf ears have never heard and the snowy massif your blind eyes have never seen and the freedom lost to you through plunder and the identity lost to you because of calumny and the failure of justice. And I restore the good which your own foolish mistakes have cheated you of. And I bring you to the love of which all other loves speak, the love which is joy and beauty, and which you have sought in a thousand streets, and for which you have wept and clawed your pillow.[10]

"Redeeming the Time": Changing the Past

But how does this work? How does God pull off this supreme trick? We do not know, but we can speculate with reason and imagination, as follows.

The "present" of *chronos*, the chronological now, is a mere point separating past and future. In *chronos* there is only past and future; nothing is present. In *kairos*, all is present; past and future are dimensions *of* the present. This is because

---

[10] Thomas Howard, *Christ the Tiger* (San Francisco: Ignatius Press, 1989), p. 151.

kairos touches eternity. Eternity includes all pasts and futures in the living present. Only eternity can "redeem the time", can heal the separation of time by touching past and future, Alpha and Omega, together.

A startling consequence is that eternity can change the past! Eternity causes everything; we in time cause only future things. The causality of eternity does not work horizontally along the time line from past to future or from present to future, but along the vertical line from eternity to time, including all time, past as well as future. The past is open to eternity, as open as the future.

For us in time, the past is dead and closed and therefore unchangeable, for it is not *present* to work on. But for those in eternity, all time is alive. The past is present. And what is present can be changed, redeemed. All the sins and mistakes and missed opportunities of the past, all the unsolvable problems and dead ends, even death itself, can be made to work backwards from eternity.[11]

Our dimensional analogy explains the paradox of changing the past. Any lower dimension can be altered in ways impossible on that dimension alone, through the causality of a higher dimension. Through the second dimension, a one-dimensional line can curve back upon itself and become a circle. Through the third dimension a surface can become both one and two: a Möbius strip. Through the fourth dimension a single body can be in two different places, if it moves through time. Through the fifth dimension (*kairos*) the fourth is modified: more can exist in less time. Finally, through the sixth dimension of eternity, even *kairos*, even a lifetime, is changed spiritually (not physically), redeemed, saved.

Lest the point seem terribly abstract and remote, here are four consequences, in practice, of the consequence-in-theory of all time being present in eternity.

[11] C. S. Lewis, *The Lion, the Witch and the Wardrobe* (New York: Macmillan, 1950), p. 133.

Fearlessness. How many times does Jesus say, "Fear not?" It is not just comforting psychology; it is accurate metaphysics. The advice of the Sermon on the Mount is exactly the opposite of the dreamy, impractical idealism most people associate with it. What could be more realistic than this: "Do not be anxious about tomorrow, for tomorrow will be anxious for itself." "Which of you by being anxious can add one cubit to his span of life?"[12]

Regretlessness. Regret is to the past what fear is to the future. We can "cast aside regret and fear [and] do the deed at hand".[13] Eternity makes regret impossible because there is nothing to regret when nothing is past, just as there is nothing to fear when nothing is future. Regret is possible only when in time we look at the dead, unchangeable past, when we say, "I believe in yesterday."

Forgiveness. God's forgiveness of sins is like His "I never knew you" toward the damned.[14] When God forgives sins, He not only forgives but forgets,[15] and what God forgets ceases to be, because God's knowledge determines its object rather than being determined by it.[16] Our knowledge follows what is, but what is follows God's knowledge. What God forgives is let go into nothingness; what God forgets *is* no more. God does not merely *cover* our sins in Christ; he annihilates them.[17]

This is why He can say to us, "you are all fair, my love; there is no flaw in you."[18] Our past sins *are* no more in

[12] Matthew 6:34, 27.

[13] J. R. R. Tolkien, *The Lord of the Rings*, vol. II, *The Two Towers* (New York: Ballantine, 1965), p. 156.

[14] Matthew 7:23; Galatians 4:4 (KJV).

[15] Psalms 25:7; 79:8; Isaiah 43:18; Jeremiah 31:34; Hebrews 8:12; 10:17.

[16] St. Thomas Aquinas, *Summa Theologiae*, I-II, 2, 3.

[17] Martin Luther, *Three Treatises* (Philadelphia: Fortress Press, 1978), p. 285; cf. Council of Trent, Decree on Justification, chap. 7 ("The Nature and the Causes of the Justification of a Sinner").

[18] Song of Songs 4:7.

eternity. Jesus brings eternity to time when he says to the dying thief on the cross, "Today you are to be with Me in Paradise." Jesus lives in Paradise, in the eternal now, in "today". Today He pronounces the judgment on the thief because today He sees the present Paradise in the thief's repentant soul. We who cling to time might resent the ease with which Jesus forgets the thief's lifetime of crime, as the Prodigal Son's older brother resented his father's forgiveness of the prodigal. Like that father, God lives in the present, not the past, so He is free to forgive. We are to enact this divine life in our lives. Our forgiveness, too, can change the past.

Prayer. "Prayer changes things", past as well as present, by touching eternity. Let me give an example from my own experience.[19] When my daughter was misdiagnosed as having a fatal, malignant brain tumor, I asked my friends to pray for her, and the prayers "worked": the tumor, surprisingly, turned out to have been benign. A skeptical friend whom I thanked for his prayers said to me, "You realize, of course, that our prayers couldn't have changed anything, really; the doctor said the tumor had been in her for years, and was benign from the beginning." I replied, "Your prayers *did* change things. God, eternally foreseeing all those prayers, decided to give her a benign tumor instead of a malignant one when He created her. Thank you."

We can pray for anything we do not know the issue of, past or present. The One we pray to is not bound by time. He can act forward, backward, and sideways.

Time-Travel in Heaven

A related consequence of all time being present in eternity is that we will be able to travel in time when we are in eternity. From eternity time is manipulable: expandable, compressible, reversible, divisible. It is silly-putty time. "With the Lord

---

[19] Peter Kreeft, *Love Is Stronger Than Death*, Appendix.

one day is as a thousand years, and a thousand years as one day"[20]; and just as He plays time like an accordion, expanding and contracting it at will, so can we when we live in Him. As an author can move backward or forward in a story, God can move in time; and so can we, once we get out of the story and into the Author.

Meeting

Still another consequence of all time being present in eternity is that all lifetimes meet there, as different roads up the same mountain meet at the top. At death, we shall meet not only in the same place but also at the same "time". If space does not separate us, neither will time. We will meet our descendants as well as our ancestors, and when we meet Abraham he will not have been waiting for four thousand years. This startling truth seems to be clearly taught in Scripture:

> For this we declare to you by the word of the Lord, that we who are alive, who are left until the coming of the Lord, shall not precede those who have fallen asleep . . . we . . . who are left, shall be caught up together with them in the clouds to meet the Lord . . .[21]

In this meeting, individuality is preserved, not destroyed, and part of individuality is individual *times*. These are not destroyed or seen through as illusory. Eternity is not Nirvana; it is the Communion of Saints. Eastern mysticism does not believe in time; Western materialism does not believe in eternity; Christianity is the paradox of eternity in time (Christ) and time in eternity (Christians).

Homecoming

"If I'm certain of anything, it's that Heaven is a coming home." Heaven is homecoming because eternity is the mother and

[20] 2 Peter 3:8.   [21] 1 Thessalonians 4:15, 17.

womb and nurturer of all times, and "mother" means "home".
Eternity is not the last point on the time line; nor is it a point
off the line; it is the whole line. All time comes home to
eternity.

We have two innate desires: to explore and to come home.
Both desires can be fulfilled by eternity, for eternity is the
co-presence of Alpha and Omega, home and exploring. Thus
Scripture describes Heaven this way: "[They shall] go in and
out and find pasture."[22] And "they shall run to and fro like
sparks among the reeds."[23] We will feel simultaneously safe
and adventurous, rooted and branching, very old and very
young when we are one with that "Beauty ancient yet ever
new".[24]

How to Find Time

No one has enough time for anything. How can we find it?
The answer is hidden in our principle that all time is present
in eternity, and in our first corollary, that of the death and
resurrection of time. He who loses his time shall gain it, and
he who keeps his time shall lose it. If you want more time,
you must go to where it is all kept: to the Eternal One, the
Lord of time. You must give Him your time, your few loaves
and fishes, and He will multiply them miraculously. He is
time's keeper and time's dispenser; He is the "householder
who brings out of his storeroom things both new and old".[25]

To be specific: on the morning of a day crammed full of
twice as many things to do as can possibly be done, you
cannot afford *not* to begin by taking time for prayer. This is
no pious platitude; it works. It has been tested and tried by
millions of people, sinners as well as saints. No miracle is

[22] John 10:9.
[23] Wisdom of Sirach 3:7.
[24] St. Augustine, *Confessions*, X, 27.
[25] Matthew 13:52 (JB).

more easily and repeatedly tested than this one. Every time time is given to God, it is transformed and tamed; every time it is not, it becomes a wild beast or a slave driver.

The reason it works is that prayer touches eternity, from which point time becomes malleable. *Kairos* transforms *chronos* only when we let eternity transform *kairos*. God gives us *kairos* freely, directly through our soul; He gives *chronos* only indirectly, through unalterable natural law. We are free to actualize or to sell our freedom; to stand in the eye of the hurricane, the still point of the turning world, or to be swept around its fringes. We are free to live in God's presence or in the presence of large, moving masses of molecules. Prayer frees us from the juggernaut, the grindstone, the cosmic wheel.

Are you skeptical about this? Then be scientific. Experiment. Honestly, open-mindedly, fairly. "But how can God bring this about in me?—Let Him do it, and then perhaps you will know." [26]

I dare you to try it.

---

[26] George MacDonald in *George MacDonald: An Anthology*, ed. C. S. Lewis, p. 99 (no. 233).

Part III

Heaven and Earth

Chapter Twelve

Does Heaven Begin Now?

Is Heaven now or after death?

If "all that seems earth is Hell or Heaven," then Heaven is now, for earth is now.

But "is that all there is?" Is Heaven only another name for earth? Then it is only a deceptive naming, a camouflage, a trick. What most people mean by "Heaven" is not just earth, however perfectly understood and appreciated. For one thing, they mean by "Heaven" an immortal life, but the life we have on earth is mortal. If Heaven is only earth, then Heaven dies.

On the other hand, if Heaven begins only at death or after death, then it is not true that Heaven is now and it is not true that "all that seems earth is Hell or Heaven."

The escape from both alternatives consists in denying their common premise: that time measures Heaven instead of Heaven measuring time. Both the "here and now" view of Heaven and the "after death" view of Heaven implicitly assume that Heaven is chronologically dateable. But Heaven is eternity, and eternity measures time; not time, eternity.

Eternity is neither *part of* time nor *apart from* time (both alternatives, you see, are measured by time), but all of time is present in eternity. From the viewpoint of eternity nothing *was* or *will be*; everything *is*.[1] From Heaven's point of view we simply *are* in Heaven, as 2 and 2 simply *are* 4; from our

[1] St. Thomas Aquinas, *Summa Theologiae*, I, 43, 4 ad 2.

earthly point of view we will be, or hope to be, in Heaven. From one point of view, a tiny baby is fully human (not an onion or a turtle!); from another, the baby has yet to become fully human. From one point of view, that da Vinci sketch is the Mona Lisa; from the other point of view, it has a long way to go to become the Mona Lisa.

This is why God says to us from the viewpoint of His eternal *now* something that to us is true only in our future, our destiny: "You are all fair, my love; there is no flaw in you."[2] That is why Jesus prophetically calls sandy Simon "Rocky" (*Petros*) long before he has become a rock.[3] That is why God is constantly changing names (that is, identities) throughout Scripture: Abram to Abraham, Jacob to Israel, Saul to Paul.[4] He is touching earth's time with Heaven's eternity. He is showing the plan of His finished masterpiece to the clumsy human brush that He is using.

So from the viewpoint of eternity, both the "here and now" and the "after death" views of Heaven are wrong—if taken literally. But they are both metaphorically right, since we may look at time as a kind of metaphor of eternity. We should not take our metaphors literally, but we should take them seriously.

We must also remember, when we ask when Heaven is, that Heaven is not first of all a place but a life, a spiritual lifeblood. The New Testament calls it *zoë*, "supernatural life", "divine life", "eternal life", "the Kingdom of Heaven". This is why the Father sent His Son: to establish the Kingdom of Heaven on earth, to begin eternal life in time, to put divinity in humanity, first in Christ and then in the Christian, first in the Head and then throughout His Body.[5]

---

[2] Song of Songs 4:7.
[3] John 1:42.
[4] Genesis 17:5; 35:10; Acts 13:9.
[5] John 1:12; 1 Corinthians 15:20, 23.

Kierkegaard calls this "the absolute paradox".[6] It is a paradox because when eternity begins in time, what can have no beginning or ending gets a beginning. This happens first in the world, by the Incarnation, and then in each individual soul that accepts it, by the "new birth". It first becomes an objective fact, then it is subjectively appropriated, believed. These are the two central events in all of history, these two comings of eternity into time. The first is the same for all, the second has a different time for each individual, but they are the same event. Our "new birth" is a microcosm of the world's; and Christ's Incarnation in Bethlehem is a prophecy of His intention to incarnate Himself in us.[7]

When we thus become "partakers of the divine nature",[8] we do not lose our human nature anymore than the world lost its nature when God entered it. To share in Christ is to share in the "hypostatic union"[9] of human and divine natures: now, in seed or shadow; after death, in fulfillment and substance.

Right now, therefore, if we believe, we are in Heaven; that is, if we accept the divine gift, we have it. Right now, in our humanity and temporality we taste "the powers of the age to come"[10]—unless we call the New Testament a lie or a fable. Right now we "can do all things" through Christ,[11] for He promised that "he who believes in me will also do the works that I do."[12]

Like His claim to divinity, this is an offense, an embarrassment. We would prefer to avoid the choice to believe it or

[6] Søren Kierkegaard, *Training in Christianity*, trans. Walter Lowrie (Princeton, N.J.: Princeton University Press, 1944).

[7] This point is the key to interpreting chapter 1 of Kierkegaard's *Philosophical Fragments*.

[8] 2 Peter 1:4.

[9] *The New Catholic Encyclopedia* (New York: McGraw Hill, 1967), vol. VII, p. 306.

[10] Hebrews 6:5.

[11] Philippians 4:13.

[12] John 14:12.

not, for believing it is "strong meat",[13] and disbelieving it is calling Christ a liar. We therefore often "reinterpret" it, water it down, explain it away, reduce it to a platitude.

Suppose we don't; what does it mean? What is the Heavenly life we have now?

Four powers, especially, of this life, four "powers of the age to come" that are now tasted as appetizers, stand out in the pages of the New Testament. These are *not* aspects of heroic sanctity or extraordinary mystical experience. They are by New Testament standards "the normal Christian life".[14] They are a part of the package deal of *zoë*. If we do not know that we have them, we need a faith-lift. We are to be *assured* of *zoë*—"I write this to you who believe . . . that you may know that you have *zoë*"[15]—and if we know we have life, we know we have the powers of that life.

First, we have an eternal, immortal life that conquers death and the fear of death. Having Christ's life, we also have His resurrection; like Him, we live through death. This claim is so central to Christianity—every single sermon in the New Testament after Christ's Resurrection centers on it—that one would think only a few could possibly be so confused as to call themselves Christians while denying it. But actuality runs far ahead of possibility, and the few have become millions. The confusion one would expect from the New Testament emphasis on the Resurrection is something like the opposite one: that of Saint Paul's Greek listeners who thought he was preaching two new gods, Jesus and Anastasis (Resurrection),[16] so central was the Resurrection to his gospel. Christianity without the Resurrection is like the Odyssey without Odysseus' wanderings: a thing without its essence. Whether that essence is true or false, whether you believe it or not, like it

[13] Hebrews 5:14 (KJV).

[14] Watchman Nee, *The Normal Christian Life* (Fort Washington, Pa.: Christian Literature Crusade, 1961).

[15] 1 John 5:13.

[16] Acts 17:18.

or not, that is what it *is*, that is its claim. "If Christ has not been raised . . . your faith is in vain."[17] That is the "Good News". The news that spread around the Mediterranean like wildfire was not "love your neighbor", but "now is Christ risen!"[18] Both are good, but the second is good *news*.

Second, as we share divine *life*, we also share divine *light*. "His anointing teaches you about everything."[19] The special "spiritual gifts" of prophecy, the interpretation of tongues, "the word of knowledge" and "the word of wisdom" are extraordinary (though widely dispersed) supernatural gifts;[20] but the gift of understanding Scripture, of having it "light up" as we read, is a universal gift of light. If we do not experience this aspect of *zoë*, we are not experiencing "the normal Christian life" according to New Testament standards.

This light is primarily simply the gift of faith, and by definition this gift (belief) is given to all believers. Faith is a way of seeing. The Christian says not "seeing is believing" but "believing is seeing". We see "through a glass, darkly",[21] but we *see* through a glass, darkly. "*Credo ut intelligam*", testified the Christian philosophers of the Middle Ages; "I believe so that I may understand."[22]

The third power of *zoë* is *agapē*, the love that only God can have by nature because it is pure gift-love, not need-love:[23] a bottomless fountain flowing out, not an emptying drain hole sucking in. Only God can have a love based on no need because only God has no needs, and God has no needs because He alone is infinitely perfect. The famous description of *agapē* in 1 Corinthians 13 is not a description of a humanly attainable

[17] 1 Corinthians 15:14.
[18] 1 Corinthians 15:20 (KJV).
[19] 1 John 2:27.
[20] 1 Corinthians 12:8–10.
[21] 1 Corinthians 13:12 (KJV).
[22] St. Anselm, *Proslogium*, 1.
[23] C. S. Lewis, *The Four Loves* (London: Collins, Fontana Books, 1965), pp. 15–22.

ideal but of a divinely revealed and given actuality: the love of Christ into which we are incorporated when we are incorporated into His body and His divine nature. Mere human nature is capable of a self-giving love, but not of a love that does not *come from* self, a love based not on self and its needs, a love perfectly selfless and self-forgetful. Even when we love, we need to love; God does not. Only His love is perfectly free.

Nature's first commandment is self-remembering, self-preservation, self-love; how could we be self-forgetful by nature? The inherent "pleasure principle" is an element in the motivation even of our natural altruism, our "herd instinct". We help others partly because we feel good when we do. Our motives are always mixed; God's are pure.

So when His *agapē* enters our soul, it is a new reality, a divine reality, even when it is mixed with our humanity. When a Christian loves you, it is Christ loving you through the Christian, the Head through the body. We are tubes designed to let God's love in at one end (by faith) and out the other (by good works, the works of love).

"Light, life, and love"; *sat, chit,* and *ananda*; the Father, the Son, and the Holy Spirit—Johannine imagery. Hindu theology of the attributes of Brahman, and Christian Trinitarian dogma all agree on the three ultimate realities and ultimate values.[24] They also happen to be the three primary human needs. (Of course; we are designed "in the image of God", designed like a glove to fit a hand.)

A fourth power of *zoë* is not a need but a glory, an extra. It is the power to work miracles, power over nature and its physical laws. This is the most empirical, most visible power of the four. It is also the *least* visible, that is, the least often seen. Perhaps that is because it is the one least believed. We are embarrassed by its high profile, its potential visibility—

---

[24] Huston Smith, *The Religions of Man* (New York: Harper & Row, 1965), pp. 25–27, 72; Heinrich Zimmer, *Philosophies of India* (Princeton, N.J.: Princeton University Press, 1974), p. 672.

or rather by its actual invisibility as a mark of the weakness of our faith. Miracles are rare partly because we do not expect them. We fear the test will fail. We expect little so that our expectations cannot be disappointed.

Yet the fact that this power is part of the whole Christian package deal of *zoë* can be seen from almost a casual skimming of the New Testament. To quote just five of many passages that promise miracles to all believers, one from each Gospel and a coup de grace from Saint Paul, see Matthew 17:20, Mark 16:17, Luke 10:19, John 14:12 and I Corinthians 3:21-23.

The history of Christianity—of *ordinary* Christianity—is full of miracles. They did not end in the first century, even though some theologians insist they should have. I have witnessed a few myself. But they are rare. Unlike *agapē*, they are not God's day-to-day policy for our life on earth. Christ Himself healed only a few blind men and lepers, not everyone in the world or even in Israel. Miracles are special foreshadowings, prophecies of the life to come, little liftings of the Heavenly curtain, appetizers, samples, signs. But they are effective signs, sacraments; they actually transmit what they signify.[25]

There are two reasons why miracles are rare. One is that our faith is much smaller than a grain of mustard seed. The other is that only when we are perfectly subject to God does God dare to let nature be perfectly subject to us. Otherwise we would surely misuse that power, just as we have misused all other, lesser powers. As we are now, "power corrupts and absolute power corrupts absolutely".[26] To keep us from such a Hell, God limits our samples of Heaven.

A chart can summarize the past, present, and future states of these four "powers of the age to come", these four aspects of Heaven. The past stage is the state of unredeemed life, *bios*, fallen Adam, the state of sin (alienation from God). The

[25] Peter Kreeft, *Heaven: The Heart's Deepest Longing* (San Francisco: Ignatius Press, 1989), p. 74; *Love Is Stronger Than Death*, pp. 60–61.

[26] Lord Acton, letter to Bishop Mandell Creighton, April 5, 1887.

Diagram 7

	past: *bios*	present: *zoë* now	future: *zoë* after death
Life:	dependent on earth, inevitable death	from God, immortal; double nature: death (*bios*) & resurrection (*zoë*)	from God, immortal; immortality given to *bios* also
Light:	reason and experience	faith	beatific vision
Love:	need-love	mixture of need-love and gift-love	pure gift-love
Power:	subject to Nature's laws; technological power	occasional miracles	physical laws are wholly subject to our will

present stage is the real but imperfect and incomplete possession of *zoë* by faith: fallen but redeemed humanity. The future stage is the complete and perfect possession of *zoë* after death.

The first stage is unstable: it must become either Heaven (the second and third) or Hell. "All that seems earth is [eventually] Hell or Heaven." The second stage is Heaven's appetizer. The third is the main course. And death intervenes between courses. But both are courses of the same "supper of the Lamb".[27] Though only a drop, even the present *zoë*

[27] Robert Farrar Capon, *The Supper of the Lamb* (New York: Doubleday, 1969).

is Heavenly wine miraculously made from our earthly water. Heaven begins now.

We only "taste" these "powers of the age to come" now, but they are actual, not just potential. A bean seed really and actually has bean life already, not just bacterial life or weed life, even though it is just a seed and quite invisible beneath the earth. It is potentially adult but not potentially bean. It is actually bean, present bean. Similarly, our *zoë*, even if invisible, is actually present: "Beloved, we are God's children now."[28]

But *zoë* is not more stagnant than *bios*. The seed of *zoë* soon pokes above ground and becomes gradually more visible to anyone who has eyes. The fruit ripens in its season. Now is history's growing season, time's spring. Our present troubles are growing pains—labor pains, in fact. Our *zoë* is a spiritual fetus, conceived (like Mary's) by the Holy Spirit. The angelic annunciation is to us too:

> The Holy Spirit will come upon you,
> and the power of the Most High will overshadow you;
> therefore the child to be born will be called holy,
> the Son of God.[29]

You cannot be partly pregnant. Ever since Heaven came to earth in Mary's womb, there have been only two choices: spiritual pregnancy or spiritual barrenness. Heaven begins now, and so does Hell.

---

[28] I John 3:2.   [29] Luke 1:35.

Chapter Thirteen

How Do We Experience Heaven Now?

Since Heaven begins now, and Heaven is eternity, we creatures in time are already participating in eternity. Eternity is one of the "powers of the age to come" that we are already tasting.

How does this make sense of our experience here in time? What difference does it make? What doors does it unlock? What are some of the experienced consequences of this idea that we in time touch eternity?

At least seven.

1. *Why We Hate Time*

For one thing, the presence of eternity in time explains why we desire eternity, why we are dissatisfied, hassled and harried by time, why there is never enough time.[1] We are not fulfilled by time, even by eons of it. We demand more—not more of the same, quantitatively more, but qualitatively more. Our heart cries out, "Is that all there is?" Thus Ecclesiastes confesses, "He has made everything beautiful in its time; also he has put eternity into man's mind [heart]",[2] that is, our desire.

---

[1] Sheldon Vanauken, *A Severe Mercy* (San Francisco: Harper & Row, 1977), pp. 199–203.

[2] Ecclesiastes 3:11.

Now we cannot desire something that we in no way know, something that in no way appears in our experience.[3] Paradoxically, we can desire only what we already have: we desire to have fully what we already have partially, or we desire as actual what we have as potential. Our desire for eternity shows that we have, here in our temporal being, an eternal dimension, a place for eternity, an eternity-shaped hole.[4] Eternity has already been present to the house of time, excavating its foundation. We are seagulls smelling the salt air of our home even here far inland.

What do we hate about time? We are harried by *clocks* but not by *sequence*. Music, dance, poetry, liturgy, playing, walking—these are sequential processes, but in *kairos* rather than *chronos*. They are fulfilling to us because they have one end in time but the other in eternity. They are anchored in eternity as they sway in time's winds. They are ways of living upside down, with our feet, our foundation, in the sky.

When we do this, life on earth becomes a liturgy, a sacred time. Liturgies are not measured by secular time; they are not measured externally, by clocks, but internally, by their events, their actions, their meaning.[5] Living liturgically means living life as "a dance, not a drill"[6]; poetry, not prose; a song, not a speech.

2. *Why Time Goes Faster as You Age*

Have you ever wondered why time seems to go faster as you get older? It seems a long time from one Christmas to the next for a child, but a short time for an adult. There is a parallel phenomenon in world-time, world-history: it too

---

[3] St. Thomas Aquinas, *Summa Theologiae*, I, 1, 1.

[4] Pascal, *Pensées*, trans. Krailsheimer (New York: Penguin Books, 1966), 117, 199; St. Augustine, *Confessions*, I, 1, 1.

[5] Robert Farrar Capon, *An Offering of Uncles* (New York: Sheed & Ward, 1967), chap. 2.

[6] C. S. Lewis, *That Hideous Strength* (New York: Macmillan, 1965), p. 149.

speeds up, its time moves faster as the world ages. More happens in less time with each era in human history. Why?

Because we learn to live in larger bites, much as a maturing reader learns to read larger and larger groups of words. This is our way of unconsciously beginning to prepare for eternity, where the "bite" is total, where we are present to all time at once.

As we approach the speed of light, scientists tell us, time itself speeds up for us and slows down relatively for others, for observers. This is a physical analogy for spirit approaching eternity. C. S. Lewis speculates along these lines:

> If movement were faster . . . and faster, in the end the moving thing would be in all places at once. . . . Well, then, that is the thing at the top of all bodies—so fast that it is at rest, so truly body that it has ceased being body at all. . . . The swiftest thing that touches our senses is light. We do not truly see light, we only see slower things lit by it, so that for us light is on the edge—the last thing we know before things become too swift for us.[7]

Even now we experience a parallel to the infinite speed of eternity where we are simultaneously present to all times: it is the power of thought, in which we are simultaneously present to any and all places.[8] Thought can bilocate, as body cannot (until spirit transmits its power of bilocation to body after the resurrection). We can be physically present only to one place at a time, but mentally present to many. In eternity we will also be simultaneously present to many *times*. And as we approach eternity by maturing, our "spirit-speed" increases; that is one reason why time seems to go faster as we get older.

[7] C. S. Lewis, *Out of the Silent Planet* (New York: Macmillan, 1965), p. 94.

[8] Pascal, *Pensées* (trans. Krailsheimer), 113.

3. Why Memory Seems Magical

Have you ever wondered, as C. S. Lewis has,[9] why memory has such magical power, why an event that seemed quite commonplace as it was occurring in your life can later become invested with great beauty and value and meaning when it is remembered? Have you wondered, as Saint Augustine has, how some past pains can be remembered without pain, or some past joys without joy?[10] The explanation is that memory gives something of a Heavenly, eternal view of our past, both individual and racial (we remember Eden).[11] Memory transforms the past; it changes the meaning of the past; it transcends the law of cause and effect that says that causality can never work backward. This is true for matter but not spirit. Memory casts an eternal light backwards on time and shows an apparently trivial and ephemeral temporal event as having an eternal significance, an "eternal weight of glory".[12] Memory gives a second life, a supernatural life to the past, as our spirit gives a second life to matter in consciousness, a life supernatural to matter, and as God gives a second, supernatural life to us when He takes us up into His own eternal life.

How does memory do this? By *fixing* a past event in memory, we create an un-fleeting picture of a fleeting event. We "redeem the time".[13] Anticipation can do this as well as memory:

> We dreamt of . . . the schooner sailing into a quiet lagoon of some far island, and the dream was charming because the *image* was without time, or time-free. In reality, there was the log

---

[9] C. S. Lewis, *The Pilgrim's Regress* (Grand Rapids, Mich.: Eerdmans, 1943), preface to third edition, pp. 7–9.

[10] St. Augustine, *Confessions*, X, 14.

[11] Pascal, *Pensées* (trans. Krailsheimer), 136.

[12] 2 Corinthians 4:17.

[13] Dante, *Paradiso*, canto III. Cf. T. S. Eliot, *Dante* (London: Faber & Faber, 1931), p. 52.

to write, the meal to get, the topsail to be mended . . . The
timelessness that seems to reside in the future or the past is an
illusion.[14]

It is an illusion because the flood of time is stemmed by the
dike of memory only for a time. Time is in memory but
memory too is in time. The rememberer must age and die.
But in Heaven every event is remembered forever. It becomes
one of the billions of pictures in God's museum—rather, God's
zoo, for they are alive there, not dead—open to inspection
with no deadlines and with total understanding.

Our lives are a picture, and death is the frame. In Heaven
we get off the picture and see it as it truly was. But time's
was is eternity's *is*. All past times are present, all dead times
are alive in eternity. Memory dimly foreshadows this; that is
why it is so magically charming.

Perhaps this also helps to explain why memory is so selective, why we remember some events and not others. Perhaps
events whose meaning will be basically unchanged in eternity,
events whose meaning we already understand, are remembered, while others are forgotten until "the healing of
memories", here or in Heaven, shines an eternal light of acceptance and understanding on them.[15] Especially painful past
events, like rejection by loved ones or wartime traumas, are
often forgotten, not only for reasons of psychic self-protection
but also for this Heavenly reason.

4. *Why We Love to Create*

Eternity in time also explains why we love to create. The
creative artist participates not only in God's love of creating
and power to create, but also in God's eternity. The creative

---

[14] Vanauken, *A Severe Mercy*, pp. 199–203.

[15] Agnes Sanford, *The Healing Gifts of the Spirit* (Nashville, Tenn.: Holman,
1976); *The Healing Light* (Plainfield, N.J.: Logos, 1972); Ruth Carter Staple-
ton, *The Experience of Inner Healing* (Waco, Tex.: Word Books, 1979).

artist lives outside the time of his creation (the drama, the musical movement, the flow of syllables) and sees all the moments, all the events of his creation at once. As creature, he is in time; as creator, time is in him.

The creative artist's work is full of *kairos*, not just *chronos*, and that work is his object; therefore he has objectified *kairos*. To objectify something, you must transcend it, you must be more than it. Therefore, to objectify *kairos*, you must transcend *kairos*. But the only dimension we know that transcends *kairos* is eternity. Therefore the creative artist creates from eternity.

But eternity is our soul's food, our fulfillment, our joy. That is why to create is a joy. And we can all be creative artists, whether we are musicians or housewives, poets or carpenters like Jesus: creative artists with our lives.

5. Why We Experience Ecstasy

The presence of eternity to our time also explains the experience of ecstasy, *ek-stasis*, standing-outside-yourself.[16]

Perhaps you have forgotten yourself completely in a great piece of music, or some beauty of nature (a sunset or a storm), or a human love, or an artistic masterpiece, or an inspired thought, or a joyful event like a birth or a healing or a conversion. Perhaps you have become so lost in it that you seemed to lose all consciousness of time as you lost all consciousness of self.[17] You seemed to become the object, to stand outside yourself in the other, not in yourself looking out at the object.

The presence of eternity in time explains this experience, for when we transcend ourselves we transcend time too. For

[16] Peter Kreeft, *Heaven: The Heart's Deepest Longing* (San Francisco: Ignatius Press, 1989), pp. 143–55.

[17] Perhaps this explains the attraction of Oriental mysticism, the "bliss" of *nirvana*. Even without an object to lose yourself in, you can through strenuous, lifelong meditation (the hard way) lose yourself, and this is blissful.

time-consciousness and ego-consciousness are two sides of the same coin. (Krishnamurti proves this brilliantly.[18]) However, I do not believe we can ever literally escape the self or see through it as an illusion, as in Buddhism, for the compelling reason that only a self can forget itself. Self-forgetfulness is good; but it is possible only if there is a real self that is forgotten and a real self that forgets.

An even commoner way of forgetting self and time is simply reading fiction.[19] Here we transcend time not to eternity but merely to another time, the time of the story. When we read a great story, we are not outside it looking in, but inside it looking out; we are outside our bodies' time and space and in the story's.[20] Whenever the spell of great fiction works, we have an out-of-the-body experience!

That is why animal languages, however complex and clever, never include fiction: animals cannot transcend time, cannot play with time. To play with something, you must transcend it. Toys do not play with themselves; people play with them. Stories play with time because storytellers transcend time. The storytelling mind stands not only in another time but also in eternity, for the story is a whole to the author, even though it unrolls part by part to the reader. But the reader too can share the mind of the author, and the reader's experience is analogous to the believer's, who through Revelation knows something of the mind of the Author of the story he is living.[21]

[18] J. Krishnamurti, *Talks and Dialogues, Saanen* (Netherlands: Servire, 1969), pp. 96–98.

[19] Mircea Eliade, *Myths, Dreams and Mysteries* (New York: Harper & Row, 1960), chap. 1.

[20] J. R. R. Tolkien, "On Fairy Stories" in *Tree and Leaf* (Boston: Houghton Mifflin, 1965), p. 37.

[21] Dorothy L. Sayers, *The Mind of the Maker* (New York: Harcourt, Brace, 1941).

6. Why Temporal Choices Determine Eternal Destiny

In this lived story, according to Christianity, our choices in time determine our eternal destiny. How can this be? How can time determine eternity?

Time is part of eternity, the beginning of eternity. In time we construct the foundation of our eternal house, the sketch of our eternal portrait. Our choices are not in *chronos* but in *kairos*, and *kairos* touches eternity; therefore, our choices touch eternity. Every choice we make has eternal repercussions. It is a brush stroke in the painting that takes on solidity and life in eternity, the painting that is our own self-portrait.

This notion, that eternity has a beginning, is what Kierkegaard calls "the absolute paradox".[22] It is the Incarnation, both in the world's history and in the individual's. Buddha knows eternity profoundly, but he does not know "the absolute paradox". Therefore he is profoundly wrong (it takes a profound thinker to be profoundly wrong) when he says so reasonably that the law of time (*samsara*) is that "whatever is an arising thing, that also is a ceasing thing".[23] There are two exceptions to Buddha's universal law: Christ's human identity and our divine identity. Both are arising things, which have a beginning in time; and both are not ceasing things, but are immortal.

The world's eternity as well as ours begins in time. The consummation of world history has begun. The great marriage between God and humanity began at the Annunciation, when Mary's *fiat* to the Father allowed the Spirit to conceive the Son in her. The bride is even now sewing her wedding garment.

[22] Cf. chap. 5, nn. 6, 7.
[23] "The Sermon at Benares", E. A. Burtt, *The Teachings of the Compassionate Buddha* (New York: New American Library, 1963), p. 31.

7. *Why We Know Eternal Truths and Values*

Finally, the presence of Heaven's eternity to earth's time explains a perennial philosophical puzzle: that of a priori knowledge[24] and absolute moral values.[25]

How can the human mind, which changes (we "change our mind" more often than we change our clothes) know changeless, eternal truths? Yet it can. Time has nothing to do with whether or not two plus two equals four, or the whole is greater than the part, or being is not non-being. Quintillions of millennia cannot change these truths. We can know them only because of what Saint Augustine called "divine illumination"[26] and Saint John called the *Logos*, "the true light that enlightens every man".[27] God's eternal mind touches every human mind that thinks such thoughts.

The experience of conscience also touches eternity; for conscience tells us "Thou shalt" or "Thou shalt not" with no ifs, ands, or buts. Our essential moral obligation is unchanging and unchangeable, whether it is formulated as "justice" (Plato), "Do good and avoid evil" (Aquinas), or "will moral duty" (Kant). Our wills and worlds change, but our "categorical imperative" does not. Here, too, Heaven visits earth in every instance of knowledge by conscience; and every acceptance increases, and every refusal decreases, our participation in Heaven.

---

[24] Plato, *Meno*, 81c; Hume, *Essay Concerning Human Understanding*, II, 13; Kant, *Critique of Pure Reason*, preface to second edition; 5a–d, 14a–108c; Hegel, *Philosophy of History*, introduction, 156d–158a.

[25] Plato, *Crito*, 48d, 54b; *Gorgias*, 467c ff.; Aristotle, *Ethics*, 341b–342c, 1097b22–1098a17–25; St. Augustine, *On Christian Doctrine*, I, 9; St. Thomas Aquinas, *Summa Theologiae*, I, 12, 1; 26, 2; 59, 1.

[26] St. Augustine, *On the Teacher*, XII, 40.

[27] John 1:9.

Chapter Fourteen

Can We Know the Joy of Heaven Now?

Joyless Christianity

The Faith is not selling well.

Faith is selling well—extremely well: faith in general, faith as an attitude, faith as positive thinking, faith in faith. Also selling well are many strange new faiths: faith in cults, faith in UFOs, faith in ICBMs, faith in The Force, faith in ancient astronauts, faith in astrology—faith in almost anything. We are an incredibly credulous age.

The reason for this is probably that "nature abhors a vacuum"[1] spiritually as well as physically. Our modern Western civilization is ready to believe in almost anything to fill the vacuum left by the de-Christianization of the last four centuries. We are on the rebound from our jilted lover, the Old God, and ready to leap into the arms of any new god that comes along.

The Old God is not selling well, in the long run, despite oft-repeated chatter about religious revivals. Compare 1990 not with 1980 but with 1280, and you will see what I mean. The British, more candid than we Americans, already call our time "the post-Christian era".

[1] St. Thomas Aquinas, *Summa Theologiae*, II-II, 35, 4 ad 2.

Why? Why is the product not selling? Millions of "salespersons" of Christianity have asked that question in the past few centuries, trying to diagnose the "decline in sales". There are only two possible answers: either because the world has changed or because we have changed. Which is it?

Do skyscrapers and atom bombs and computers somehow make it less reasonable to believe in God? Has the discovery of the age of the universe or the structure of the brain or the genetic code disproved the Creator of the universe and the brain and the genetic code? Surely the change is not so much in the world we face as in the face with which we face the world. We change our world before it changes us; the changes in our world did not come from angels or insects but from us. If they have changed us, we have changed ourselves through them. So we must look to ourselves to find out why God is not selling; to psychology, not physics.

What needs of the human consumer are fulfilled by the divine product? What holes in human nature does the Faith fill?

For one thing, we need to know the truth. We want to live in the true world, not in a fabrication of someone's imagination. The Faith claims to be a divine revelation of what is true. Have we been let down by the Faith here? Have its dogmas been proved false? Is it intellectually bankrupt?

Certainly not. The Church's understanding of her "deposit of faith" has changed by addition, not subtraction; it has deepened impressively. Between Jesus and ourselves stand Paul, Augustine, Aquinas, Pascal, Newman, the popes—a great growth both of the Mystical Body of Christ and of her own self-understanding: progress, not regress, in the intellectual area.

A second area is the moral one, and a second human need is goodness. What about that aspect of the Faith: its morality, its sanctity, its life practice? Here too there has been great progress; between Jesus and ourselves stand millions of saints, known and unknown, whose lives are an even more impressive selling point for the Faith than the great theologians' minds.

But there is a third human need: joy. And here is the let-down. While our intellectual and moral images of God and Heaven have grown in respectability and attractiveness, our sense of beauty, glory, wonder, awe, magnificence, triumph—these have shrunk. We associate these qualities with medieval rather than modern times. It seems that while the Christian mind and the Christian will have grown, the Christian heart and imagination have not. Our images of God and of Heaven are joyless.

A simple syllogism demonstrates this. Whatever seems joyful sells. And the Faith is not selling. Therefore the Faith must not seem joyful.

Honestly, I really hate to play this role, the Prophet of Doom. But we should not "cry 'Peace! Peace!' when there is no peace"[2]—or "Joy! Joy!" when there is no joy. I was flabbergasted when an editor suggested to me that I add a chapter to this book to point out that the joy of Heaven is available to us here on earth. "Surely that is the most obvious platitude", I objected; "surely every Christian knows that already? Why waste time telling people what they already know?"

"Because they *don't* know it."

"That's ridiculous. I can't believe that." (I am often very naïve about the forms of foolishness people will follow.)

"You don't believe it? Look around you. Talk to the average Christian. Go into the churches. See all the joy? Everyone knows it already, right?"

I saw his point. To find a joyful Christian is so unusual that when we find one we entitle an anthology of his writings *The Joyful Christian* precisely because he is so distinctive.[3]

When I look around me—more, when I look inside me—I see such ridiculous joylessness that it seems as if the Good News was never preached. The common Christianity in the

[2] Jeremiah 6:14; 8:11.
[3] *The Joyful Christian: 100 Readings from the Works of C. S. Lewis* (New York: Macmillan, 1977).

land is: "God exists and love your neighbor." This is not the Good News; in fact, it is neither good nor news, but a poor platitude inexplicably encumbered by a transcendental mystification. It is what Kierkegaard describes in his *Attack upon Christendom*:

> The common Christianity in the land I want to place alongside the New Testament in order to see how these two are related to one another. Then, if it appears, if I or another can prove, that it can be maintained face to face with the New Testament, then with the greatest joy I will agree to it. But one thing I will not do, not for anything in the world. I will not by suppression, or by performing tricks, try to produce the impression that the ordinary Christianity in the land and the Christianity of the New Testament are alike.[4]

One of the crucial differences between the Christianity of the New Testament and "the ordinary Christianity of the land" is the difference between the crazy, total joy of the former, the joy that put songs on martyrs' lips, and the joylessness of the latter. The story is told of the English vicar who was asked by a colleague what he expected after death, and replied: "Well, if it comes to that, I suppose I shall enter into eternal bliss, but I really wish you wouldn't bring up such depressing subjects."

If the very joy is depressing, where is the joy? "If then the light in you is darkness, how great is the darkness!"[5] "If salt has lost its taste, how shall its saltness be restored?"[6]

How to recover joy? There can be no gimmick, no trick, no technique. Just look at reality. Joy is not something to work up, or imagine, or strive to attain. It *is*. It is not first of all a human feeling but a divine reality, not a future earthly

---

[4] Søren Kierkegaard, "What Do I Want?" in *Attack upon Christendom*, trans. Walter Lowrie in *A Kierkegaard Anthology*, ed. Robert Bretall (New York: Modern Library, 1947), p. 439.

[5] Matthew 6:23.

[6] Matthew 5:13.

goal but a present Heavenly achievement. And the Kingdom of Heaven has come to earth. *That* is the Good News.

Christ is the God Who has come, and He is joy. Our God is also Jove, Jupiter, the God of Joy. God is all the gods and more, not less—all that the human mind has imagined, all that the human heart has desired, and more. He is certainly not less jovial than Jove. Joy bubbles and brims at the heart of God, the heart of reality. God is an overflowing fountain of joy, a volcanic explosion of joy, a trillion burning suns of joy, a joy that would utterly break our hearts if we touched even a drop of it at its source. He is the joy that *does* break our hearts with love and longing whenever we catch a taste of it in human love or see the shadows of it in the beauties of nature or hear the remote echoes of it in great music. Even here in the valley of the shadow of death that is our life we are overcome by its traces:

> The faint, far-off results of these energies which God's creative rapture implanted in matter when He made the worlds are what we now call physical pleasures; and even thus filtered, they are too much for our present management. What would it be to taste at the fountain-head that stream of which even these lower reaches prove so intoxicating? Yet that, I believe, is what lies before us. The whole man is to drink joy from the fountain of joy.[7]

That is the Good News. The two ingredients in "the ordinary Christianity in the land" are a kind of faith (God exists) and a kind of charity (love your neighbor) but *hope* is missing, and it is hope that brings the joy of running toward a beautiful goal.

How Christian Joy Revolutionizes Living

This joy is not an ideal but a given reality. It is given not only to saints and mystics but to all Christians. It is not to read

[7] C. S. Lewis, *The Weight of Glory* (New York: Macmillan, 1949), p. 14.

about, envy, and sigh after; it is utterly free, utterly available. For it is God. God does not *give* joy; God *is* joy. And He gives Himself (and therefore joy) without limit, without stinginess. The only limit is on our part, and that limit is not our merit but our desire. God does not say, "Let him who is *worthy* come and take joy", but rather, "Let him who is *thirsty* come, let him who *desires* take the water of life without price."[8] Heavenly joy is for beggars, not the rich; "Those who are well have no need of a physician, but those who are sick; I came not to call the righteous, but sinners."[9]

Please notice that I have deliberately been identifying (1) joy, (2) God Himself, (3) the Kingdom of Heaven, and (4) Christ, God incarnate. Joy is the very life of God, the spiritual bloodstream into which we are plunged when we accept Christ as Plunger. Saint Paul says, "All is yours, and you are Christ's, and Christ is God's."[10] Christ connects us to divine joy because Christ is God (and thus *is* divine joy) *and* He is us: second Adam, fully human, Head of the Body that we are.

The practical point of this theology is that since Christ *is* our joy (not just *gives* it), and since we always have Him ("Lo, I am with you always"[11]), therefore *we always have joy*, whether we feel it or not. We are in Heaven already, whether we know it or not, just as a fetus is already in the world, though the womb masks it from his eyes. How do we know this is true? Simply because God has repeatedly told us so. We know it by faith—faith means simply believing what God says. We do not see it, but "Blessed are those who have not seen and yet believe."[12] Nor do we feel it, but feeling is only another kind of seeing. What we need is not just a seeing and

---

[8] Revelation 22:17 (emphasis added).
[9] Mark 2:17.
[10] 1 Corinthians 3:22–23.
[11] Matthew 28:20.
[12] 1 John 20:29.

not just a feeling but a fact, a reality: God Himself. *And this we have.* This we are guaranteed. Jesus is the glue, the having. He is the Mediator by Whom we have God and God has us.

Once we believe this—that we already have the joy we want even if we do not feel it—the feeling follows. It is like earthly happiness: grab after it and it escapes you; forget the feeling and seek the good instead of happiness, and feelings of happiness come unsought. The same law operates here on a higher level. Stop sighing after joy, relax in the assurance not of your own heart but of God's word that you now have God as your secure and complete possession, and the joy will come. We are to know this for sure, according to the New Testament:

> We know that we have passed from death unto life. . . . We know that we are of the truth, and shall assure our hearts before Him. For if our heart condemn us, God is greater than our heart, and knoweth all things.[13]

The consequences of believing this are inexpressibly revolutionary. This faith transforms the whole of our lives, especially the dimension of ethics, goodness, holiness. It becomes not just duty but joy. Obeying God's will is not the artificial, external, constricting, repressive straitjacket that it seems to those who do not *do* it; it is the path to joy. Uprightness is not uptightness. Even the good pagan Plato knew that: the central thesis of the greatest work in the history of philosophy, the *Republic*, is that "Justice [goodness] is more profitable [happy, joyful] than injustice."[14] How dare Christians be less certain of that than pagans?

It is so shatteringly simple that a child can understand it. In fact, only a child can understand it. That is why "unless you . . . become like children, you will never enter the kingdom of heaven."[15] The same simplicity refracted into

[13] I John 3:14, 19–20 (KJV).
[14] Plato, *Republic*, I, 354a.
[15] Matthew 18:3.

different words tells us that God loves us, therefore wills only our joy, therefore to live in His will *is* to live in joy. The only difficulty in understanding it is that it is much too simple. I have had brilliant students who could not understand that $X = X$ was necessarily true. They keep looking for a way out, something to argue about. They hate to become little children and just shut up and smile. All right then, if you are like that (and we all are sometimes), let's make the same point in a more roundabout way; a critical, rational, logical way; an argument.

An Unanswerable Argument for Joy

It seems too good to be true. Yet here is a proof. Think about each step and ask yourself whether you can deny any step of the argument. If not, there you are: in total joy.

First premise: God wills only what is Godlike, not what is anti-Godlike: good, not evil; light, not darkness; truth, not falsehood.

Second premise: God is joy—not despair or pain or panic or anger or any of the opposites of joy.

Conclusion: therefore God wills only joy, everyone's joy.

Let us be sure about this. Let us prove the same conclusion from different premises.

First premise: God is love.

Second premise: Love wills the joy of the beloved.

Third premise: You are God's beloved. That is the Gospel, the Good News. God loves you, not because you are lovable, but you are lovable because God loves you.

Conclusion: God wills your joy.

Of course. The more you love someone, the more you want joy for them. Is God any less loving than you are?

So far we have proved only that God *wills* your joy. But when we put this conclusion together with the truth that God is all-powerful, and therefore infallibly gets what He wills, the conclusion becomes that you *will* find joy. *You* are not powerful enough to give joy infallibly even to those you love best. But God is.

But, you object, why then do I not know this joy and experience it and live in it? Is it because I'm not good enough? Because I don't try hard enough? No. Only because you don't believe it.

We persist in believing instead the First Lie, the lie that lost us Eden, the Devil's lie that sin is fun and sanctity is not, that following "My will be done" is joy and following "Thy will be done" is not. The Devil teaches us this primal lie about the separation between our will and God's to make us think of God as our enemy, to make us fear Him instead of trusting Him, so as to keep us from our joy.

Satan hates us and loves to take away our joy. He hates God even more, but he cannot take away God's joy. But he *can* take away ours, if we let him. Even that, however, he can do only indirectly, by deceiving us with the two false pictures of God's will as joyless and our own as joyful. We believe his pictures instead of God's. This is the origin of sin. Sin begins in the area of belief, not action. All sin follows this pattern from the first sin:

> *Now the serpent . . . said* to the woman, "*Did God say,* 'You shall not eat of any tree of the garden'?"
> And the woman said to the serpent, "We may eat of the fruit of the trees of the garden; *but God said,* 'You shall not eat of the fruit of the tree which is in the midst of the garden, neither shall you touch it, lest you die.'"
> *But the serpent said* to the woman, "You will not die . . . you will be like God." [16]

We must begin here, then: what do we *believe* about joy? What we must believe is extremely simple; that is why we find it so hard to believe, and why only a saint or a child can believe it. It is that God is infinitely simple-hearted; that He loves us simply, without qualification; that He wills only our

[16] Genesis 3:1-5 (emphasis added).

joy—not joy mixed with something else, not joy withheld, but pure, simple, absolute joy: His own joy. God is no miser. He gives as much as we can take, as much as we want. Saint Francis of Assisi's disciple Brother Giles put it very simply: "Who, thinkest thou, is the readier, our God to grant us His grace, or we to receive it?"[17]

God gives without calculating merit, without judging, without condemning, in total forgiveness, just as He asks us to give to each other. Indeed, how could He possibly command behavior from us that He does not practice Himself? Most Christians worship a God Who is an omnipotent hypocrite, Who does not practice what He preaches, Who withholds from us the total love and forgiveness that He commands us not to withhold from each other.

Now this joy is present, not just future. He has already given it to us: it is Christ, it is the Kingdom of Heaven, it has come to earth. Therefore the pattern of prayer Christ teaches us is present too:

> I tell you therefore: everything you ask and pray for, believe that you *have it already*, and it will be yours.[18]

I dare you: Think simply and clearly about Brother Giles' question for just a moment, with full attention: Who do you think is readier? God to give joy or you to receive it? Don't stop with mere words, a correct verbal answer. Look at the facts. Look at the face of God.

There is simply no way out. God is pure love and God is infinite power, and if you dare touch those two truths together like flint and steel, the spark comes out that everything in all creation, the motion of every molecule, every event in history and in our lives, every pebble, every cavity, every birth, every death, every tragedy, is part of God's perfect plan for our

[17] *The Little Flowers of St. Francis* (New York: Dutton, Everyman's Library, 1934), p. 173.
[18] Mark 11:24 (JB).

joy, is working together for our joy. That is what the Bible says: "*all* things work together for good to them that love God."[19] Nothing in all creation, Saint Paul goes on to say in the most triumphant and all-conqueringly joyful words ever written, neither death nor life nor angels nor devils nor things present nor things to come will ever be able to separate us from our joy because our joy is Jesus Christ, the Kingdom of Heaven Who has come to earth, to us. We are in Him *now*, this second.

All the saints say this. They see through the Devil's illusion. They see joy everywhere, even in suffering. They believe it even when they do not feel it. Why don't we?

Obstacles to Joy

If it is not our mind that holds back, if we believe God and His Word, then it must be our will, our desire. Fear is the opposite of desire. What fear holds back our natural desire for joy?

Perhaps the ultimate fear, the fear of death. Believing that God's will is our joy, is a kind of death: a death to self-will. Something in us whispers: "Watch out! Don't let God get too close. He's a killer, you know." The voice is right. God *is* a killer, a purifying fire, a surgeon, an illusion-destroyer, an awakening from a dark dream, and the dream fears its annihilation.

But it is this very death of self-will that is joy. This is so in three ways. First, it is a *road* to joy: it leads to Heaven. Even if it were not in itself joy (which it is), its seeming sufferings "are not worthy to be compared with the glory which shall be revealed in us".[20] The most horrible lifetime on earth, seen from the viewpoint of Heaven, will look like only one bad cold.

[19] Romans 8:28 (KJV).
[20] Romans 8:18 (KJV).

Second, the death of self-will not only leads to future joy, it is present joy. "In His will, our peace", writes Dante;[21] the greatest line ever written, comments T. S. Eliot. You don't believe it? There is only one way to find out. Try it, you'll like it.[22]

Third, the very difficulty we encounter in obeying, the very shrieks of the fallen Adam in us, the very death-agony of our selfish ego, is a joy. In the midst of this death, we find life. The death of self-will is like stripping off hot, dirty clothes or like being cured of cancer.

Perhaps this is why the Lady Julian said "sin is behovable", or good for something.[23] The Easter liturgy makes the same shocking statement: "O happy fault!"[24] Unless there were sin, we would never experience the joy of dying to sin; so even sin can contribute to our joy through the golden door of repentance. This sounds shocking, but it is logical: God would not allow *any* evil to come into any of His works, argues Saint Augustine, unless His goodness and power were such as to bring out of it an even greater good.[25] This applies to all evil, the evil of sin as well as the evil of suffering, the evil we do as well as the evil done to us, moral evil as well as physical evil. God could prevent this too with great graces; God could turn us into saints this very moment by zapping us with Instant Beatific Vision. There is only one possible reason why Pure Love would not do this: the same reason Pure Love does everything—for love. (Love is very simple-hearted.)

[21] T. S. Eliot, "Ash Wednesday", IV, stanza 4.

[22] Cf. the words of the old hymn, "Trust and obey/For there's no other way/To be happy in Jesus/But to trust and obey" (J. H. Sammis; copyright 1915 by D. B. Towner, Hope Publishing Co.).

[23] Lady Julian of Norwich, *Revelations of Divine Love* in F. Happold, *Mysticism* (Baltimore, Md.: Penguin, 1964), p. 297.

[24] "Exultet" in the Easter Vigil of the Roman liturgy, *St. Andrew Bible Missal* (New York: Darton, Longman & Todd, 1960), p. 477.

[25] *Enchiridion*, 11.

God does not have a Universal Instant Beatific Vision-Zapping Policy because He is enlarging our eyes and our hearts by the present surgery of suffering and even the surgery of allowed sin and repentance, so that eventually those eyes and hearts can contain even more of Him and more of joy.

We see how it works in a few selected scriptural examples: Joseph, Jacob, Job. The sins of Joseph's brothers in selling him into slavery saved the Jews from starvation years later.[26] Jacob's greed and grasping were used by God to make a saint, and Jacob learned to grapple with God.[27] The greatest saints are often made from the greatest sinners. Job's sufferings and also his rebellion under them were used as the road to his wisdom and his beatitude in meeting God face-to-face.[28] And finally, the greatest sin ever committed, deicide, saved the world.

We see this only seldom: how evil works out for good. God gives us a few examples in Scripture to make it easier for us to believe it, as He gives us a few miracles to show us more clearly what He always is and does. But faith must go beyond sight and proof, for love's sake; no lover proposes to his beloved with syllogisms.

All is love. Nothing escapes. Nothing happens by chance when God's back is turned. No fly settles on His painting, no gust of wind spills His ink bottle. Every wart is part of the masterpiece.

That includes our free will and its free choices. God did not take a chance and lose; God did not create a world half under His control and half not. God's providence includes our free will as surely as it includes the revolution of the planets and the growth of weeds. And this absolute divine sovereignty does not take away our free will, it includes it; it constitutes our free will just as it constitutes planets and weeds

[26] Genesis 50:20.
[27] Genesis 32:24-32.
[28] Job 42:5.

as different parts of its perfect plan. As Saint Thomas Aquinas
puts it,

> It pertains to divine providence to produce every grade of
> being. And thus it has prepared for some things necessary
> causes, so that they happen of necessity; for others contingent
> causes, that they may happen contingently [dependent on our
> free choices]. . . . The effect of divine providence is not only
> that things should happen somehow, but that they should
> happen either by necessity or by contingency. Therefore what-
> soever divine providence ordains to happen infallibly and of
> necessity, happens infallibly and of necessity; and that happens
> from contingency which the plan of divine providence con-
> ceives to happen from contingency.[29]

Then How Is Hell (Refusal of Joy) Possible?

God is absolutely inescapable,[30] and God is joy. Therefore
what-is-in-objective-fact-joy is inescapable. But we need not
experience joy as joy. The very fires of Hell are the love and
joy of God experienced as wrath and torment by the soul that
hates the light and its purifying fire. (We have seen this in
Chapter 10). But that *is* a kind of escape, as the ostrich sticking
its head in the sand *escapes* the hunter, or rather, escapes *seeing*
the hunter. How is even this possible? How can we be so
stupid?

The question here is not: How is Hell possible if God is
love? That is the question of Chapter 9. Our question here
is: How is Hell possible if man is sane? Why do we refuse joy?

It *is* possible; that much is clear. For it is actual; it happens.
And whatever is actual is possible. But how?

It seems impossible, for everyone seeks happiness—in seeking anything, we are seeking happiness. Happiness is the last
end, ultimate good, or *summum bonum* of everyone. No one

---

[29] St. Thomas Aquinas, *Summa Theologiae*, I, 22, 4.
[30] St. Augustine, *Confessions*, X, 2.

seeks happiness as a means. No one wants happiness in order to attain riches, or power, or pleasures of the senses, or a good conscience, or knowledge; but we do seek all these things because we think they will make us happy. As Pascal puts it, "this is the reason why one goes to war and why another does not. It is the motive for all that we do, including those who go and hang themselves."[31]

It must be, then, that happiness is not the same as joy. For all seek happiness, but not all seek joy. It is shocking to recognize that not all seek joy, but it must be true, for (1) all who seek joy find it—God guarantees that[32]—and (2) not all find joy. There is Hell. God has told us that too.[33] It necessarily follows, then, that not all seek joy.

But how can this be? How can we understand this conclusion that has just been squarely deposited in our startled laps by a scriptural syllogism?

It must lie in the difference between joy and happiness. There are at least five differences, which explain why all desire happiness but not all desire joy.

First, we can control happiness, but not joy. Joy always comes as a surprise. And some of us insist on control and resent surprises.

The second reason explains the first: joy is a surprise because joy is bigger than ourselves, while happiness is smaller. Happiness is in us, but we are in joy: "Enter thou into the joy of thy Lord."[34] And some of us resent what is bigger than ourselves, just as Satan does.

Third, since joy is bigger than ourselves and happiness smaller, the *desire* for joy is therefore different from the desire for happiness. We can *have* happiness, but we cannot have joy; we can only let it have us. And some of us resent "being had".

---

[31] Pascal, *Pensées*, trans. Krailsheimer (New York: Penguin Books, 1966), 148.

[32] Matthew 7:8 (JB); Luke 11:10; Romans 14:17.

[33] Matthew 25:31–46.

[34] Matthew 25:21 (KJV).

Fourth, to let joy "have" us, we must die to ourselves, our expectations and desires. Happiness makes no such demands; it fulfills our expectations and desires. We shrink from death; that is why we shrink from joy.

Fifth, we must grow by shrinking to enter the Kingdom of Joy. Only a child can enter the Kingdom because its gate is tinier than the needle's eye (to connect two images of Jesus).

The old Adam in us refuses joy. But even this has been taken care of by God: "Our old self was crucified with him [Christ]."[35] All that remains for us to do is to believe, to accept the finished work,[36] the gift already given, which is Christ Himself: "If you knew the gift of God . . . who it is that is saying to you, 'Give me a drink', you would have asked him, and he would have given you living water."[37] It is free for the asking: "Let him who is thirsty come, let him who desires take the water of life without price."[38]

Why Bother?

One last problem that bothers many people: if God is all-loving and all-powerful, so that all things ultimately work together for good, why bother? No matter what we do, it is part of God's perfect plan, right? If there is no escape, then not only is there no point in trying to escape, there is also no point in trying to get in or stay in.

A first answer is that all things work together for good *only to those who love God*. It is not automatic. Heaven includes earth, yes; but so does Hell. "All that seems earth is Hell or Heaven." There is an either-or.

But what about the saved? Why should *they* bother? Once you are in Noah's ark, why swim? The answer is that there

---

[35] Romans 6:6.
[36] John 19:30.
[37] John 4:10.
[38] Revelation 22:17.

is no reason to swim, but there is reason to clean the animals. The "bother" here is not to gain salvation, to buy an entrance ticket to Heaven. No good works, care, or even earthly love can force God's hand. The ticket is free. Our work is therefore also free (this is Luther's great liberating discovery), free of the burden of "making it" to Heaven, free of worry about not making it, free of performance anxiety before God. God is a loving Father and we are his toddlers; He delights in every teetering step and laughs when we fall out of weakness. Why bother, then? Why does a toddler want to learn to walk? To be like his father. God's goodness is the supreme beauty and joy; the more we know it, the more we love it and want to be like that. We do not do good to get to Heaven; we do good because Heaven has already got to us. We do not work to make everything work together for good; we work because everything works together for good. It is our part in the good play.

Third, even if we cannot understand how both halves of the paradox of divine sovereignty and human free will can be reconciled, we must embrace both halves of the paradox. The Orient tends to give up the human free will and human works half and to become passive; Western secularism tends to give up the divine providence half and to become frantic. Both halves are essential for the drama, just as in classical Greek drama it is only the doubleness of the divine and human points of view that makes for the dramatic tension, interest, and meaning.

Jesus, at any rate, softens neither half of the paradox. His moral urgency is extreme; His severity of warning to the wicked is in excess of every Old Testament prophet (and this aspect of His teaching has been conveniently ignored by our fashionably comfortable and comfort-mongering age); on the other hand, almost equally unendurable and equally shocking is the extremity of His tenderness and unlimited eagerness to forgive.

Fourth, not only does it make an infinite difference whether or not I accept God's free offer of Heaven, but once I do, it still makes a tremendous difference, an eternal, Heavenly difference to me, what kind of person I become in time, how great a capacity for God I develop on earth.

I do this not by playing God but by playing John the Baptist for Him: "Prepare ye the way of the Lord." My efforts are needed not to create joy but to move into the stream of God's joy.

Two Ways You Can Avoid Joy

Most readers will respond to this chapter as follows:

This is all very inspiring but I don't feel this joy I'm supposed to feel. Therefore either there's something wrong with me or with the theory, the ideal. Either my faith is terribly weak, in which case all this wonderful stuff about joy is just another reason for me to feel guilty; or the ideal is simply not practical for me, only for saints or mystics or monks, impractical people with their heads in the clouds.

The answer is first of all that joy is not a feeling. It simply does not matter whether I feel joy or not; I have it. God's word says so. So there.

Second, the ideal is utterly practical and not for people with their heads in the clouds (saints, mystics and monks do *not* have their heads in the clouds, by the way). Joy is not a nice feeling. Joy is a fact. Joy is Christ. There is nothing more real, more realistic, more practical, more here and now. Come out of your precious little feelings into the world of hard, enormous fact; forget your feelings of joy and "enter into the joy of the Lord".

Part IV

Heaven and Hell

Chapter Fifteen

Is There Really a Hell?

I am deeply distressed to have to write this chapter. I can truthfully say with C. S. Lewis that

> . . . there is no doctrine which I would more willingly remove from Christianity than this, if it lay in my power. But [1] it has the full support of Scripture, and, [2] especially, of Our Lord's own words; [3] it has always been held by Christendom [thus three arguments from authority]; and [4] it has the support of reason.[1]

Let us investigate in this chapter the support of reason for the doctrine of the existence of Hell. In the next chapter we will speculate about the nature of Hell. For now let us merely define it as the eternal separation from God.

Hell is certainly the most unpopular of all Christian doctrines. It scandalizes almost all non-Christians. How shall we judge it? By counting heads? The democracy of truth is, of course, nonsense, both in principle (it is the facts that make an idea true, not the number of people who believe it) and in practice (most great truths were discovered by those who swam against the stream). As a matter of fact, even democracy supports Hell if only we extend the franchise to the dead by tradition.

---

[1] C. S. Lewis, *The Problem of Pain* (New York: Macmillan, 1962), p. 118.

Human authority thus votes for Hell. Divine authority (Scripture, Christ, and Church) votes for Hell. Reason votes for Hell, as I shall try to show. Only one vote is cast against it, that of modern fashion. But it must be reason or authority that judges fashion, not vice versa. Yet this is the rarest of phenomena: reason judging fashion. I can only ask the reader to try very hard to be truly honest and open-minded, not merely repeating the shibboleths but enacting the intellectual labor.

Is the question really important, though? What difference does it make? We began this book with that question, to justify the whole enterprise; perhaps we should do the same with this chapter.

Hell makes an infinite difference. The height of the mountain is measured by the depth of the valley. The greatness of salvation is appreciated against the awfulness of damnation, what we are saved *from*. C. S. Lewis notes that "I have met no people who fully disbelieved in Hell and also had a living and life-giving belief in Heaven."[2]

To see the difference anything makes, we can always make the thought-experiment of removing it and seeing what happens. With no Hell, all roads lead to the same place, whether that place is Heaven, or death, or reincarnation, or a mythic shadow-land. And if all roads lead to the same place, it makes no ultimate difference which road we take. But if they lead to two infinitely different places, it makes an infinite difference which one we take. According to Christianity,

We are not living in a world where all roads are radii of a circle and where all, if followed long enough, will therefore draw gradually nearer and finally meet at the centre: rather in a world where every road, after a few miles, forks into two,

[2]C. S. Lewis, *Letters to Malcolm* (New York: Harcourt, Brace & World, 1964), p. 76.

and each of those into two again, and at each fork you must make a decision.[3]

Yet we must avoid a popular trap here. Both orthodox Christians (who believe in Hell) and Modernists (who do not) often fall into it. It is the trap of deciding whether or not to believe in any given idea on some other ground than that it is *true*—for example, on the ground of it being interesting, or safe, or popular, or comforting, or challenging, or fitting in well with previously held ideas. One form of this is the argument *for* Hell often found in anti-Modernist polemic: if you do not believe in Hell there will be no deterrent to immorality on earth and we will have Hell on earth. "It was thought that if the fear of eternal punishment were removed, . . . society would collapse into an anarchical orgy."[4]

There are three weaknesses to this argument. First, we do not really know such consequences. Second, servile fear is not a moral motive, though it is an effective one, as every tyrant knows. But God is not a tyrant but a lover, and "perfect love casts out fear".[5] Third, it is simply dishonest; it is the trap mentioned above, believing an idea because of something other than its truth. In this case, the reason is better than popularity or comfort or interest—it is that it is a deterrent to immorality. But it is still dishonest.

The same sort of dishonesty is often used to justify the modernist's disbelief in Hell. "It inspires servile fear rather than genuine love." Perhaps it does (and then again, perhaps it does not—it certainly doesn't in the saints). But even if it does, that does not prove it isn't *true*. "This is a gun pointed at your head" inspires servile fear, but it may be true nevertheless.

---

[3] C. S. Lewis, *The Great Divorce* (New York: Macmillan, 1975), pp. 5–6.
[4] Daniel Pickering Walker, *The Decline of Hell* (London: Routledge, 1964), p. 4.
[5] I John 4:18.

You see, both sides can and often do produce dishonest and irrelevant arguments that you should believe or disbelieve because of the consequences of believing or disbelieving, not because it is true or false. These two sets of "arguments" simply cancel each other out, and we are left with the original question: is it true?

The Modernist has one argument left, though, which we should consider before turning to the substantive question. It is that Hell is part of exoteric (public, popular) teaching, but not part of the esoteric (private, hidden) truth known to the spiritually mature. The refutation of this idea is, first, that the theologian is ignoring the fact that Christianity, unlike Eastern religions, is *not* esoteric but open to all, one of the three "religions of the Book" together with Judaism and Islam. Also, to say that Hell should be taught only to the masses who need deterrents to immorality is to assume that the speaker is a saint with pure motives who needs no deterrents!

The defense against the charge of dishonesty is usually that Hell is not a lie but a myth. But once someone can distinguish between the factual and the mythical, it is a lie to tell him the myth as a fact. Once children ask: "Is Santa Claus real or just a story?" it is a lie to tell them it is literally, not just mythically, true. Once we ask: "Are Hell and Heaven and Incarnation and Ascension and Resurrection and the supernatural in general real?" it is a lie to answer yes and think no. Either these teachers have contempt for the intelligence of the masses, placing them at the believing-in-Santa-Claus level, or they are liars.

The majority of Modernists, I think, are honest enough to want to "emancipate" instantly all of humanity from belief in Hell simply because it is false. With such people we can have an honest argument.

Reasons for Believing in Hell

The strongest reason, for the Christian, is that Jesus believed in it, and taught it strongly, clearly, and frequently. There is a strangely popular idea around that Jesus taught a gentle, "acceptable" message and Saint Paul toughened it up with things like Hell. All that idea shows is how little its proponent has read the New Testament. Almost all the Hell-fire comes from the lips of Jesus, almost none from Saint Paul. It is Paul, not Jesus, who seems to flirt with universalism.[6]

Even Jesus' most popular, compassionate, and loving saying talks about Hell: John 3:16. Hell is mentioned five times in the Sermon on the Mount. If there is no Hell, or even if there are only a tiny few in it so that there is very little practical danger for ordinary people, then Jesus is scaring us just for the Hell of it, and is a bad teacher, not a good one.

Suppose one says that Jesus never taught Hell, that some parties unknown added all the Hell passages. Who? His disciples? They all misunderstood or perverted His message *that* radically, and then died for the lie? It is utterly arbitrary to pick out the sayings of Jesus that you happen to like and to construct a version of "Christianity" based only on them, then invent some unhistorical hypothesis of apostolic fakery or ecclesiastical forgery to disqualify all the passages you happen not to like! One does not need to know Freud to suspect rationalization here. We *like* to construct a Christ in our own image rather than reconstructing ourselves and our ideas in His image; to judge rather than to be judged. It saves us the trouble of truth. Truth is often very troublesome. For instance, the truth of Hell is very troublesome.

There is only one rational argument for Hell. No argument that seeks to prove that Hell is necessary because of some fundamental dualism in the universe, or by a yin-yang notion of good and evil, or even by the absoluteness of divine justice,

---

[6] 2 Timothy 2:4; 1 Corinthians 15:22; 1 Timothy 4:10.

will work, for the simple reason that Hell is *not* necessary, not a structural part of the universe. It is freely chosen, even freely created, by human and angelic spirits. The free will is the only convincing reason for the existence of Hell.

Scratch freedom and you find Hell. Everyone wants there to be free will and no one wants there to be Hell, yet if there is either one there must be the other. For life is a game, a drama, not a formula, and "if a game is played, it must be possible to lose it".[7]

> If the happiness of a [free] creature lies in [free] self-surrender [to God], no one can make that surrender but himself (though many can help him to make it) and he may refuse. I would pay any price to be able to say truthfully "All will be saved." But my reason retorts, "Without their will, or with it?" If I say "without their will" I at once perceive a contradiction: how can the supreme voluntary act of self-surrender be involuntary? If I say "with their will", my reason replies "How if they *will* not give in?"[8]

But, you reply, God forgives all sins, even sins of pride and refusal of self-surrender. Surely. But "forgiveness needs to be accepted as well as offered if it is to be complete",[9] like any gift. We either accept that gift or refuse it. To refuse it is Hell. "The doors of Hell are locked on the inside."[10] Love locks no doors, and God is love. But perhaps we are not.

To anticipate the next chapter's essential picture of the nature of Hell in this connection, C. S. Lewis says it is proper to think of Hell

> not as a sentence imposed on him but as the mere fact of being what he is. The characteristic of lost souls is "their rejection of everything that is not simply themselves" (von Hügel). Our imaginary egoist has tried to turn everything he meets into a province or appendage of the self. The taste for the *other*, that

---

[7] C. S. Lewis, *The Problem of Pain*, p. 118.
[8] Ibid.   [9] Ibid., p. 122.   [10] Ibid., p. 127.

is the very capacity for enjoying good, is quenched in him
except in so far as his body still draws him into some rudimen-
tary contact with an outer world. Death removes this last
contact. He has his wish—to live wholly in the self and to
make the best of what he finds there. And what he finds there
is Hell.[11]

As a matter of fact, this Hell is God's greatest compliment
to human free will and responsibility. God does not say to
us, "You are creatures of your heredity and environment, for
which *I* am ultimately responsible, not you. I cannot expect
you to prefer good to evil, altruism to egoism, self-surrender
to self-glorification and gratification. You are an innocent,
unfree victim of circumstances. I cannot blame you *or* forgive
you, for there is nothing to forgive." Instead, He says, "You
are like a god: free to create. Your heredity and environment
I gave you as your raw material, and of course I will justly
take them into account in judging you. But ultimately it is
not them *and not I*, but you, who choose your character and
your destiny."

The reason God does this astonishing thing, you see, is that
He is not a puppet master but a Father.

Objections to Hell

1. Retributive punishment is not moral. It is vindictive and
unworthy of God.

Answer: It is objective justice, not subjective vindictiveness
or vengeance, that necessitates punishment. More, it is even
God's love that constitutes the punishment, as we shall see in
the next chapter: the fire of God's love (which is His essence
and which He cannot turn off) is what tortures those who
hate Him in Hell. The loveless seek their own element,
lovelessness, and are tortured by the element most foreign to
them, love.

[11] C. S. Lewis, *The Problem of Pain*, p. 123.

2. How can finite sins merit infinite punishment?

Answer: How can one little foot slipping off a cliff "merit" loss of one's whole life?

Furthermore, the punishments of Hell are not infinite but finite, and proportioned to the sins, just as Heaven's rewards are proportioned to the sanctity. But an unending *time* awaits us all, simply because of the fact that we are immortal.

3. The awful pains imagined in Scripture are barbaric, crude, primitive, and horrible.

Answer: Indeed they are. Though the fire and the gnashing of teeth are imagery, what they image is indeed horrible. This is not an objection; this is simply a true observation. The observation becomes an objection, an argument, only by assuming that what is so horrible cannot exist. But how can that be proved? Very horrible things *do* exist. Pain to the point of panic and insanity exists. Insane delight in cruelty exists. The Holocaust existed. The objection is not an argument but a confession of naïveté.

4. How could God let a being created in His image go to Hell? How could He destroy His masterpiece? It would be an eternal failure.

Answer: God does not destroy His human image in Hell because God does not destroy and because the thing that destroys itself in Hell is no longer human but spiritual garbage. The Hebrew word for Hell, *Gehenna*, was the name of the garbage dump outside the holy city, which had been used for human sacrifice by pagan tribes, so the Jews used it for the most degrading thing possible: burning garbage.

> In all our experience . . . the destruction of one thing means the emergence of something else. Burn a log and you have gases, heat and ash. *To have been* a log, means now being these three things. If soul can be destroyed [and Hell means eternal death, not life; and death of soul, not body, which has died on earth], must there not be a state of *having been* a human soul? . . . in the parable, the saved go to a place prepared *for them*, while the damned go to a place never made for men at

all (Mt. 25:34, 41). To enter Heaven is to become more human than you ever succeeded in being on earth; to enter Hell is to be banished from humanity. What is cast (or casts itself) into hell is not a man; it is remains.[12]

5. Wouldn't the known pains of the damned spoil the Heavenly bliss of the saved?

Answer: First, how could God let grief eternally blackmail joy?[13] Second, there are no *people* in Hell, only "remains". All *people* are loved. Third, Heaven and Hell do not coexist in time, like Earth and Mars. Heaven's eternity has the cosmic monopoly on all lived times. Heaven includes all *kairos*; Hell includes none. There are no *lives* in Hell to pity. Fourth, there is no common space either. Heaven is a real place, but Hell is not. Heaven is gloriously real; Hell is a state of mind.[14] Fifth, the blessed, like God, know and love all, and *that* love is experienced as torture by the damned. Finally, like God, the blessed love and care and pity only actively, not passively (to use a distinction that has already proved useful).[15]

6. If in a God-created universe "all that is, is good", then either Hell *is* not, or Hell is good.

Answer: In one sense, Hell *is* not, as blindness *is* not. They exist, but only as privations. Darkness is not a thing, like light, but the absence of a thing. The joylessness, purposelessness and meaninglessness of Hell are not positive being, but the *absence* of joy, purpose, and meaning.

In another sense, Hell is good. The good and proper thing to do with garbage is to burn it. God would not tolerate Hell unless it were proper, and best, and just, and even consonant with His love. Thus Aquinas' boldly consistent reasoning draws the conclusion that the blessed rejoice over the justice

---

[12] C. S. Lewis, *The Problem of Pain*, p. 125.
[13] C. S. Lewis, *The Great Divorce*, p. 120.
[14] Ibid., pp. 68–69.
[15] Chapter 2, section 6, pp. 37–38, above.

of God manifested in Hell[16]—not because they lick their vindictive chops, but because "all that is, is good"[17] and they see and praise the good in everything.

7. The main objection to Hell is surely God's tremendous, surprising, miracle-working love. Couldn't this love do *something* about this problem of Hell? If God is infinitely good and infinitely powerful, how can He allow Hell?

Answer: This is the same problem as the problem of evil on earth. If God is infinitely good and infinitely powerful, how can there be evil? For if He is infinitely good, He wills only the good, and if He is infinitely powerful, He can do all that He wills. The answer to the problem of evil is the same on earth and in Hell: free will.

In fact, the answer to the question "If God is love how can there be Hell?" is that only *because* God is love can there be Hell! God's love created the highest creatures, free creatures, creatures who were also creatures of their own destinies, and some of them created Hell.

God did not have to create free creatures. He could have limited Himself to infallibly obedient plants and animals. But love plays dangerous games, and love holds nothing back. Love gives what it is, and love is free, therefore love gives freedom.

The only reason we know that God is love is divine revelation: Jesus, Scripture, and the Church. But all three also assure us that there is Hell. Both doctrines are surprises. Revelation infinitely extends our expectations in both directions, the heights and the depths. It shows us as potential gods and goddesses *and* potential fiends; it shows us "Christ in you, the hope of glory"[18] and the "Hitler in ourselves".[19]

---

[16] St. Thomas Aquinas, *Summa Theologiae*, III (Supplement), 94, 3.

[17] Ibid., I, 5, 3.

[18] Colossians 1:27.

[19] Max Picard, *Hitler in Ourselves*, trans. Heinrich Hauser (Hinsdale, Ill.: Regnery, 1947).

8. If Hell is involuntary, if God forces us into it against our will, then God is neither just nor loving. But if Hell is voluntary, then we must be insane to make that choice. What is more insane than preferring Hell to Heaven? But the insane are not responsible for what they choose; and it is uncharitable, unjust, and unnecessary to punish them for their ignorant choices. Whoever chooses Hell must be mentally sick, not wicked.

Answer: This is Plato's old saw about evil being only ignorance. It simply contradicts experience, first of all our experience of our own wickedness. The argument here posed against Hell applies equally to earthly sin, and the solution is the same. Sin exists; we do make foolish and wicked choices. Evil is not mere ignorance, or sickness; for we are not responsible for sickness, but we are responsible for evil. If evil is only sickness, we are not responsible and not free.

The deepest problem of Hell, then, is psychological, not theological. We got God off the hook, but how can we get man off the hook? How can we understand "the mystery of iniquity"?[20] Is there real, free, responsible evil? Worse, is it in ordinary people, not just sadists? Worst of all, is it in me?

The best and wisest of us are the surest that it is. It is always the saints who insist they are the worst of sinners. When *we* see a Hitler, we say, like the Pharisee, "God, I thank thee that I am not like other men."[21] The saint says, "There but for the grace of God go I."

Now either the saints are greater fools than we, or greater sages. Either sanctity is a pious delusion, or it is wisdom. Either the closer we get to God the farther we get from true self-knowledge, or the closer. The choice is hardly up for grabs.

How unthinkably arrogant we would have to be to patronize the saints, to tolerate their delusions with a smug and

[20] 2 Thessalonians 2:7 (KJV).
[21] Luke 18:11.

snobbish assurance that they were only exaggerating. They have looked long and deep into the human heart; do we know that heart better than they do? Worse, do we know it better than God, who says "the heart is deceitful above all things, and desperately wicked"?[22]

Our picture of wickedness is usually incredibly childish and simplistic. We seldom really feel anything but physical cruelty to be evil, perhaps because we seldom feel anything but physical pleasure to be good.[23]

If your imagination as well as your faith needs to be convinced, read the most frightening book I have ever read, Charles Williams' *Descent into Hell*. It is a psychologically sophisticated and credible picture of an ordinary man choosing Hell. It may well convince you of the real possibility of Hell *for you*.

How is it possible to prefer Hell to Heaven? Let us see. What we understand depends on what we love. Only if we will God's will, will we understand His teaching.[24] Similarly, only if we love our friend, will we understand him.

Now when we are selfish, when our *summum bonum* is the satisfaction of our own will (and this is our natural state!), we tend to believe the philosophy of selfishness. We believe that Hell is more desirable than Heaven because Hell is pure selfishness and Heaven pure selflessness.

We are not saints because we believe sanctity is joyless, onerous, and inhuman. We separate goodness and joy and prefer joy. The greatest work of non-Christian thought in history, Plato's *Republic*, was written to convince us of exactly the opposite, that justice (goodness) is always more profitable (happier, healthier, more joyful) than injustice.

But the devil is a deceiver, and he can make us not only *be* selfish but *believe* in selfishness, confusing Heaven and Hell.

[22] Jeremiah 17:9 (KJV).
[23] C. S. Lewis, *The Problem of Pain*, p. 40.
[24] John 7:17.

Take this little bit of Hell to its logical conclusion, and you have the motivation for our preferring Hell to Heaven. That is why faith is so necessary. Our experience, conditioned as it is by our fallenness, is not reliable. It is open to demonic deception. Satan tells us the forbidden fruit of "my will be done" will make us happy. God tells us it will kill us.[25] The first question is: Whom do we believe? Plato was half right: if we really believed holiness always made us happiest, we would be holy.[26] Plato's mistake was to seek to remedy our ignorance merely by reason, not faith. Plato also forgot that our ignorance was in turn caused by evil;[27] it is not invincible but vincible and culpable ignorance.[28]

9. If nothing will be able to separate us from the love of God,[29] then how can Hell separate us?

Answer: It doesn't. It only makes us closed to it, it makes love feel like wrath and joy feel like torture. God's love is inescapable. It is everywhere, even in Hell. "If I make my bed in hell, thou art there."[30] God loves the garbage in Hell. But it does not love Him. That is what makes its condition Hell rather than Heaven.

Psychological Reasons for the Loss of Hell

Hell is usually the first of Christian doctrines to be abandoned, for there are at least six strong psychological pressures in the direction of its abandonment in the typically modern mind.

[25] Genesis 2:17.

[26] Plato, *Republic*, II, 357–88.

[27] St. Thomas Aquinas, *Summa Theologiae*, I-II, 76, 2; I-II, 6, 7; Jacques Maritain, *St. Thomas and the Problem of Evil* (Milwaukee, Wisc.: Marquette University Press, 1942); A. E. Taylor, *Socrates* (New York: Doubleday, 1956), pp. 140–47.

[28] *New Catholic Encyclopedia*, vol. IX, pp. 354–56.

[29] Romans 8:39.

[30] Psalm 139:8 (KJV).

1. Progress is our new myth, our overall structuring concept, our uncriticized assumption. This accounts for such spontaneous "refutations" of Hell as: "Are you living in the Twentieth Century or the Dark Ages?" What is behind the rhetoric is a dying but still dominant humanism, a faith in man despite Auschwitz, Hiroshima, the Gulag, Cambodia, and Jonestown. We are shocked when we hear about such things. Previous generations were not; they believed in evil. We are still Chamberlain at Munich when it comes to the soul.

2. We do not believe in dualism, especially moral good-evil dualism. That is why Eastern religions are so popular in the modern West: they are monistic. They, like we, do not believe in sin or Hell. This entails loss of belief in free will, for free will can choose only between two really distinct objects. If all roads lead to the same place, we can only accept and not reject; all are inevitably blended into one Heaven. That is also why totalitarianism, collectivism, and communism are popular today; as in Eastern religions, the individual and his terrible burden of responsibility and freedom are removed.

3. We do not believe in objective values. Our picture of the objective world is merely that of science: matter, time, and space. Everything else, including good and evil, is subjective. Our model for objective reality is a rock rather than God, matter rather than spirit. Without objective spirit, objective values have no place, no home. How could a value be "out there" like a stone?

4. We think of ourselves as having progressed in our appreciation of the value of love. But this is counterbalanced by our subjectivizing and sentimentalizing of love as mere kindness or tolerance. Thus we think of love as the rival of justice, and forget the necessity of justice.

It is true that justice without love is hardness of heart; but love without justice is softness of head. We usually have a "straw man" concept of justice as mere legalism, or else an unjust concept of justice as equality of result rather than of opportunity, sameness rather than hierarchy and harmony: the "justice" of a mass age.

If love is reduced to kindness and justice to sameness, of course God could not allow Hell.

5. Loss of belief in the supernatural entails loss of belief in Hell, both directly, and indirectly through the link of loss of belief in the divinity of Christ. If Christ is a mere man, He can be patronized away as a child of His time on the Hell issue. But if His wisdom is not merely ancient, or merely Jewish, but eternal and universal; if He is Who He claims to be (and if He isn't, then He is insane)[31]—why, then, He must know.

If there is no Hell, there is no need for salvation, only good teaching and example—thus the humanists' Christ. Salvation from ignorance needs only a man; salvation from Hell needs a God.

6. A final reason for the decline of belief in Hell is simply its unpopularity coupled with modern popularism: believing whatever is popular rather than whatever is revealed. John describes it candidly: "they loved the praise of men more than the praise of God."[32] The purely practical argument of Pascal's "wager",[33] as a last resort, should hold the dikes of sanity against this madness; but few are as sane or sensible as Christopher Hollis, who concludes his autobiography thus:

> I believe without hesitation in Purgatory and am more doubtful about hell. The only reason why I am hesitant about complete repudiation is the fact that there are some strange and violent threats in the Gospels of which at any rate the apparent meaning is that we cannot be indifferent to the threats of what the Mass calls "final damnation." Whoever has the arranging of the Last Judgment it will not be me. So it is of little importance what I

[31] Peter Kreeft, *Between Heaven and Hell* (Downers Grove, Ill.: InterVarsity Press, 1982).
[32] John 12:43.
[33] Pascal, *Pensées* (trans. Krailsheimer), 418.

may think about it. My friend Smitt-Ingerbretsen was the Chairman of the Religious Committee of the Norwegian Government. It fell to him to give advice to the King what doctrine the King as head of the State Lutheran Church should pronounce about hell. His natural instinct was to be liberal, but then he reflected on the possibility that, if he denied all possibility of damnation, "my constituents, they will go to the Last Judgment, and they will say, 'Mr. Smitt-Ingerbretsen said it would be all right,' and Almighty God, He will say, 'Who the hell is Mr. Smitt-Ingerbretsen?' and I shall look like a bloody fool." He was a very sensible man.[34]

[34] Christopher Hollis, *The Seven Ages* (London: The Catholic Book Club, 1975), pp. 233–34.

Chapter Sixteen

Is Hell Fire or Loneliness?

Hell Is Not External

Just as Heaven is not a mercenary reward of physical pleasure for spiritual success, so Hell is not a mercenary punishment of physical pains for spiritual failure. First, it is not physical, or external;[1] second, it is not a mercenary, super-added punishment;[2] third, it is not brought about by failure: even failures can enter Heaven, through the gracious gate of repentance.

The *images* of Hell in Scripture[3] are not to be taken literally, that is, as something other than images. But they are to be taken seriously, because they point to something more, not less, horrible than the literal images denote.[4]

Hell is a state of mind. Nothing on earth has as much potency for good or evil, pleasure or pain, joy or horror, as

---

[1] C. S. Lewis, *The Problem of Pain* (New York: Macmillan, 1962), p. 123; *The Great Divorce* (New York: Macmillan, 1975), p. 69.

[2] C. S. Lewis, *The Weight of Glory* (New York: Macmillan, 1949), pp. 2–3; *The Problem of Pain*, p. 123. See Plato, *Republic*, 362e–67c, 588a–91c, 608b–21d.

[3] Matthew 5:22; 7:23; 8:12; 10:28; 18:9; 13:42; 22:13; 25:41; Mark 9:42, 48; Luke 3:17; 16:22–23; 2 Thessalonians 1:9; Hebrews 10:29–31; Revelation 14:9–11; 20:15.

[4] George MacDonald in C. S. Lewis, ed., *George MacDonald: An Anthology* (New York: Macmillan, 1978), p. 10 (no. 22): " 'But this is only a figure.' True. But is the reality intended less or more than the figure? "

the mind. Unlike Heaven, Hell is *only* a state of mind. In fact,

> . . . every state of mind, left to itself, every shutting up of the
> creature within the dungeon of its own mind—is, in the end,
> Hell. But Heaven is not a state of mind. Heaven is reality
> itself. All that is fully real is Heavenly.[5]

In reality, the damned are in the same place as the saved—in
reality![6] But they hate it; it is their Hell. The saved love it,
and it is their Heaven. It is like two people sitting side by side
at an opera or a rock concert: the very thing that is Heaven
to one is Hell to the other. Dostoyevski says, "We are all in
paradise, but we won't see it."[7]

Hell is not thrust upon us from without. Hell grows up
from within, a spiritual cancer. It emerges from our freedom
and eats away that freedom, just as a cancer eats its host.

Hell is not literally the "wrath of God". The love of God
is an objective fact; the "wrath of God" is a human projection
of our own wrath upon God, as the Lady Julian saw[8]—a
disastrous misinterpretation of God's love as wrath. God really
says to all His creatures, "I know you and I love you", but
they hear Him saying, "I never knew you; depart from Me".
It is like angry children misinterpreting their loving parents'
affectionate advances as threats. They project their own hate
onto their parents' love and experience love as an enemy—
which it is: an enemy to their egotistic defenses against joy.[9]

The existence of a Hell and the nature of Hell as something
other than external punishment of fire and brimstone are both

---

[5] C. S. Lewis, *The Great Divorce*, p. 69.

[6] H. G. Wells, "The Country of the Blind" in *The Country of the Blind and
Other Stories* (London: Nelson, 1911); C. S. Lewis, *The Last Battle* (New
York: Macmillan, 1956), chap. 13, "How the Dwarfs Refused to Be Taken
In"; G. K. Chesterton, "They Haven't Got No Noses" in *The Flying Inn*, p.
482.

[7] Dostoyevski, *The Brothers Karamazov*, p. 343 (part II, bk. VI, chap. 2(a)).

[8] F. Happold, *Mysticism* (Baltimore, Md.: Penguin, 1964), p. 293.

[9] C. S. Lewis, *The Great Divorce*, pp. 69–70.

confirmed by the medically dead and resuscitated.[10] These "death-travelers", especially suicides, often found themselves in a place strikingly similar to the "grey town" in C. S. Lewis' *Great Divorce* (which none of them, apparently, had read): a dreary place in which all the earthly problems they had tried to escape were intensified—naturally, since our problems are never merely outside us but inside us, and we can never escape ourselves.

Hell Is Sin

Hell is not just punishment for sin; Hell is sin itself in its consummation. Sin is its own punishment just as "virtue is its own reward".[11] It is the state of spiritual death.[12] The wages of sin is sin.

The popular concept of Hell is eternal life with pain rather than eternal *death*. The popular concept comes from Greek philosophy, which believes the soul cannot die[13] because it is its own source of life,[14] a little god. Scripture derives the soul's life from God.[15] Thus souls can die when cut off from God, just as bodies can die when cut off from their source of life, the soul.

When the soul leaves the body, the body is neither annihilated nor remains a body; it is transformed into a corpse. And

[10] Maurice Rawlings, M.D., *At the Hour of Death* (New York: Bantam, 1979), chap. 7; Raymond Moody, *Reflections on Life after Life* (New York: Bantam, 1977), pp. 18–22.

[11] "*Ipsa quidem virtus sibimet pulcherrima merces*", Silius Italicus (ca. A.D. 25–99), *Punica*, bk. XIII, line 663; in Diogenes Laertius, *Plato* XLII; Prior, *Imitations of Horace*, bk. III, ode 2.

[12] In Scripture, Hell is not eternal *life* with pain, but eternal *death*: see n. 3, and Romans 6:23.

[13] Justin Martyr, *First Apology*, I, 198; *Dialogue* 8; Hippolytus, *The Refutation of All Heresies*, bk. I, chap. 16.

[14] Plato, *Phaedo*, 105b–6a.

[15] Deuteronomy 8:3; Proverbs 8:35; John 1:4; 14:6; Colossians 3:3; 1 John 5:11.

when the life of God leaves the soul, the soul is neither annihilated nor remains a soul; it dies.[16] It becomes spiritual garbage, and Hell is the dump where the garbage is burned.

Sin—Hell—spiritual death—the three terms mean the same thing: separation from God. *Sin* means only in the second place specific acts of disobedience ("actual sin"). It means in the first place the state of "original sin" that underlies particular acts of sin: spiritual sterility, lifelessness.

God's life is offered us every moment. He says to each as He said to Mary: May My Spirit impregnate you with My life so that My Son can be born in you?[17] The Annunciation is for all, not just Mary, for Mary is a type of the Church, that is, us.[18] If we repeat Mary's *fiat*, it is done; Heaven enters the soul, Christ is reproduced in us. If not, not. And this "not" is Hell. If a free proposal is made, a free refusal is possible.

> O Jerusalem, Jerusalem, killing the prophets and stoning those who are sent to you! How often would I have gathered your children together as a hen gathers her brood under her wings, and you would not![19]

He stands at the door and knocks.[20] If the door remains locked, it becomes the door of Hell. C. S. Lewis shows how this can happen to an ordinary person in his short story, "The Shoddy Lands".[21] Peggy's egocentrism shuts her off from "the taste for the other".[22] At one point, as she hears her boyfriend pleading, "Peggy, Peggy, let me in", she also hears (perhaps

---

[16] Ezekiel 18:4; Matthew 10:28.

[17] Luke 1:29–33.

[18] *Documents of Vatican II*, Decree on "The Church", chap. 2.

[19] Matthew 23:37.

[20] Revelation 3:20.

[21] C. S. Lewis, "The Shoddy Lands" in *Of Other Worlds* (New York: Harcourt, Brace & World, 1967).

[22] Gilbert Meilaender, *The Taste for the Other: The Social and Ethical Thought of C. S. Lewis* (Grand Rapids, Mich.: Eerdmans, 1978).

in the first voice) Another standing at her door and knocking,
Someone Who is

> soft as wool and sharp as death, soft but unendurably heavy,
> as if at each blow some enormous hand fell on the outside of
> the shoddy sky and covered it completely. And with that
> knocking came a voice at whose sound my bones turned to
> water, "Child, child, child, let Me in before the night comes."

Hell is the refusal of this divine guest of the soul. Hell is
our declaration of independence against our divine husband.
It is not a passive suffering but an active rebellion. Even Hell's
pains are active, not passive. Even earthly pains are active:
the fear or hatred or rebellion of spirit against the knife, not
the knife itself. When drugs or yoga stop the inner rebellion,
the pain is no longer pain. If even earthly pains are active
attitudes of spirit, how much more the pains of Hell.

Here is a very practical consequence of the notion that Hell
is sin: If Hell is sin, sin is Hell. We have all been in Hell—at
least its porch, its outer borders—many times (and, by the
grace of God, out again). The practical difference this makes
is that if believed, it is a great deterrent against sin. We sin
because we see sin as a bargain. We unconsciously calculate
that it's worth it, that it pays, that "justice is *not* more profitable
than injustice". Sin seems to be simply a choice between alternative life-styles on earth. But if we recognize that all sin is
Hellish, if we see sin as Hell wearing an earthly mask, we will
fly to the Father in fear. Such fear is not a bad thing: "while
there are wild beasts about, it is better to be afraid than secure." [23]

The Consequences of Lifelessness: Lovelessness

Since God is love, since love is the essence of the divine life,
the consequence of loss of this life is loss of love. In Hell

[23] George MacDonald, *Unspoken Sermons*, first series (London, New York:
Rutledge, 1873), p. 4.

there is only hatred and refusal—of everything, of all four things that exist, all four things we can either love or hate: God, ourselves, others, and the world.

The damned hate God because God demands they repent, and that hurts their pride, it is the death of their egotism. They see God as the enemy of what is dearest to them: their own demand to be their own God and create idols to worship. It is very easy to hate God. God is a killer.[24]

Hatred of God leads to hatred of oneself, for the self—the true self—at its heart is the image of God, is a God-shaped vacuum, is a love and longing for God. The damned hate this in themselves because they hate God, just as the blessed love themselves because those selves love God: the blessed love themselves for God's sake and the damned hate themselves for God's sake.[25] Even here on earth the good hate their own love of evil, and the evil hate their love of good.

Others are equally images of God and equally hated for this reason by the damned. Others are also part of the world and hated for the same reason the whole world is hated: the world is God's love made visible.

Though the damned do not love God, God loves them, and this is their torture. The very fires of Hell are made of the love of God! Love received by one who only wants to hate and fight thwarts his deepest want and is therefore torture. If God could stop loving the damned, Hell would cease to be pure torture. If the sun could stop shining, lovers of the dark would no longer be tortured by it. But the sun could sooner cease to shine than God cease to be God.

[24] Thus the universal ancient tradition of sacrifice; thus the popularity of Shiva and Kali among Hindus [Heinrich Zimmer, *Philosophies of India* (Princeton, N.J.: Princeton University Press, 1951), and C. S. Lewis, *The Great Divorce*, pp. 98–104].

[25] On love of self for God's sake as the final stage of learning to love, see St. Bernard of Clairvaux in Elmer O'Brien, *Varieties of Mystic Experience* (New York: New American Library, 1964). On self-hatred in sinners, cf. St. Thomas Aquinas, *Summa Theologiae*, II-II, 25, 7; III (Supplement), 98, 3.

"Our God is a consuming fire."[26] All that can be consumed, will be consumed, so that only the unconsumable will remain.[27] Self must be consumed, must die, in order to rise. There is no other way to eternity.[28] The blessed embrace that blessed death of the sinful self they hate, and it is to them supreme bliss. The damned refuse it (but that does not make it any less necessary; the fire burns on whether we feel it as life-giving warmth or destructive pain), and it is their supreme torture. Thus Heaven and Hell are the very same objective reality, the only one there is, the only game in town: the fire of God's love, which is His essential being. In a sense, everything is Heaven. Earth is Heaven as a seed. Purgatory is Heaven's kindergarten. Hell is Heaven refused. Heaven is Heaven accepted.

The Consequences of Lovelessness: Lightlessness

The lovelessness of the damned blinds them to the light of glory in which they stand, the glory of God's fire. God is in the fire that to them is Hell. God is in Hell ("If I make my bed in Hell, Thou art there."[29]) but the damned do not know Him. For when it comes to knowing a person, knowledge depends on love: only when we love a person do we really know him. The damned do not know God because they do not love Him.[30] It is the "pure in heart", the lovers, who see God.[31] The sun of God is in Hell too, but He is eclipsed by the moon of hate.

We know God only when we freely affirm our being-known

[26] Hebrews 12:29.
[27] Hebrews 12:25–27; cf. George MacDonald in C. S. Lewis, ed., *George MacDonald: An Anthology*, pp. 1–2 (2–3).
[28] John 12:24–25; C. S. Lewis, *The Great Divorce*, pp. 97, 104.
[29] Psalm 139:8 (KJV); St. Thomas Aquinas, *Summa Theologiae*, I, 8, 1–3.
[30] St. Thomas Aquinas, *Summa Theologiae*, III (Supplement), 98, 8.
[31] Matthew 5:8.

by God, when we willingly stand in the light, when we "confess"[32] like the Psalmist in Psalm 139. C. S. Lewis says:

> We are always completely . . . known to God. That is our
> destiny whether we like it or not. But though this knowledge
> never varies, the quality of our being known can. . . . When
> we assent with all our will to be so known, then we treat
> ourselves, in relation to God, not as things [objects] but as
> persons [subjects]. We have unveiled. Not that any veil could
> have baffled this sight. The change is in us. The passive changes
> to the active. Instead of merely being known, we show, we
> tell, we offer ourselves to view. . . . By unveiling, by con-
> fessing our sins and "making known" our requests, we assume
> the high dignity of persons before Him.[33]

As Augustine says, "If I would not confess to You. . . . I should only be hiding You from myself, not myself from You."[34]

But suppose we do flee instead of confessing? Then we will cry out to the mountains to fall on us and the rocks to hide us[35] from the inevitable and irresistible divine gaze that becomes our torture, our Hell. Job flirts with Hell when he says:

> What is man, that you should make so much of him,
>   subjecting him to your scrutiny,
> that morning after morning you should examine him
>   and at every instant test him?
> Will you never take your eyes off me
>   long enough for me to swallow my spittle?
> Suppose I have sinned, what have I done to you,
>   you tireless watcher of mankind?[36]

---

[32] Romano Guardini, *The Conversion of Augustine*, trans. Elinor Briefs (Chicago: Regnery, 1966).

[33] C. S. Lewis, *Letters to Malcolm* (New York: Harcourt, Brace & World, 1964), pp. 20–21.

[34] St. Augustine, *Confessions*, X, 2.

[35] Luke 23:30.

[36] Job 7:17–20 (JB).

Sartre embraced Hell when, as he relates in his autobiography, he felt the presence of God "only once" and "flew into a rage . . . whirled about . . . blasphemed . . . [until] He never looked at me again"[37] and when he repudiates Daniel's conversion in *Le sursis*—Daniel is converted when he recognizes he is an object to God's knowledge.[38] That is precisely Hell to Sartre, because he believes that when others know us, they objectify us, reduce us to an object, deny our freedom; thus "Hell is other people."[39] In contrast, Jane in C. S. Lewis' *That Hideous Strength* overcomes this natural rebellion against being an object to God. Jane had thought that

> "Religion" ought to mean a realm in which her haunting female fear of being treated as a thing, an object . . . would be set permanently at rest and what she called her "true self" would soar upwards and expand in some freer and purer world. For still she thought that "Religion" was a kind of exhalation or a cloud of incense, something steaming up from specially gifted souls toward a receptive Heaven. Then, quite sharply, it occurred to her that the Director never talked about Religion; nor did the Dimbles nor Camilla. They talked about God. They had no picture in their minds of some mist steaming upward; rather of strong, skilful hands thrust down to make and mend, perhaps even to destroy. Suppose one were a *thing* after all—a thing designed and invented by Someone Else and valued for qualities quite different from what one had decided to regard as one's true self?[40]

Being a real self is a matter of degree. The more we endure God's gaze, the more real we are. Adam became less real, less authentic, less solid and substantial after the Fall when he hid

---

[37] Jean-Paul Sartre, *The Words*, trans. B. Frenchtman (New York: G. Braziller, 1964), p. 102.

[38] Jean-Paul Sartre, *Le sursis* (Paris: Gallimard, 1951).

[39] Jean-Paul Sartre, *No Exit and Three Other Plays* (New York: Vintage, 1957), p. 47.

[40] C. S. Lewis, *That Hideous Strength* (New York: Macmillan, 1965), p. 318.

from God. God could hardly see him when He called, "Where are you?"[41] Adam was fading, getting a little closer to the Hell of hearing "I never knew you". Hiding from God, he then hid from Eve, by covering his nakedness and by passing the blame ("The woman whom thou gavest to be with me, she gave me fruit of the tree, and I ate"[42]).

If God's gaze is your Hell, if truth is your Hell, then you are in Hell everywhere and everywhen and forever, for truth is everywhere and everywhen and forever.

[41] Genesis 3:9.   [42] Genesis 3:12.

Chapter Seventeen

How Many Roads to Heaven?

Can you get to Heaven without being very good?

If you can't, then none of us will get there. For it is the best of us who know how bad they are.

Can you get to Heaven without being religious?

If you can't, then the Bible missed the boat. It never tells us, "Be religious." It hardly ever talks about "religion".[1] It talks instead about something infinitely more interesting: God. Jesus insists that the way into the Kingdom of Heaven is not to trust "religion" but to trust Him.[2]

The real question, then, is: Can you get to Heaven without believing in Jesus?

If you can, what becomes of His claim that you can't? Not once but many times He says the equivalent of: "I am the way . . . no one can come to the Father except through me."[3]

If you can't, isn't God absurdly unfair to the good pagan who never had the good fortune to hear about Jesus? How could God consign Socrates to Hell?

If the answer is halfway between these two, if you can believe in Jesus in some vague way, "in spirit" or in good intention, then just how clear and explicit must the vague

---

[1] Acts 17:22; James 1:26–27. See Wilfred Cantwell Smith, *The Meaning and End of Religion* (New York: New American Library, 1964); C. S. Lewis, *That Hideous Strength* (New York: Macmillan, 1965), pp. 234, 315–18.

[2] John 6:28–29.   [3] John 14:6 (JB).

belief be? How right of spirit or good of intention do you have to be? Where is the cutoff point? Does God send you to Hell if you score a 69.9 but to Heaven if you score a 70?

This question of the salvation of non-Christians is not just a theoretically interesting question in "comparative religion" (a good way to be comparatively religious), but the practical question: "What must I do to be saved?"[4] Who makes it to Heaven and who doesn't?

This question is closely connected with another question, which we must drop as soon as we have raised it, because it is not solvable; and unless we distinguish our question from this second question, our question will be similarly unsolvable. The second question is one about comparative population statistics of Heaven and Hell: How many are saved?

We must drop that question because Jesus did:

> Someone said to him, "Lord, will those who are saved be few?"
> And he said to them, "Strive to enter by the narrow door."[5]

He was referring to Himself: "I am the door."[6] The reply "strive to enter in" is as single-mindedly practical as Buddha's similar reply to his disciple's similar question in the "Arrow Sermon", a question that Buddha calls a "question not tending to edification".[7] Spiritual masters are always practical, not theoretical; they teach only the knowledge that is necessary or useful for our salvation, not for our curiosity and certainly not for our diversion.

The right answer to the disciple's question is: None of your business. We not only do not know, we have no business knowing, how many are saved. Both medieval and modern expectations are wrong, not because of their answer but because of their question. The medievals may have been right to suppose that the majority end up in Hell. Moderns may be right to suppose that the majority end up in Heaven. But

---

[4] Acts 16:30.   [5] Luke 13:23–24.   [6] John 10:9.
[7] Majjhima-Nikaya, Sutta 63.

the business of both is not to speculate "Lord, what about this man?"[8] but to "follow me".[9]

But wait, *Don't* we know? Hasn't Jesus told us? Doesn't the following passage bear out the medieval expectation?

> Enter by the narrow gate; for the gate is wide and the way is easy, that leads to destruction, and those who enter by it are many. For the gate is narrow and the way is hard, that leads to life, and those who find it are few.[10]

The answer is that the words "many" and "few" in this passage are addressed to the will, not the curiosity, and are uttered by love, not scientific knowledge. By the standards of a loving Heavenly Father, even one out of a hundred of His sheep that wanders away from the fold is *too many*, and the ninety-nine safe at home are *too few*. If a parent loses one out of twelve children in a tragic accident, that is one too many, and the eleven left are one too few.

In a similar way the prophetic message about the Second Coming, "I am coming soon",[11] does not mean a calculable number of years. It means that all the events between the First and Second Comings are qualitatively unimportant compared to these two events, and that we must be ready at every moment.[12] If we knew the exact date, we would not be ready at every moment, only the last. Not all knowledge is good for us, and supernatural population statistics fall into that category. If we knew most were damned, we would be harsh and judgmental; if we knew most were saved, we would be lazy and uncaring. And, in fact, both ages that thought they knew have fallen into those traps.

[8] John 21:21.
[9] John 1:43; 21:19; 21:22.
[10] Matthew 7:13–14.
[11] Revelation 3:11.
[12] Matthew 24:44; Vernard Eller, *The Most Revealing Book in the Bible* (Grand Rapids, Mich.: Eerdmans, 1971).

But though Jesus did not give us population statistics, He did give us a road map. We may not know *who* goes there, but we know *how*. The only question, then, is whether we can deduce the *who* from the *how*. The *how* is the One Who said, "I am the Way." Let's look at the way before turning to the pilgrims.

A Road Map to Heaven

There is a famous Vermont farmer joke about the city slicker who got lost in the back roads of Vermont and asked a farmer, "Which way to Boston?" The farmer thought a while and said, "Well, now, let's see . . . if ye keep a-goin the way yer a-goin, ye'll end up in Canada. If ye take the right fork, ye'll land in my corn field. And if ye take the left fork, ye'll go . . . no, that road's out, ye'll land in the crick. Boston, eh? Ye cain't git thar from here."

Heaven may seem even more unreachable if there is no road. What is the road?

In one sense the answer to that question is very simple: objectively, Jesus is the Way. In another sense, the answer is mysterious and tricky: What subjective relationship must one have with Jesus in order to be on the right Way? Are there "anonymous Christians"?[13] Are Hindus, Buddhists, Mau Maus, agnostics, and atheists saved too?

First of all, we simply do not know. That is the most important thing we know. All the rest must be in that context.

Second, it *seems* the answer is yes. The "liberal" interpretation of other religions—or, rather, of individuals who believe other religions—seems strongly suggested by quite a few passages in the New Testament, such as Saint Paul's sermon to the Athenians about the Unknown God they were already

[13] Karl Rahner, *The Christian of the Future* (New York: Herder & Herder, 1969), p. 85.

worshiping,[14] and his affirmation in Romans of a universal
natural knowledge of God from nature and conscience,[15] as
well as John's statement that "he who abides in love [*agapē*]
abides in God, and God abides in him".[16] Also, Jesus' sayings
include: "I have other sheep, that are not of this fold",[17] and
"he that is not against us is for us".[18]

The character of God as revealed by Christ would surely
seem to require the most loving answer possible. "[God is]
not willing that any should perish."[19] If there is any way for
God to take Socrates to Heaven—and Xanthippe too—then
the God we know through Jesus certainly will. The problem
then becomes: How? Is there any side road around Jesus?

No. There's the snag. Clearly not. The same God Who
revealed His universal love revealed the "narrow way". To
rely on divine authority for either one of these two teachings
and to dismiss or ignore the other is inconsistent, even dishonest: not facing all the evidence. "One Way" is not sectarian
human invention, but clear divine revelation.[20] If "One Way"
is bigotry, then it is Jesus Who is the bigot. He smacks us
full in the face with the stark either-or of acceptance or rejection. No side roads.

But we do *not* know whether this One Way is or is not
present anonymously where He is not named and known
clearly. Presence is not limited to conceptual clearness. Perhaps
there is an "unknown Christ of Hinduism".[21] Perhaps a Hindu
is really worshiping Christ when he thinks he is worshiping
Krishna. Perhaps. We simply do not know.

But we can distinguish what we know from what we do
not know. We can distinguish the objective question from the
subjective question. I do not see how a believer in the Bible

---

[14] Acts 17:23.   [15] Romans 1:19–20, 32.   [16] 1 John 4:16.
[17] John 10:16.   [18] Mark 9:40.   [19] 2 Peter 3:9 (KJV).
[20] John 14:6.
[21] Raymond Panikkar, *The Unknown Christ of Hinduism* (London: Darton,
Longman & Todd, 1964).

can avoid the most strict and narrow answer to the objective question: all other gods are idols. But I also do not see how such a believer can avoid the most liberal and broad answer to the subjective question, if he knows God's tricky mercy in soulmanship. In other words, even though Hindu*ism* is not a second way to God, *Hindus* can be saved by the "One Way" Christ. They can know Him even though they do not know *of* Him.

The Salvation of Non-Christians

To know Christ, He Himself insists, is the only way to know the Father,[22] and to know the Father is the only way to have eternal life.[23] So we must know Christ to have eternal life. How does a non-Christian know Christ?

Perhaps in the same way an Old Testament Jew did. Perhaps it is hope in the God to come.

Perhaps it is in the way suggested by John 1:9, through the universal pre-incarnate Logos, or divine mind, that enlightens everyone. Thus any choice for or against truth is a choice for or against Christ.

Perhaps in the way suggested by Saint Paul's sermon on Mars Hill about the Unknown God. Not only the Greeks but in a sense all of us, including Christians, worship an Unknown God. We are saved not by our knowledge but by God. How much knowledge must we have? We too lack knowledge; what we know about God, though tremendously more than the pagans knew, is still a flea compared with the elephant God is, even if their knowledge was a molecule compared with our flea. If we can be saved, knowing God so slightly, perhaps they can too, knowing Him even more slightly.

However, even such a "liberal" interpretation of salvation is bound to appear illiberal, even imperialistic, to

[22]John 14:8–9; 1 John 2:23; John 6:46.
[23]John 17:3.

non-Christians. They will quite properly point out that it means that when a Jew or a Buddhist dies, he finds out that he had been wrong (in his head, if not in his heart) and that Christianity was right. It is still One Way.

The Christian answer can only be: Yes, it is. That is not our or Paul's or Augustine's or the Church's invention. It is what we bump up against when we honestly listen to Jesus. It is one of His "hard sayings".[24] To each time and culture a different set of His sayings is hard. To many of His contemporaries, His mercy was the scandal; to us, it is His severity.

I think the five teachings of Jesus that most scandalize the modern mind are: (1) sin, especially Original Sin, (2) Hell, (3) His claim to divinity, (4) miracles, and (5) the "One Way" exclusivism; and of the five, I think the last is most odious of all to modernity.

Why? Why do we prefer a religion of (1) the natural goodness of man, (2) universal salvation, (3) a merely human Christ of (4) natural rather than supernatural deeds, and above all (5) the essential equality of religions? It is the fifth that accounts for the other four; it is in the name of the equality of religions that we seek common teaching, and the second set of teachings is much more common, more popular, more universal than the first.

But this attitude, however good-hearted it may be, is impossibly soft-headed. (How hard and rare to combine a soft heart and a hard head, like Jesus!) Religion claims to deal with things as they really are, to tell us what is true, not just comforting. So when different religions tell us contradictory things, both simply cannot be true. No one believes in the equality of all scientific theories or historical accounts or common sense hunches or newspaper stories. We test them to find out which are false and which are true, and no one thinks this is narrow-minded, bigoted, or illiberal. Why do

[24]John 7:60; William Neil, *The Difficult Sayings of Jesus* (Grand Rapids, Mich.: Eerdmans, 1977).

we think differently about religion? Because we do not think religion is about truth, about objective reality. We embrace the equality of religions only because we embrace the equality of myths. Santa Claus may be as good as Zeus, but little green men from UFOs are not as good as little green worms from apples because in the latter case we claim to know something *true*. Christianity claims to be a truth stranger than UFOs. If it is *not* true, it is a lie, not a myth, and Jesus is not a good teacher but a deluded egotist claiming miracles and divinity and salvation when in fact he is only someone like us. How can he be a good teacher if his teachings are not true?

Why Only One Way?

Jesus' "only One Way" teaching makes no sense if religion is for subjective comfort, not for objective truth. It also makes no sense if religion is a human way up to God, not a divine way down to us. For most human things are at root equal: races, civilizations, politics, arts, cultures. It is sheer imperialism to insist that only one man-made road up the divine mountain is the right road and all others are wrong. But Christ does not claim to be a man who became God but God become Man. "No one has ascended into heaven but he who descended from heaven, the Son of man." [25] Christianity claims to be the road God made down, not the road we made up. That's why the "One Way" claim is necessary: because we are only repeating the message God gave us—we are mailmen, not authors.

It makes sense for God to make just one road. He starts from unity, from the top of the mountain. We start from diversity, from the bottom. Diverse human religions are indeed equal: equally failures. "You can't get there from here." The mountain is simply too high. We have jumped into the

[25] John 3:13.

quicksand and can no longer stand on a solid platform to support the leap out. All our Babels collapse because their foundation is only ourselves.

> We are floating in a medium of vast extent, always drifting uncertainly, blown to and fro; whenever we think we have a fixed point to which we can cling and make fast, it shifts and leaves us behind; if we follow it, it eludes our grasp, slips away, and flees eternally before us. Nothing stands still for us. This is our natural state, and yet the state most contrary to our inclinations. We burn with desire to find a firm footing, an ultimate, lasting base on which to build a tower rising up to infinity, but our whole foundation cracks and the earth opens up into the depth of the abyss.[26]

All human Babels reach only reachable gods, therefore false gods. There is *no* way up. But there is one way down: the Man Who called Himself Jacob's ladder,[27] the ladder God let *down* from Heaven. For a mere particular man to be the universal Savior is nonsense; but for the universal Logos, the divine light that lightens every man,[28] to become a particular man, is "the foolishness of God", which is "wiser than men".[29]

So How Do I Get to Heaven?

When God appears at the golden gates and demands to know why He should let me in, what do I say? It is only the most important question in the world, and it bears endless repeating even though Scripture is quite clear about it, because there are millions of people who have read Scripture till it comes out of their ears and still haven't got the point. I have repeatedly taken polls and surveys in college classrooms and adult education classes, and the percentage of people who believe the world's most pervasive superstition, that good

[26] Pascal, *Pensées*, trans. Krailsheimer (New York: Penguin Books, 1966), 199.
[27] John 1:51.   [28] John 1:9.   [29] 1 Corinthians 1:25.

guys go to Heaven and bad guys go to Hell, is always well over 50 percent, often over 90 percent. This popular religion is really legalism, though none of its believers call it that. They are deceived by the looseness or liberality of their law. But even an easy law is still a law. Even a subjective law is a law. Even an ethic that revises "Be ye holy, for the Lord thy God is holy" to "Try to be nice and to behave in socially acceptable ways, if it doesn't threaten your self-actualization" is still a law, a blueprint for self-salvation.

Jesus tells us two shocking things about getting to Heaven. We often hear the second without the first. The second shock is the good news that Heaven's door is open; that only accepting the gift by faith, hope and love is required; that the gift is Christ, who takes the whole scraggly, clownish, raga-muffin, confused and bickering crowd of sinner-saints piggyback to Heaven. But the first shock is the bad news that all other ways are absolutely impotent, whether good works or good intentions or meditation or mystical enlightenment or asceticism or social service or any kind of spiritual athleticism. Modern preachers, listening to the nearly total consensus of modern psychology instead of to God and the psychology of the saints, insist that we should not be told that "all our righteousnesses are as filthy rags".[30] God disagrees. It is not a good investment to disagree with God.

Jesus says, "Apart from me, you can do nothing."[31] Dare we patronize Him? Dare we pat Him on the head and say, in our superior way, "There, there, now; we know you have to exaggerate a bit to put the fear of God into the uneducated peasants of your unfortunate, benighted era. But we know better. We are The People, and wisdom will die with us. At least, it was born with us. We know there *must* be other ways. Everyone says so. How dare we put all our eggs in one basket—your basket—as you demand? It's not a reasonable investment."

[30] Isaiah 64:6 (KJV).   [31] John 15:5.

No. It is not. One does not get to Heaven by making reasonable investments. One does not even get to Everest, or Gothic architecture, or Beethoven by making reasonable investments. One does not fall in love by making reasonable investments. One falls in love by giving one's all. That is what He demands. Love will not settle for anything else.

"All" includes our trust in all His words, even His shocking words about Hell and about Himself as the only way to the Father. His claim is total on our mind as well as our heart; for He claimed not just to show the truth but to *be* the Truth. His claim is total on our life because He claimed not just to show the way but to *be* the Way. Remember where all human ways lead: into the valley of the shadow of death. How can we expect to endure *that* way alone? Only One has passed that way and lived: the One Who uttered the heart-stoppingly incredible claim, "I am the Life."

Appendix

How Can We Know
What Heaven Is Like?

The "how" question, the question of method, has called forth oceans of ink in every field of study, and you may well ask the question: How on earth can we know anything about Heaven?

Although the question of method is usually treated first, I have relegated it to an Appendix for three reasons. First, I do not think it is as *interesting* a question as the substantive questions. I would rather know whether there *is* music in Heaven, for example, than know how one *knows* whether there is music in Heaven. Knowledge is secondary to being. Secondly, this chapter came last in fact, as a reflection on what I had already written, rather than first, as a road map. Third, this is the natural order of things because (as Aristotle put it) actuality precedes potentiality.[1] We know how a thing is possible only after it actually happens and we know it is actual. And method deals with the possible; it tells us how it is possible to do something.

I believe we must use at least five methodological principles in theologizing in general and in theologizing about Heaven especially. These five may not be sufficient, but they are necessary. We may need more, but we cannot make do with less.

---

[1] Aristotle, *Metaphysics*, IX, 8 (1049b5).

Each of the five is traditional. Saint Thomas Aquinas, for instance, practices all five consistently. Yet, despite modern theologians' concentration on methodology, they seldom practice these principles as Aquinas did.

The five principles are:

1. Ask concrete, specific questions, not just abstract, general ones.

2. Combine faith, reason, and imagination.

3. Begin with data: divine revelation.

4. Use earthly analogies, remembering they are *only* analogies.

5. Remember the Socratic wisdom of "learned ignorance".

First Principle: Ask Specific Questions

Philosophers and theologians often hide behind safe generalizations, thus avoiding embarrassingly specific questions like: Do cats eat cat food in Heaven? The Sadducees were better theologians than that when they asked Jesus the excellent question: Whose wife would the woman who had seven husbands be in Heaven?[2] Jesus knew the false motives of the questioners—they didn't really want to know the truth about the matter but just wanted to trap Jesus and show the foolishness of His belief in Heaven—but He still answered their question because it was a good question.

Another example of an embarrassingly good question that no one dares ask today is the famous medieval question: How many angels can dance on a pinhead?[3] To the modern mind, this has become a stock example of a foolish question. That only shows who the real pinheads are. For this is in fact an excellent question: to answer it, you must test your general ideas about the nature of spirit (angels) and matter (pinheads)

[2] Matthew 22:23–33.

[3] I have been unable to find this question in any mediaval philosopher; I believe it is a Reformation cannard.

and their relationship by applying them to this specific case. It is also a good question because it is practical and relevant to us. It is just the opposite of a fantastic or escapist question. It is in fact about our essence; *we* are essentially a mysterious union of spirit and matter, angel and pinhead. A contemporary equivalent of the question might be: Can more than one mind use the same brain at the same time? Is multiple personality or spirit possession possible?

This may sound irreverent, but one of the most fruitful theological discussions I have ever heard—in fact, the one that made me fall in love with theology for life—began with the question, posed in a college dormitory: Did Adam burp before the Fall? It proceeded to the question: Will we ever burp in Heaven? And we soon realized that these half-serious questions were indeed half *serious*, and that they could not be answered without facing great questions about the historicity of Adam and Heaven, the relation between the resurrection body and the immortal soul, the relation between physical objects and aesthetic pleasure, the objectivity or subjectivity of beauty, and the nature of human perfection. It was four in the morning before we gave up.

Will my dead cat be alive in Heaven? If not, how can I be happy there? If so, will it eat cat food? If it doesn't, how can *it* be happy there? If it does, where will its food come from? [4]

Will we have sexual organs in Heaven? If we will not, will we all be neutered? If we will, what will we use them for if we no longer copulate?

What language will we speak?

Will we be able to listen to Beethoven's Ninth?

Ninety-nine out of a hundred contemporary theologians would not touch such questions with a ten-foot pen. I propose to you a daring experiment. Let's turn back the clock and

---

[4] If you insist on an answer, I think cats are in Heaven as part of the "new earth" (Revelation 21:1), and that they need not eat there any more than we (Augustine, *City of God*, XIII, 22–23).

become medievals or children again. (Turning back the clock is a very progressive thing to do when the clock starts keeping the wrong time.)[5] The questions a child asks, the questions the childhood of the human race asked, are the profoundest and best questions. Adults often don't have answers to them, so they pretend they are not the profoundest questions. Out with pretense! Even if we don't have all the answers to such questions, let's explore them rather than the "grown-up" questions, the safe, respectable questions, the questions you already know the answers to.

Now—*how* do we explore such hard questions? This brings us to our

Second Principle: Combine Faith, Reason, and Imagination

All three are faculties of knowing and gifts of God. Yet they are seldom combined. Especially, reason is seldom combined with imagination. Rational philosophers and theologians seem suspicious of the imagination, and poets and storytellers suspicious of reason—as if imagination would pollute the purity of reason or reason kill the liveliness of imagination.[6] Jesus is the great counterexample, of course, and it is strange that so few Christian theologians follow Him here. Augustine, Pascal, Kierkegaard, and C. S. Lewis are four of the few.

Two of these three things were combined throughout the Middle Ages: faith and reason, Christianity and philosophy. Some Christians refuse even this synthesis and pray, "forgive us our syntheses", seeing philosophical questioning as a threat to their faith and faith as an irrational leap in the dark. But Christian philosophers like Saint Thomas Aquinas who deliberately synthesize faith and reason have always been in the mainstream of the Christian tradition.[7]

[5] C. S. Lewis, *Mere Christianity* (New York: Macmillan, 1960), p. 36.

[6] Robert P. Roth, *Story and Reality* (Grand Rapids, Mich.: Eerdmans, 1973).

[7] St. Thomas Aquinas, *Summa contra Gentiles*, I, 1–9; Etienne Gilson, *Reason and Revelation in the Middle Ages* (New York: Scribner's, 1938).

However, the reason for combining the truths of faith with the truths of reason also justifies the inclusion of the truths of imagination in the synthesis. This reason is the great principle enunciated by Aquinas at the beginning of his *Summa contra Gentiles*, a principle so extremely simple that no Christian could deny it, yet so weighty with consequences that no one could exhaust them. It is simply that "all truth is from God."[8]

One of the consequences Aquinas immediately deduces from this principle is that there is no possibility at all, ever, of anything validly proved by reason contradicting anything revealed by God and believed by faith. Whenever there appears to be a conflict, the apparent proof is not really a proof and can therefore be refuted.[9] This means that *all* objections to revealed truths can be refuted by reason. For instance, the Trinitarian nature of God cannot be proved. But all objections to it (e.g., that it is self-contradictory to call God both one and three) can be refuted (e.g., by distinguishing person and nature: God is three persons in one nature, not three persons in one person).

The reluctance of many people today to accept such a logically necessary consequence of the principle that all truth is from God—the reluctance of even many believing Christians to believe that every objection against the Christian faith can be answered by reason—is an index of the fractured condition of the modern mind. We chop our minds, as we chop our lives, into isolated pieces, and we use a different method for each piece: faith for religion, reason for philosophy, imagination for literature. We forget that they are united,

[8] St. Thomas Aquinas, *Summa contra Gentiles*, I, 7.

[9] "From this we evidently gather the following conclusion: Whatever arguments were brought forward against the doctrines of faith are conclusions incorrectly derived. . . . Such conclusions do not have the force of demonstration: they are arguments that are either probable or sophistical. And so, there exists the possibility to answer them" (St. Thomas Aquinas, *Summa contra Gentiles*, I, 1–9).

because we forget where they are united: we forget that truth is one.

The Bible does not forget. It uses imagination—the drama of a Job, the parables of Jesus—and reason—the startling simplicities of the Sermon on the Mount, the complex *midrash* of Saint Paul's exegeses—as well as sermonizing, prophesying, and promising, which are appeals to faith. So should we.

But in what order?

Third Principle: Begin with Divine Revelation

First things first. We should begin with data. The data for a believer is what God has revealed, just as the data for a scientist is what nature reveals.[10]

Christian theology is defined by the medievals as *fides quaerens intellectum*, faith seeking understanding.[11] This is not a merely medieval, historically relative definition, but a definition of the unchanging essence of what Christian theology is and always in this life must be.[12] For a Christian is one who believes that God has revealed Himself in Christ, and in the Body of Christ, the Church, and in her Scriptures. So a Christian theologian is one who (1) begins with that common Christian data and then (2) seeks to (a) explore its meaning, (b) demonstrate its truth, or (c) draw out its applications and implications. In other words, Christian theology is (1) faith (2) seeking the understanding of its own (a) nature, (b) causes (reasons), and (c) effects (consequences).

Christian theologizing is simply exploring the revealed mysteries in these three ways. The mysteries of faith are like a truckload of balls that have been delivered into our ball park by God; all we do is play with them, juggle them, feel them,

---

[10] Christopher Derrick, *Church Authority and Intellectual Freedom* (San Francisco: Ignatius Press, 1981), chap. 2.

[11] St. Anselm, *Proslogium*, preface.

[12] Josef Pieper, *Scholasticism* (New York: McGraw-Hill, 1964), chap. 12.

squint at them from different angles and in different lights. We don't make them rational, or relevant, or systematic, or acceptable, or anything they aren't; we do not improve on them. The data are not mere raw material for our shaping; they are the thing itself, the truth, the Good News. In fact, the theologian doesn't do very much. He is like a fly crawling on an elephant.[13] This is a great blow to our vanity, that we really don't do very much. Perhaps that is why our last two points are so rarely preached or practiced. The fourth principle tells us simultaneously how much we can know and how much we can't know about Heaven; the fifth reminds us how inadequate is even what we *do* know.

Fourth Principle: Use Earthly Analogies

To understand this principle, consider a specific question (thus already using our first principle): Is there sunlight in heaven?

There are three possible kinds of answer to such a question. First, there is the simple, literal answer yes or no. This implies that our words about Heaven have a literal meaning, the same meaning they have when we apply them to earth. The technical term for this is that they are *univocal* terms, terms with a single meaning.

A second answer says, instead, that all our language about Heaven is equivocal (double-meaninged) because we cannot reach beyond our earthly horizons of meaning. No answer can be given; the question is impossible. If the first kind of answer was dogmatic, the second is skeptical.

Our method, following Saint Thomas Aquinas,[14] will take a third position, avoiding both extremes. Words about Heaven, like words about God, are neither univocal nor equivocal but analogical: partly the same and partly different.

---

[13] Robert Farrar Capon, *Hunting the Divine Fox* (New York: Seabury, 1974), chaps. 1–5.

[14] *Summa Theologiae*, I, 13.

They are neither nonsense nor photographic reproductions, neither simple lies nor simple truths. They are symbols, metaphors, images of the real thing.

To apply this principle to our sample question, the light of Heaven is real light, but it is not the same kind of light as earth's because Heaven's sun is not a ball of burning gas but God Himself, who manifests Himself not through the sun but through the Son. Heaven's sunlight is Sonlight. But it is meaningful to use the word not because of the pun (that's equivocation) but because there is a real analogy between the two lights.

But the analogy works the opposite way from what we usually think. Instead of the Heavenly light being symbolic and earthly light, literal light, it is the Heavenly light that is the true light and earthly light that is its symbol or image. Heaven is earth's model, earth is Heaven's image.

That idea comes from Scripture. Saint Paul calls God's fatherhood the true fatherhood and earthly fatherhood is named after it, not vice versa.[15] When Jesus tells His worried disciples that He has enough food in the wilderness because His food is to do His Father's will, He says "This is true food."[16] This is what food really means. This (doing God's will) is that of which eating physical food is an image. Body food is an image of soul food as body is an image of soul, and God's will is our soul food.

We are the metaphors, the images of God. That is why our language must be metaphorical. The analogical method of speaking about Heaven is founded on the metaphysical fact that earth is an analog to Heaven.

Saint Thomas also says that we can know what God is *not* in an univocal way—for example, God is not temporal, material, imperfect, and so on.[17] We can know what God is *not* and what God is *like* but not what God *is*; we can have negative

[15] Ephesians 3:14–15.   [16] John 4:34.
[17] *Summa Theologiae*, I, 3, preface.

univocal knowledge or positive analogical knowledge but not positive univocal knowledge of God. The same applies to Heaven: we must choose between the negative and the analogical way, as Jesus did when answering the Sadducees' question about the woman with seven husbands. First He said (negatively) that "they neither marry nor are given in marriage" in Heaven; then He used an analogy, "they are like angels". (He did not say that they *are* angels, but that they are *like* angels in not marrying.)

Negative and analogical knowledge must continually correct and supplement each other. Otherwise, we fall into two popular unbiblical pictures of Heaven: sheer immateriality (mere negation of earth) or mere worldliness (mere extension of earth).

We see these two popular pictures of Heaven in different world religions. The Buddhist *nirvana*, the Hindu *moksha* or *mukti*, and the Zen *satori* are ineffable, mystical states of immaterial spirituality that have nothing in common with earth or the ego-self. In fact, they abolish both world and ego as illusory. And they are reached not by natural desire but by abolishing all desire (*tanha*), thus dissolving the illusion of desiring ego and desired world together. At the opposite extreme from this unworldliness, we have the "happy hunting grounds" of the American Indian and the Islamic pleasure garden where you get all the pleasures you were denied here, including a harem. Such heavens are materialistic and the desire for them is ordinary materialistic desire.

Within Christianity, modernists sometimes approach the first concept and fundamentalists the second, but traditional Christian orthodoxy sees earth as neither simply removed nor simply extended but radically transformed. As Scripture puts it, there will be "a new heaven *and a new earth*". And this new Heaven and earth will satisfy only our unselfish desires for goodness and truth and beauty, not our selfish desires. Desire, like self and world, is neither simply denied nor simply affirmed but transformed. Heaven transforms lust to love, greed to goodness, perspiration to aspiration, the desire to possess the world to the desire to be possessed by God.

Fifth Principle: Remember the Socratic Wisdom of "Learned Ignorance"

Socrates was declared by the Delphic oracle of Apollo to be the wisest man in the world. He interpreted this to mean that even though he had no wisdom at all, he had the wisdom to know that he had no wisdom, while all others, who also had none, thought they did. "So I am wiser than them by only this trifle, that what I do not know, I do not think I do."[18] This "trifle" is the difference between wisdom and foolishness, between the apparent foolishness of Socrates, which is really wisdom, and the apparent wisdom of the world, which is really foolishness.[19] In other words, there are only two kinds of people: the wise, who know they are foolish, and the foolish, who think they are wise. It is a perfect parallel to the moral division of people into the saints, who all know they are sinners, and the sinners, who think they are saints. The Socratic purpose of this book is not to understand Heaven, but to keep exposing the illusion of having understood Heaven.

Suppose God were to read and mark this book! I think the most charitable grade would be a good laugh. What would be left in it to take seriously except that laugh? But let's pursue the thought, follow it through. Suppose God said, "I'll divide your book into four categories. (1) I'll leave all your true and adequate insights white; (2) I'll yellow-pencil your essentially true but inadequate insights, which need only fine tuning; (3) red-pencil your molehills of understanding that rest on mountains of misunderstanding, your glimmers of truth twisted almost beyond recognition; and (4) I'll blacken out

---

[18] Plato, *The Apology of Socrates*, 21d.
[19] 1 Corinthians 1:15-25.

your sheer falsehoods." How much do I honestly think would fall into each of these four categories, not by the judgment of some earthly book reviewer as ignorant as myself but by the Heavenly review?

It is a useful exercise thus to reverse our habitual perspective from "What do we think about God?" to "What does God think about us?" because it amounts to the shift from opinion to truth.[20] Of course, we have only our guesses, our opinions, about what His opinions of our opinions would be. My guess is that His colored-pencil review would show very little if any white, and only a little more yellow—a few sentences, perhaps, hardly enough for a page, much less a book. There would be enormous blotches of red, with (I hope) as little black as white.

Saint Thomas Aquinas called his *Summa Theologiae* "straw" compared with the light he had seen in mystical contemplation.[21] If the *Summa* is straw, this is gossamer. But we have little else to build with. Our confidence is not in our building but in our foundation:

> For no other foundation can any one lay than that which is laid, which is Jesus Christ. Now if any one builds on the foundation with gold, silver, precious stones, wood, hay, stubble—each man's work will become manifest; for the Day will disclose it, because it will be revealed with fire, and the fire will test what sort of work each one had done.[22]

When the big bad wolf of death blows all our houses down and we meet in that Day in the real Heaven, we will look back and have a good laugh at our houses of straw, our imagined Heavens.

We are warned with proper severity by that truly Socratic thinker C. S. Lewis to "give no poor fool the pretext to think

[20] C. S. Lewis, *The Weight of Glory* (New York: Macmillan, 1949), p. 10.

[21] Jacques Maritain, *St. Thomas Aquinas* (New York: Meridian, 1959), p. 54.

[22] I Corinthians 3:11.

ye are claiming knowledge of what no mortal knows".[23] Like Lewis' thoughts on Heaven, mine are "guesses, of course, only guesses. If they are not true, something better will be."[24]

But as Lewis also says, "'something better' is almost the definition of the thing"[25]—the thing "no eye has seen, nor ear heard, nor the heart of man conceived, what God has prepared for those who love him."[26]

[23] C. S. Lewis, *The Great Divorce* (New York: Macmillan, 1975), p. 127.
[24] C. S. Lewis, *Letters to Malcolm* (New York: Harcourt, Brace & World, 1964), p. 124.
[25] C. S. Lewis, *The Problem of Pain* (New York: Macmillan, 1962), p. 149.
[26] 1 Corinthians 2:9.

INDEX